# WINNING THROUGH
# INNOVATION

**THE MANAGEMENT OF INNOVATION AND CHANGE SERIES**
Michael L. Tushman and
Andrew H. Van de Ven, Series Editors

*Emerging Patterns of Innovation: Sources of Japan's Technological Edge*
Fumio Kodama, with a Foreword by Lewis M. Branscomb

*Crisis & Renewal: Meeting the Challenge of Organizational Change*
David K. Hurst

*Winning through Innovation: A Practical Guide to Leading Organizational Change and Renewal*
Michael L. Tushman
Charles A. O'Reilly III

*Imitation to Innovation: The Dynamics of Korea's Technological Learning*
Linsu Kim

# WINNING THROUGH

# INNOVATION

## A PRACTICAL GUIDE

## TO LEADING ORGANIZATIONAL

## CHANGE AND RENEWAL

## MICHAEL L. TUSHMAN
GRADUATE SCHOOL OF BUSINESS,
COLUMBIA UNIVERSITY

## CHARLES A. O'REILLY III
GRADUATE SCHOOL OF BUSINESS,
STANFORD UNIVERSITY

HARVARD BUSINESS SCHOOL PRESS

Boston, Massachusetts

Tushman, Michael.
　　Winning through innovation : a practical guide to leading
　organizational change and renewal / Michael L. Tushman, Charles A.
　O'Reilly III.
　　　p.　cm.
　　Includes bibliographical references and index.
　　ISBN 0-87584-579-7
　　1. Organizational change—Management.　　I. O'Reilly, Charles A.
　II. Title.
　HD58.8.T885　1997
　658.4′063—dc20　　　　　　　　　　　　　　　　96-2805
　　　　　　　　　　　　　　　　　　　　　　　　　　　CIP

This book is dedicated to
Marjorie,
Ulrike,
and Bernie

# CONTENTS

# PREFACE AND ACKNOWLEDGMENTS

This book reflects twenty years of our collaboration; it also reflects our continuing desire to link organizational research to managerial practice. Over these two decades, our work on managing innovation, culture, leadership, and change has been shaped by two powerful forces: the evolution of our academic fields and our close interactions with thousands of managers. Research and practice have actively informed and shaped each other. Mike's early research on communication networks in R&D settings and organizational designs for innovation complemented Charles's early work on decision making, communication, and culture. These ideas first found expression in the development of Columbia University's Executive Program on Managing Strategic Innovation and Change. This program initially provided us with a platform to interact with practicing managers and to extend our work on managing innovation, culture, and change.

As we have taught over the years, managers have often told us that our approach to managing innovation and change helped them understand the tension between meeting today's performance demands *and* preparing their organizations for future innovation. It offered managers a systematic way of approaching the topic. The combination of our contact with managers, who have pragmatic concerns, and our colleagues, who are more interested in research, has shaped our work and helped us focus on the tensions inherent in managing innovation. Mike's research evolved into understanding technology cycles, executive teams, and organizational evolution, and Charles's into culture, demography, and human resources. Our teaching, executive education, and consulting work also evolved—we became intensively involved in helping managers and organizations grapple with the issues of winning through innovation.

Recently, a colleague and friend at the Graduate School of Business at Columbia, Don Hambrick, gave his presidential address at the Academy of Management. In this address, he observed that too often the research on management had only limited impact on the practice of management. Don challenged his academic colleagues to make their research more accessible and useful to managers. We agree with him. In our experience, research in organizational behavior can be extraordinary valuable to managers, but often academics don't understand the pressures facing practicing managers and don't know how to convey their research in ways that can be applied. Hambrick's admonition and our own desire to make a difference in real organizations triggered the writing of this book.

Over the past decade we have been helped and encouraged by literally thousands of managers from around the world. They have sharpend, extended, and improved on our ideas. We owe all of them a debt of gratitude. In a real sense, they are coauthors. Mark Twain once observed that a person who undertakes to carry a cat home by the tail learns ten times as much as the person who simply watches. In this sense, we have watched carefully and learned an immense amount from them. While they carried the cat home, we wrote this book.

In writing, we have attempted to take research on innovation, technology, and change, and present it in a friendly and useful way. We hope that this book will make a difference to those who read it, both managers and students of organizations. We want readers to both *understand* the dynamics of innovation and change and effectively manage this process—*get it done*. Our challenge has been to write in a way that reflects the concerns and constraints of practicing managers and to bring relevant theory and research to bear in an engaging way.

A number of colleagues have been instrumental in this book's evolution. The single person without whom the book would not have been written is Guido Spichy from Ciba-Geigy (now Novartis). Guido supported our efforts through his energy and enthusiasm. He provided opportunities for us to test our ideas within Ciba. He has been the product champion for this effort. Other Ciba managers have been instrumental in helping refine our ideas, including Alex Krauer, Francois L'Eplatinier, Kurt Huber, Michael Jacoby, Rolf Meyer, Uwe Eisenlohr, Dieter Wyrsch, Glenn Bradley, Michel de Rougement, Robert Spoerry, and Pierre Urech. They, and over five hundred other Ciba managers, have taught us about innovation and change. Other important contributors have included John Lane at Data General, Russ Demers at Bristol-Myers Squibb, Jerry Abarbanel at Dun & Bradstreet, John Elias and C. K. Chow at BOC, Sandy Quesada at IBM, John Whitehead at Technicon, Tracy Koon at Intel, Rod Spence and Johan Swanepol at Anglo American, Peter Lindwall at Ericsson, Ron Bossert at Johnson & Johnson, Dan Cole at SciMed, Dan Reid at Citibank, Cory Billington and Ed Feitzinger at Hewlett-Packard, Fabio Corno at the Centro Studi d'Impresa in Italy, Joan Burke at John Hancock, Dean Hayakawa at The Nomura School of Advanced Management in Tokyo, Kathy Esslinger at the American Electronics Association, Rauno Puskala at the Nordic Management of Technology Group, Soren Sjolander at Chalmers University, Al Bean at Lehigh University, and Nick Nichols at Caltech. Without their help and encouragement this book could not have been written.

Our work has also been shaped by a remarkable set of colleagues, friends, and students. Jeff Pfeffer at Stanford and David Nadler at the Delta Consulting Group have been great friends and critical supporters over the past twenty years. Their ideas pervade the book. Elaine Romanelli, Phil Anderson, Sara Keck, and Lori Rosenkopf were Mike's Ph.D. students. Dave Caldwell, Jenny Chatman, and Jim Wade were Charles's students. They are now valued colleagues. Their enthusiasm, creativity, and energy were a constant source of insight and challenge.

Ralph Katz, Andy Pettigrew, Don Hambrick, Kaye Schoonhoven, Jeff Pfeffer, Andy Van de Ven, Jenny Chatman, Bala Chakravarthy, Charlie Galunic, Linda Johanson (formerly Linda Pike), and Martin Gargiulo have read early versions of the manuscript and given us important feedback. Our students at Columbia, Stanford, Berkeley, MIT, and INSEAD have also been constant challengers and shapers of our ideas. Without great students our lives as professors would certainly be less fruitful and interesting. Institutional support has also been crucial in our work. Without Columbia's long-term support for Mike and Stanford's and Berkeley's support for Charles, this book could not have been written. The faculty and administrators at these institutions value great research and the translation of this research into material that managers can use.

Still others have helped this book see the light of day. At Harvard Business School Press we were blessed with a team of supremely competent professionals—Carol Franco, Hollis Heimbouch, Barbara Roth, Natalie Greenberg, and Nindy LeRoy were great to work with. They helped craft our book to better communicate with managers. Joy Glazener's administrative and editorial support helped Mike's writing and productivity in innumerable ways. Alan Gistrak and Murray Bilmes provided some of the fundamental insights that enabled this book to get written. They were more helpful than they know. Their professionalism and support were invaluable for this book.

Perhaps most fundamentally we would like to thank our most important supporters and personal anchors, our families. To Rachel and Jonathan, Mike's children—"The book is finally done." Thanks for all your patience and love. Marjorie Williams's support, professional insight, emotional energy, spirit, love, and encouragement provided Mike with the space and context to both write this book and love his evolving life. Anne and Brant Wenegrat offered the same unstinting support to Charles. Ulrike Schaede made it all enjoyable.

# C H A P T E R 1

# THE TYRANNY OF SUCCESS

IN 1972, IBM, GENERAL MOTORS, AND SEARS RANKED number one, four, and six, respectively, in the *Fortune* 500 listing. In 1983, they were listed among the country's most admired firms. In fact, in 1982, IBM was the most admired corporation in the survey. Yet, by 1992, each firm was struggling and none ranked among the top 20 *Fortune* firms. Cumulatively, they lost a total of $32.4 billion in 1992 alone. How could this happen? How could presumably smart managers, who were extraordinarily well paid to prevent failure, allow these great firms to lose their competitive advantage?[1]

In 1963, Thomas Watson, Jr. arguably one of America's most famous executives, addressed a group of MBAs at Columbia University. He pointed out that only two of the top 25 industrial corporations in the United States in 1900 were still in that category and went on to say, "Figures like these help remind us that . . . success—at best—is an impermanent achievement that can always slip out of hand."[2] Less than 30 years later the truth of that statement applied directly to IBM itself. In the mid-1980s,

IBM accounted for 40 percent of sales and 70 percent of profits in the computer industry. As a company, it possessed immense technological, financial, marketing, and human resource skills. Just as Xerox owned the reprographics market in the 1970s, IBM dominated the computer market. Yet between 1986 and the end of 1994, IBM was forced to lay off almost 200,000 employees. A total of $14 billion in hardware profits had evaporated, and in 1993 alone it reported a loss of $8.1 billion.[3]

In the 1980s, the business press was filled with accounts of the managerial prowess of firms like Toyota, Apple, and People Express. Today, People Express is gone, Apple is a shadow of its former self, and European automakers like Mercedes are using Ford, not Toyota, as their benchmark. In the 1980s, managers raced to implement techniques like quality circles, just-in-time inventory, and lean manufacturing. Today, we read articles about the failure of total quality management (TQM) and the dangers of reengineered, anorexic organizations. Firms like ABB, GE, and Microsoft are now celebrated in business and academic journals. If history is any guide, a decade from now the business press may well report on the decline of many of these same firms.[4]

This pattern—success followed by failure; innovation followed by inertia—is common across firms and industries and over time. It isn't an American, European, or Asian phenomenon; it is a global disease and can strike managers at all levels of organizations. Whether it is the demise of great U.S. firms like Singer Sewing Machines, International Harvester, or Western Union (at one time the most successful technology company in the world), or the current struggles of companies like Philips, Nissan, or Fiat, the lesson is clear: success—staying on top—can be tenuous.

Yet success need not be paralyzing. The most successful firms are able to capture the benefits of short-term advantage even as they build organizational capabilities for long-term strategic renewal. They transform themselves through proactive innovation and strategic change. Proactive firms are able to move from today's strength to tomorrow's strength by setting the pace of innovation in their industries.[5]

To succeed both today and tomorrow, managers must play two different games simultaneously. First, they must continually get better at competing in the short term, which requires increasing the alignment among strategy, structure, people, culture, and processes. This efficiency game requires mastering the basics. Yet efficiency alone will not ensure long-term success. In fact, today's success may actually increase the chances of tomorrow's failure. For sustainable success, managers must also master another game: understanding how and when to initiate revolutionary innovation and, in turn, revolutionary organizational change.

Organizational renewal demands mastering the dynamics of innovation and organizational change. Great managers are able to manage for today and for tomorrow simultaneously. The ability to play both games is crucial for long-term survival and success. The tools necessary to master these are understandable and implementable by managers everywhere. These tools help managers become architects of their organizations, constantly managing the contexts in which people operate. They also help managers understand the dynamics of innovation and organizational change more deeply.

## THE TYRANNY OF SUCCESS: AN AGE-OLD PROBLEM

Managers, faced with changing competition, new technologies, and shifting markets often feel as though they are meeting challenges never dealt with by their predecessors. They are both right and wrong. They are right in that markets and technologies are changing, often in new and unpredictable ways, but the fundamental dynamics of these changes are largely the same across industries, countries, and time. So, while the specifics of the competitive environment may be unique, the way in which they affect managers and organizations is not.

Let's begin our exploration of the dynamics of innovation and organizational change, not by looking at the latest in biotechnology or the information superhighway in the 1990s, but by going back a hundred years to one of the oldest recorded examples of how managers reacted when faced with the challenge of innovation and change. As you read the following account, imagine how the story might play out in your organization today.

Elting Morison was neither a manager nor a professor of management. He was an historian of technology.[6] He wasn't even interested in business. Yet, his careful account of how the U.S. Navy came to develop and adopt a relatively simple innovation could be a parable of innovation in many organizations today. Morison describes how continuous aim gunfire, a new way to aim and fire naval guns, found its way into the U.S. Navy about the turn of the century. This innovation provided dramatic improvements in the navy's ability to accomplish one of its most important tasks: accurately hit and destroy opposing ships. Yet, the innovation almost did not happen.

In 1898, gunfire at sea was notoriously inaccurate. In one study, the Bureau of Ordnance (the navy's R&D group) found that out of 9,500 shots fired, only 121 found their mark! Firing a gun fixed to the deck of a pitching and rolling ship and hitting another moving vessel is not easy. Indeed, the navy was doing fine. It had just helped win the Spanish-American War, and any comparison of accuracy and hit rate would have shown that the American navy was the standard of excellence. Any criticism of its "inaccuracy" could be answered by noting that there was simply no navy better at naval gunfire.

Inaccuracy was simply accepted as part of the complexity of naval warfare and continued until Admiral Percy Scott of the British navy noticed a gunner on his ship who was far more accurate than the norm. Upon close observation, Scott saw how the gunner unconsciously used the roll of the ship to help his aim. So the admiral fitted the gun to elevating gears, which made adjustment easier, and added a telescopic sight. With this new technique (the gun and the associated subsystems), the hit rate on Scott's ship increased more than 3,000 percent.

Admiral Scott was by nature an inventor, not a product champion. He retrofitted his ship but had no interest in persuading others within the British navy to make the change. Scott, however, did share his innovation with a young American naval officer, Lt. Sims. Sims was serving aboard a U.S. ship also patrolling in the South China Sea. A conscientious young officer, Sims was interested in improving the accuracy of his gunners. He quickly became convinced that Scott's new approach was vital to the U.S. Navy. Who could object to a 3,000 percent improvement in the accuracy of his gunfire? He went on to champion the innovation by gathering extensive data on its efficiency and accuracy. Sims carefully compiled his data and sent detailed reports to the Department of the Navy and the Bureau of Ordnance in Washington, D.C. He expected a quick and positive response.

He was disappointed. Sims waited but heard nothing from Washington. The navy's and the Bureau of Ordnance's response to Sims's new product was, initially, to do nothing. They simply ignored his reports. After all, does a junior lieutenant 7,500 miles from headquarters know more about naval gunnery than senior officers and ordnance experts? Not one to let his innovation die, Sims continued to gather more data and send more reports to the bureau and the larger Washington military community. In his view, any rational person had to see the benefits of continuous aim gunfire. Believing that the technologists in the Bureau of Ordnance would respond to data, Sims sent even further reports documenting the efficacy of the innovation. His reports were still ignored.

In the face of this silence, Sims escalated his efforts. He wrote in a more strident tone. He began to distribute his reports widely among other gunnery officers. He soon became too big a pest to ignore. Too many people knew of his outlandish claims, so the Bureau of Ordnance felt compelled to respond. First it rationally pointed out why the innovation could not possibly work the way Sims claimed. Further, it stated, there was no problem with accuracy in the U.S. Navy. The navy had the best technology in the world and had recently used it to win a war. If there was a problem, it was with the gunners and their training, not with the equipment.

This response infuriated Sims, so he escalated the conflict with even more data, reports, and pungent language. In the face of this increasingly public controversy, the bureau was compelled to test Sims's notion of continuous aim gunfire. The experiment used a gun platform located on dry ground. Because it did not allow for the rolling of a ship at sea, the results predictably "proved" that continuous aim gunfire was, as the navy and the bureau had claimed all along, impossible. The result was a period of name calling among Sims, the navy, and the Bureau of Ordnance.

By this time Sims's career was over. He had challenged the highest authorities in the navy, cast aspersions on their motives and competence, and generally made an extraordinary pain of himself. He finally took the remarkable step of documenting the entire case and sending the record directly to the president of the United States, Theodore Roosevelt. Amazingly, the president, an ex-Rough Rider and ex-secretary of the navy, read Sims's report and realized the potential of this new approach. Violating navy practice and usurping the entire hierarchy, he brought Sims to Washington and made him inspector of target practice. Roosevelt mandated the use of continuous aim gunfire throughout the navy and charged Sims with ensuring that his order was accomplished.

It is crucial to note that this innovation was implemented solely because a product champion was willing to sacrifice his career for the principle involved. It was implemented in spite of its demonstrated superiority. Those resisting were precisely those who an observer might think would be the most knowledgeable about its advantages. Finally, it was implemented because the head of the organization, for reasons that remain unclear, took time to read a report and was willing to override his senior advisers. This is decidedly not the way to introduce innovation in organizations, but it is illustrative of the processes that make innovation and change so difficult.

We have discussed Sims's story with managers from Asia, Europe, and the Americas, and found that the same dynamics occur in their organizations today. The challenge has not changed. Unfortunately, neither has the response of many organizations.


## LEARNING FROM THE PAST

Before we consider the managerial lessons to be learned from Morison's account, we need to understand why there was such resistance to what was unequivocally an important new product for the navy. Opposition was so remarkable that Morison describes it as "dynamic conservatism," referring to the active efforts by the naval hierarchy to preserve the status quo. Morison suggests several reasons. First, Sims as the product champion was a deviant. He was a low-level officer on the periphery of the organization (literally 7,500 miles away). He was also intolerant of the navy's bureaucracy and hierarchy; he did not fit the culture and traditions of the navy, which valued loyalty and obedience. Because Sims had little credibility and was unable to form alliances with more credible officers, he was quickly labeled a "crackbrained egotist" and a "falsifier of evidence."

Second, continuous aim gunfire was resisted because it solved no pressing organizational problem (according to the naval hierarchy). Further, the service had recently been rocked by a series of other technological changes, including the introduction of steam turbines and electric motors. The combination of a glorious, successful history, no clear hit-rate problem, benchmarked excellence, and other more pressing changes colluded to drive Sims and his innovation away.

Third, the navy as an organization had a strong, proud, conservative culture, one that valued courage, bravery, and closing with the enemy. Were continuous aim gunfire implemented, naval battles would be fought coldly and at a distance. The innovation would shift the strategy and tactics of naval warfare. Naval core values would become less important.

Fourth, should the new gun be adopted, the relevance of historically crucial navigational skills and, in turn, the power of the captain and his navigational officers would be threatened by the newly acquired expertise of the gunnery officer. In this new world, all that would be required of the captain and the navigators would be to maneuver the ship so the gunners could see the target. Navigation and bravery, the very competencies associated with success in the navy, would be rendered worthless should the new technology be adopted.

Finally, the Bureau of Ordnance was the official repository of expertise about the technology of gunnery. It, too, was proud of its competence, but it was not in close contact with its "customers." To adopt a new gun, especially one that produced such a massive increase in accuracy, the navy would have to admit that it was less competent than it believed it was. That the development of such a product came from a junior officer, much less one known to be nontraditional, was an added insult. Because the new gun was not invented with the official authorization of the navy, by the bureau's logic, it could not be effective.

The navy, as an historically successful organization, had developed structures, systems, culture, and a mode of leadership that were all aligned. Members of this society had learned what worked and thought they knew what was important and feasible. The simple introduction of a seemingly important innovation, however, would threaten that alignment, so it was met by resistance and inertia—not because the "managers" were pigheaded or stupid, but because they had been steeped in a particular culture and had been successful. Sims and his innovation threatened the status quo. This success syndrome, this active resistance to innovation and change, trapped the U.S. Navy in its distinguished past.

Morison uses this example to develop his core hypothesis, an hypothesis that pervades our book. He suggests that because of "limited identification" (focusing on the product rather than the process), successful organizations are dynamically conservative; they actively try to preserve their core competencies. This conservatism can make it very difficult for any successful organization or system to reform itself. In Morison's example, reform was forced on the navy by an outside actor, the president, and a protagonist, Sims, who violated the existing culture.

The issues of limited identification and dynamic conservatism are applicable today, not only in the U.S. Navy, but in most successful firms. Paradoxically, a firm's history and its current strategy, structure, people, and culture often combine to dampen innovation and adaptive change. The challenge to the navy at the turn of the century, and to managers today, was to balance the need for strong alignment among strategy, structure, people, and culture to win today's war with the need to carry out the periodic revolutionary changes required to win the next one. Do this at the wrong time, and, as we shall see, failure can follow. Don't do it, and failure will surely follow.

## LESSONS FOR TODAY'S MANAGERS

Before leaving the nineteenth century, let us draw several other lessons from Sims's case—lessons that still characterize the experience of managers:

1. The 3,000 percent increase in accuracy was not a result of basic research or a new technology. Rather, this breakthrough innovation was a result of the creative use of existing technology. What was new was the insight, which came from a practitioner not a scientist, that existing technologies could be linked together and used to generate significant performance improvements.

2. Continuous aim gunfire resulted from the combination of a chance event and a prepared, motivated manager. Admiral Scott commanded a ship where gunners felt free to experiment. This experimentation, this trial and error, led to the particular trial that Scott observed and used to develop his new gun. Scott's unit had a maverick culture, not one that emphasized strict hierarchical authority, but one that promoted innovation and change.

3. As long as there is no gap between expectations and performance, a successful system will actively attempt to remain

stable. Managers of successful organizations learn what
works and are able to incorporate their learning into the firm's
formal and informal structures and processes. In order to be
effective, these lessons often require uniformity and conformity. Yet, if the learning emphasizes today and yesterday, the
organization runs the risk of being trapped in the present.
Generals are said to always be prepared to fight the last war.
Managers are often most prepared to compete in yesterday's
markets.

To avoid the tyranny of success, managers must sometimes create performance gaps or opportunities during periods of success. Sims attempted to do this with data, but facts
are often a function of the historical and political context. In
the absence of a crisis, an improvement in accuracy was not
viewed as pressing enough to overcome the navy's inertia.
Yet, had Sims's navy been losing ships because of enemy
gunfire, the response of the organization to a gun that increased accuracy 3,000 percent would have been different. In
the absence of problems, successful organizations become
proud and, in turn, vulnerable.

4. It is also worth noting that the roots of the resistance Sims
   encountered were systemwide. Resistance was not centered
   in a single person or small group of individuals opposed to
   the change. Rather, the entire navy's structure, culture, traditions, processes, and people resisted the threat of the innovation. Careers were based on conformity, respect for authority,
   and seamanship; in such a culture, Sims was a fortunate
   anomaly. The navy's leaders were men who had succeeded
   under the old system and had devoted their lives to ensuring
   its success. But to champion innovation and change successfully, managers need a way to diagnose dispassionately the
   systemwide root causes of resistance to innovation and
   change.

5. Observe that organizationwide innovation and change came
   quickly when the senior manager (in this case, the president)
   acted. As we discuss later, when faced with revolutionary

change, 90 percent of organizations that adapt do so under the guidance of a new top management team. A recent McKinsey & Company study of 85 large firms facing difficulties found that two-thirds of senior managers had been replaced before the businesses were revived.[7] It is uncommon for the existing leadership of an organization to be able to manage the revolution. In the most successful firms, however, the existing management provokes the change. These findings underscore the importance of managers learning how to engage in both evolutionary and revolutionary innovation and organizational change.

6. While managers must be wary of resistance to change, they also must appreciate the substantial benefits that accrue to a robust, stable, reliable organization. Such order, stability, and discipline win both military and commercial wars. A navy filled with too many officers like Sims might lack the coordination to be effective. Change can paralyze an organization. Most senior managers have many product champions who are only too willing to transform the organization. Indeed, of 100 brilliant product champions in real time, ex-post we know that only 10 are likely to be true champions. Ninety may be the "crackbrained egotists" some officers believed Sims to be. Unfortunately, managers often cannot know who is the champion and who is the fool, and thus, successful organizations have good reason to protect themselves from the Simses of the world. Dynamic conservatism is important. So, too, is the trial-and-error learning that seeds major innovation.

## A PRACTICAL GUIDE TO LEADING ORGANIZATIONAL CHANGE AND RENEWAL

The lessons Morison highlighted are part of a much larger phenomenon. The problems Lt. Sims faced a century ago are similar to those countless managers face today. Consider the list of industries shown in Table 1.1. Are there underlying commonalties? At first glance, not many. How can financial services be similar to athletic equipment? But there is a disturbing theme common to each. In every industry, a set of leading firms, faced with a period of rapid change, often became losers. Whether it is the watch, automotive, motorcycle, tire, banking, airline, reprographic, athletic shoe, or financial services industry, competition has quickly moved from domestic to global; product development cycle times have sharply decreased; and quality, delivery, and service as well as innovation have become key competitive requirements. Furthermore, across diverse industries, winners too often become losers as product class conditions change. The number of managers who fail to make the transition as competitive demands shift is far larger than those who succeed (see Table 1.2).

Such failure is not only the case in declining industries, with firms playing exit strategies; on the contrary, in all these examples, product classes were being transformed and market opportunities were expanding. Furthermore, those declining firms did

---

**TABLE 1.1**

**INDUSTRIES IN WHICH LEADING FIRMS RAPIDLY LOST MARKET POSITION**

| | |
|---|---|
| Watches | Food processors |
| Automobiles | Microwave ovens |
| Cameras | Athletic equipment |
| Stereo equipment | Semiconductors |
| Medical equipment | Industrial robots |
| Color televisions | Machine tools |
| Hand tools | Optical equipment |
| Radial tires | Consulting services |
| Electric motors | Computer hardware |
| Photocopiers | Textiles |
| Ship building | Airlines |
| Software | Financial services |

not lack the technology to succeed. Often, internally developed innovation, like continuous aim gunfire, is squandered. Rather, these organizational failures result from senior managers' inability to lead innovation and change. But organizational inertia need not hold successful organizations hostage to their past. Long-term success stories abound—GE Medical Systems, Intel, Microsoft, Ericsson Radio, Alcoa, Ciba Vision, Hewlett-Packard Printers, and BOC Gases—have all proactively moved from today's to tomorrow's successes through innovation and change.

This paradoxical pattern in which winners often become losers, in which firms lose their innovative edge, is a worldwide phenomenon. Whether exemplified by the struggles of IBM, Apple, or General Motors in the United States, Michelin in France, Philips in Holland, EMI, or British Gas in England, or Mazda in Japan, leading firms often fall victim to their past successes. These paradoxical patterns are driven by managerial actions and organizational processes in the face of discontinuous change—not by the invisible hand of the market or public policy. Managers make the decisions that lead to success or failure, and

**TABLE 1.2**

**THE TYRANNY OF SUCCESS: PRODUCT CLASS WINNERS WHO FELL VICTIM TO THEIR SUCCESS**

| | |
|---|---|
| ICI (chemicals) | SSIH (watches) |
| IBM (personal computers) | Oticon (hearing aids) |
| Kodak (photography) | Bank of America (financial services) |
| Sears (retailing) | Goodyear (tires) |
| General Motors (automobiles) | Polaroid (photography) |
| Ampex (video recorders) | Bausch and Lomb (vision products) |
| Winchester (disk drives) | Smith-Corona (typewriters) |
| U.S. Steel (steel) | Fuji Xerox (copiers) |
| Syntex (pharmaceuticals) | Zenith (TVs) |
| Philips (electronics) | EMI (CT scanners) |
| Volkswagen (automobiles) | Harley-Davidson (motorcycles) |

with them lie the remedies that will counteract the tyranny of success.

There are similarities across countries and industries that separate long-term winners from losers. To understand this phenomenon, we need to appreciate how technological change affects cycles of innovation, how industry standards emerge, how periodic changes in technology demand equivalent changes in management and organization, and how organizational culture can be a major help or hindrance in the managerial response to these changes. To avoid being trapped by success, it is critical that managers appreciate how to avoid the pitfalls of these dynamics.

But long-term competitiveness requires more than an awareness of changing strategic demands. Managers also need to understand how success can be a double-edged sword; how short-run effectiveness can sow the seeds of organizational failure by hindering long-term adaptability. While flexibility, speed, innovation, and responsiveness are crucial as product classes evolve, so, too, are characteristics such as consistency, reliability, and efficiency. Too much of the former, and organizations may fail to capture the value of their early innovations. Too much of the latter, and firms may develop toxic levels of resistance and inertia. Managerial competencies that stimulate both innovation and efficiency are an important ingredient in differentiating between organizational success and failure over long periods.

The managerial challenge is clear but daunting. Long-term organizational success requires streams of innovation—systematically different kinds of innovation over time. These *innovation streams* run counter to forces for organizational inertia. Given these contrasting forces for change and stability, managers need to create ambidextrous organizations—organizations that celebrate stability and incremental change as well as experimentation and discontinuous change simultaneously. As we discuss, in the most successful firms, managers encourage tight alignment among strategy, structure, people, and culture to ensure today's success and periodically promote revolutionary change for tomorrow's renewal. Ambidextrous organizations create organizational capabilities for excelling both today and tomorrow.

The issues of performance gaps, resistance to change, organizational inertia, and incremental innovation hampering breakthrough innovation haunt organizations today as much as they did the navy at the turn of the century. Given the increased pressure on managers for efficiency as well as innovation and flexibility, we must do better today than the U.S. Navy did at the beginning of the century. We present managers with an integrated set of tested tools to enhance their understanding of and ability to shape both innovation streams and organizational dynamics. While we offer no easy answers, we do furnish a proven process to help managers adapt their leadership styles as well as build teams and organizations to lead change and renewal through streams of innovation.

Our book focuses on managing both for today's requirements and for tomorrow's possibilities. Excellence in both is required for winning over time. Chapter 2 sets the stage by illustrating how profound, and global, are the challenges of innovation and organizational renewal. Chapters 3, 4, 5, and 6 concentrate on managing for today—building organizational capabilities, structures, competencies, and, in particular, cultures that can exceed the performance of today's competition. Chapter 3 focuses on setting strategy, objectives, and vision and on establishing performance and opportunity gaps. Chapter 4 presents a congruence-based problem-solving approach, a proven method for getting at the roots of today's performance or opportunity gaps, while Chapters 5 and 6 focus on organizational culture—a particularly crucial ingredient for winning through innovation.

Chapters 7 and 8 discuss innovation streams and discontinuous organizational change as ways to renew the firm. Chapter 7 introduces technology cycles, the importance of innovation streams, and building ambidextrous organizations, while Chapter 8 focuses on getting it done—the role of managers and their teams in implementing organizational changes associated with innovation streams. Chapter 9 pulls together our core themes on winning through innovation.

# AMBIDEXTROUS ORGANIZATIONS: LEADING EVOLUTIONARY AND REVOLUTIONARY CHANGE

IN THE MID-1950S, VACUUM TUBES REPRESENTED roughly a $700 million market. Leading firms in the then state-of-the-art technology of vacuum tubes included such great technology companies as RCA, Sylvania, Raytheon, and Westinghouse. Yet from 1955 to 1982, there was almost a complete turnover in industry leadership, a remarkable shakeout brought on by the advent of the transistor. By 1965, new firms such as Motorola and Texas Instruments had become important players while Sylvania and RCA had begun to fade. Over the next 20 years still other upstart companies like Intel, Toshiba, and Hitachi had become the new leaders, and Sylvania and RCA exited the product class (see Table 2-1).

What happened to companies like RCA? RCA was initially successful at making the transition from vacuum tubes to transistors. But within RCA, bitter disputes raged about whether the company should enter the transistor business and risk cannibalizing its profitable tube business. Some made reasonable arguments that the transistor business was new and the potential

TABLE 2.1

## SEMICONDUCTOR INDUSTRY, 1955–1995

| 1955 (Vacuum Tubes) | 1955 (Transistors) | 1965 (Semicon- ductors) | 1975 (Integrated Circuits) | 1982 (VLSI) | 1995 (Submicrons) |
|---|---|---|---|---|---|
| RCA | Hughes | TI | TI | Motorola | Intel |
| Sylvania | Transitron | Fairchild | Fairchild | TI | NEC |
| General Electric | Philco | Motorola | National | NEC | Toshiba |
| Raytheon | Sylvania | GI | Intel | Hitachi | Hitachi |
| Westinghouse | Texas Instruments | GE | Motorola | National | Motorola |
| Amperex | GE | RCA | Rockwell | Toshiba | Samsung |
| National Video | RCA | Sprague | GI | Intel | TI |
| Rawland | Westinghouse | Philco | RCA | Philips | Fujitsu |
| Eimac | Motorola | Transitron | Philips | Fujitsu | Mitsubishi |
| Lansdale | Clevite | Raytheon | AMD | Fairchild | Philips |

SOURCE: Richard N. Foster, *Innovation: The Attacker's Advantage* (New York: Summit, 1996), p. 133. Adapted with the permission of Simon & Schuster from *Innovation* by Richard Foster. Copyright © 1996 by McKinsey & Co., Inc.

profits from it uncertain. Others, without knowing whether transistors would catch on, felt that it was risky not to pursue the new technology. But even if RCA were to enter the solid-state business, thorny organizational issues would have to be worked through. How could the firm manage both technologies? Should the new solid-state division report to the head of the electronics group and to a manager steeped in the old culture of vacuum tubes? With its great marketing, financial, and technological resources, RCA decided to enter the sold-state business, but in the absence of a clear strategy and an understanding of the cultural differences required to compete in both the solid-state and vacuum tube markets, RCA failed.

Notes Richard Foster, a director at McKinsey & Company, "Of the 10 leaders in vacuum tubes in 1955 only two were left in 1975. There were three variants of error in these case histories. First is the decision not to invest in the new technology. The second is to invest but picking the wrong technology. The third variant is cultural. Companies failed because of their inability to play two games at once: To be both effective defenders of what quickly became old technologies and effective attackers with new technologies."[1] Firms like Intel and Motorola were not saddled with internal conflict and inertia, and, as they grew, were able to re-create themselves. Other firms, like RCA, were unable to manage these multiple technological approaches; they were trapped by their successful pasts.

In contrast to RCA, consider Hattori-Seiko's watch business. Although Seiko was the dominant Japanese watch producer in the 1960s, Japanese firms were small players in the global watch market (see Table 2.2). Driven by an aspiration to be a global leader in the business and informed by internal experimentation among alternative oscillation technologies (quartz, mechanical, and tuning fork), Seiko's senior management team made a bold bet. It spearheaded Seiko's transformation from merely a mechanical watch firm into a quartz and mechanical watch company. This move into low-cost, high-quality watches triggered wholesale change within Seiko and, in turn, within the worldwide

**TABLE 2.2**

**WORLDWIDE WATCH PRODUCTION**

a) **Number of Firms and Workers in the Swiss Watch Industry, 1950–1985**

|  | Number of Firms | Employees |
|---|---|---|
| 1945 | 2,500 | 80,000 |
| 1950 | 1,863 | 60,239 |
| 1955 | 2,316 | 70,026 |
| 1960 | 2,167 | 74,216 |
| 1965 | 1,927 | 83,922 |
| 1970 | 1,618 | 89,448 |
| 1975 | 1,169 | 62,567 |
| 1976 | 1,083 | 55,182 |
| 1977 | 1,021 | 54,825 |
| 1978 | 979 | 52,669 |
| 1979 | 867 | 46,716 |
| 1980 | 861 | 46,998 |
| 1982 | 730 | 38,200 |
| 1985 | 600 | 32,000 |

SOURCE: Adapted from M. Porter and E. Hoff, "Hattori Seiko and the World Watch Industry in 1980." Case 9-385-3000. Boston: Harvard Business School, 1985. Copyright © 1985 by the President and Fellows of Harvard College. Reprinted by permission.

b) **Export of Watch Movements and Completed Watches, 1951–1980 (thousands of units)**

|  | Japan | Switzerland |
|---|---|---|
| 1951 | 31 | 33,549 |
| 1955 | 19 | 33,742 |
| 1960 | 145 | 40,981 |
| 1965 | 4,860 | 53,164 |
| 1970 | 11,399 | 71,437 |
| 1975 | 17,017 | 65,798 |
| 1980* | 68,300 | 50,986 |

*Includes movements [21].

SOURCE: Reprinted from Amy Glasmeier, "Technological Discontinuities and Flexible Production Networks: The Case of Switzerland and the World Watch Industry." *Research Policy,* 20, 1991, with kind permission from Elsevier Science-NL, Sara Burgerhartstraat 25, 1055 KV Amsterdam, The Netherlands.

watch industry. Even though the Swiss had invented both the quartz and tuning fork movements, they chose to reinvest in mechanical movements. But ultimately the quartz movement won the oscillation battle to become the industry standard. As Seiko and other Japanese firms prospered, the Swiss watch industry suffered drastically (see Table 2.2). By 1980, SSIH, the largest Swiss watch firm, was less than half the size of Seiko. Only when SSIH and Asuag, the two largest Swiss firms, went bankrupt and were taken over by the Swiss banks and transformed by Nicholas Hayek into SMH, would the Swiss move to recapture the watch market.[2]

## PATTERNS OF ORGANIZATIONAL CHANGE

Organizations are filled with sensible people and usually led by smart managers. Why, then, are innovation and change so difficult for successful organizations? And why are the patterns of success and failure so prevalent across industries and over time? How can a manager know when evolutionary or revolutionary change is called for?

Both the RCA and the Seiko examples illustrate the pattern by which organizations evolve: long periods of incremental change punctuated by revolutionary, or discontinuous, change. These organizational discontinuities are driven either by performance crises or by technology, competitive, or regulatory shifts. Whereas less successful firms (e.g., SSIH, RCA) react to environmental jolts, the more successful ones proactively initiate innovations that reshape their market (e.g., Seiko).[3]

### Growth through Evolution

For many years, biological evolutionary theory proposed that the process of adaptation occurred gradually over long time periods. The process was assumed to be one of variation, selection, and retention. Variations occurred naturally within species across generations. Those variations that were most adapted to the environment would, over time, enable a creature to survive and reproduce.[4] For instance, if the world became colder and snowier, animals that were whiter and had heavier coats would be more likely to survive. As climatic changes affected vegetation, those species with longer necks or stronger beaks might do better. Variation led to adaptation and fitness, which were subsequently retained through later generations. The environment changed gradually and species adapted slowly to these changes.

But this perspective did not consider a crucial question: What happened if the environment was characterized, not by gradual change, but by periodic discontinuities? What about rapid changes in temperature or dramatic shifts in the availability of food? Under these conditions, reliance on gradual change was a one-way ticket to extinction. Discontinuities required a different version of Darwinian theory—that of punctuated equilibria, in which long periods of gradual change were interrupted periodically by massive discontinuities. Survival or selection went to those species with the characteristics needed to exploit the new environment.

So it seems to be with organizations. Research on organizations has demonstrated many similarities between populations of the animal kingdom and those of organizations as diverse as wineries, newspapers, automobiles, biotech companies, and restaurants.[5] The results confirm that populations of organizations are subject to environmental pressures: They evolve through periods of incremental adaptation punctuated by discontinuities. Variations in organizational strategy and form are more or less suitable for different environmental conditions. Those organizations and managers most able to adapt to a given market or competitive environment will prosper. Over time, the fittest survive—until there is a major discontinuity, at which point, unlike the impersonal selection processes that occur in nature, managers are faced with the challenge of reconstituting their organizations to adjust to the new environment. Managers who try to adapt to discontinuities by making only incremental change are unlikely to succeed.[6]

The familiar S-curve, shown in Figure 2.1, describes organizational growth. For example, at its inception, Apple Computer was not so much an organization as a small group of people trying to design, produce, and sell a new product, the personal computer. With success came the beginnings of a formal organization, visible in a functional organization—assigned roles and responsibilities, some rudimentary systems for accounting and payroll, and a culture based on the shared expectations among employees about innovation, commitment, and speed. Success at this stage was seen in terms of congruence, or "fit," among the strategy, structure, people, and culture. Those who fit Apple's values and subscribed to its cultural norms stayed. Those who found Steve Jobs's and Stephen Wozniak's vision too cultish, left. Apple's early structure was aligned with the strategy and the critical tasks needed to implement it. Success flowed not only from having a new product with desirable features but also from the ability of

**FIGURE 2.1**

**ORGANIZATIONAL EVOLUTION VIA PUNCTUATED EQUILIBRIA: INCREMENTAL AND REVOLUTIONARY CHANGE AT APPLE**

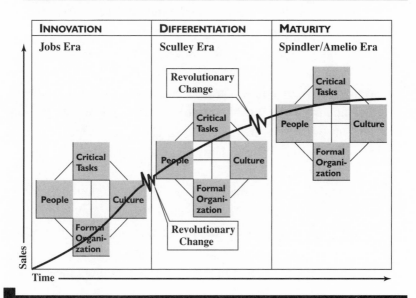

the organization to design, manufacture, market, and distribute the new PC. The systems in place tracked those outcomes and processes that were important for the implementation of a single product strategy.

As the firm continued its successful growth, several inexorable changes occurred. First, it got larger; more structure and systems were added. Although this trend toward professionalization was resisted by Jobs (who referred to professional managers as bozos), the new structures and procedures were required for efficiency and control. Without them, chaos would reign. As Apple got older, new norms were developed about what was important and acceptable and what would not be tolerated. The culture changed to reflect the new challenges.[7]

Inevitably, even Apple's strategy had to change. What used to be a single product firm selling the Apple PC and its successor, the Apple II, became a vendor of a broader range of products in increasingly competitive markets. Instead of a focused strategy, the firm shifted to a marketwide emphasis. Not only was Apple selling to personal computer users, but also to educational and industrial markets. This strategic shift required further adjustment to the structure, people, culture, and critical tasks. The well-publicized ouster of Jobs by Apple's board of directors reflected its judgment that John Sculley had the skills necessary to lead a larger, more diversified company.

As the personal computer industry continued to evolve, IBM PCs and the clones emerged. Microsoft's Windows operating system loosened Apple's grip on the easy-to-use graphical interface and triggered a battle among three incompatible operating systems—the Mac, IBM's OS/2, and Windows. Once Windows became the industry standard in operating systems, the basis of competition shifted to cost, quality, and efficiency. Faced with these realities, Apple managers once again had to rebalance the congruence among strategy, structure, people, and culture. The board of directors replaced Sculley as CEO in 1994 with Michael Spindler, who was seen as having the operational skills needed to run the company in a mature market. Spindler's task was to emphasize the efficiencies and lower margins required in today's markets and to establish Apple software as the industry standard in operating systems. With Apple's performance stagnant, its board chose a turnaround expert, Gil Amelio, to finish what Spindler could not accomplish.

Notice how Apple evolved over a 20-year period. Long periods of incremental change were punctuated by discontinuous, revolutionary change. Whereas the first discontinuity—the movement from selling one product to selling a whole line of products—was made proactively, the second discontinuity—the drive to compete in mature markets and to reestablish market leadership—resulted from a performance crisis. Both revolutions were initiated by new senior teams. Incremental changes were needed to increase the fit among strategy, structure, people, and culture in the short term. But while absolutely necessary for short-term success, incremental change is not sufficient for long-term success. Different stages of a product class require very different competencies, strategies, structures, cultures, and leadership skills. As we discuss in Chapter 7, in emerging markets, new technologies, innovation, and flexibility are critical. In mature markets, by contrast, cost, efficiency, and incremental innovation are key. These transitions must be navigated by discontinuous organizational change—either proactively or reactively. It is not by chance that Steve Jobs was successful at Apple until the market became more differentiated and demanded the skills of John Sculley. Nor is it surprising that, as the industry consolidated and competition emphasized costs, operations-oriented managers, Michael Spindler and, in turn, Gil Amelio, were selected to reorient Apple.

## Growth through Revolution: The Dynamics of Technology Cycles and Innovation Streams

Although organizational growth by itself can lead to a periodic need for discontinuous change, another, more fundamental, process also results in discontinuous change. This is a pervasive phenomenon that occurs across industries: the dynamic of technology cycles and innovation streams. The emergence of industry standards (or dominant designs) and subsequent radical departures from them (product substitutions) together make up a technology cycle (Figure 2.2). Technology cycles consist of fundamentally different kinds of innovation, or what we call innovation streams, that are found across all markets. To win over time, managers must not simply manage innovation, but manage streams of innovation.[8]

Whether in computer chips, automobiles, baby diapers, or cash management accounts, a technology cycle begins with a proliferation of innovation as a new product or service gains acceptance. For instance, at the turn of the century, bicycles and horse-driven carriages were threatened by the horseless carriage,

**FIGURE 2.2**

**PATTERNS OF INNOVATION OVER TIME**

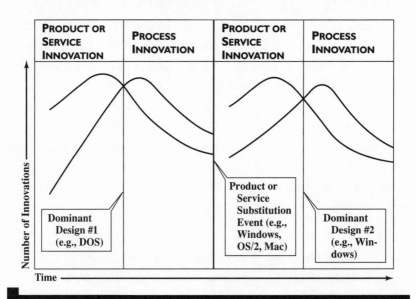

soon to be called the automobile. Early in this new product class there was substantial competition among alternative technologies. There were several competing alternative energy sources—steam, battery, and internal combustion engines—and different steering mechanisms and arrangements of passenger compartments. In a fairly short period of time, however, a dominant design emerged epitomized by the Model T Ford. This design consisted of an internal combustion engine, steering wheel on the left, brake pedal on the right, and clutch on the left. Once this standard emerged, the basis of competition in the automaking industry shifted from variations in how an automobile was powered and what it looked like to what features it had and how much it cost. The closing on the Model T at Ford was, in turn, associated with systemwide organizational change. At this point, the imperative for managers at Ford was to proactively change their strategy and organization to re-create this market.

A period of incremental change, based on the Model T design, lasted until 1919 when General Motors introduced a radically new concept in cars—the fully enclosed steel automobile. Within a few years, the fully enclosed auto became the industry standard. In response, Ford had to temporarily shut down its famous River Rouge production facility in order to retool it to produce a fully enclosed car. Ford's single-minded attention to incremental change and increased productivity had stunted its ability to quickly imitate General Motor's innovation.[9]

With a little imagination, any manager can feel the challenges in managing technology cycles and innovation streams. Holding aside the pressures of growth and success, managers must continually readjust their strategies and realign their organizations to reflect, or ideally proactively shape, the underlying dynamics of technological change in their markets. As we describe in more detail in Chapter 7, profound shifts in innovation streams (for example, the introduction of fully enclosed automobiles) trigger fundamental change in the bases of competition. These different bases of competition, in turn, demand revolutionary rather than incremental organizational change. Winning through innovation hinges on understanding the dynamics of technology cycles and innovation streams and being able to proactively shape innovation streams through discontinuous organizational change. The danger is that, facing a discontinuous change, successful firms may suffer from life-threatening inertia, which results from the very congruence that had made them successful.

## CONGRUENCE AS A MANAGERIAL TRAP

Successful companies learn what works well and incorporate this knowledge into their operations. During periods of evolutionary change, managers engage in continuous, incremental change, constantly refining the organization to better accomplish its mission. As these changes are comparatively small, the incongruence they introduce is controllable (e.g., an expansion in sales territory, a shift in emphasis among products in the product line, a new logistics package, or improved processing technology in production). The process of making changes of this sort is well known and the uncertainty created for people affected by such changes is tolerable. Opportunity is provided to anticipate and learn what is new. The overall system adapts.[10]

But there is a dark side to this success. As firms grow, they develop structures, processes, and systems to handle the increased complexity of their work. These structures and systems are interlinked, making proposed changes difficult, costly, and time-consuming to implement. Structural inertia—a resistance to change rooted in the size, complexity, and interdependence in the organization's structures, systems, and formal processes—sets in (see Figure 2.3).

Quite different from and significantly more pervasive than structural inertia is the cultural inertia that comes with organizational age and success. As organizations mature, part of their learning is embedded in the shared expectations about how things are to be done. These expectations are manifest in the informal norms, values, social networks, and in myths and heroes that have evolved over time. The more successful an organization has

**FIGURE 2.3**

**CONGRUENCE AS A MANAGERIAL TRAP:
THE SUCCESS SYNDROME**

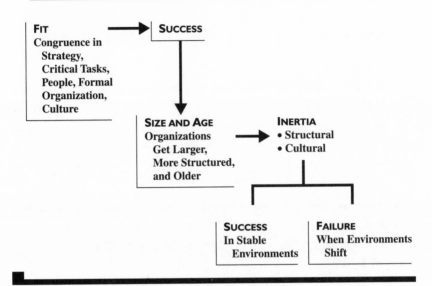

been, the more institutionalized or ingrained this learning becomes, further increasing cultural inertia and organizational complacency. In relatively stable environments, the firm's culture is a critical component of its success. Culture provides an effective way of controlling and coordinating people without elaborate and rigid formal control systems. Yet, when confronted with discontinuous change, the very culture that fostered success can quickly become a significant barrier to change. When Lou Gerstner took over as CEO at IBM, he recognized that simply crafting a new strategy was not the solution to IBM's predicament. In his view, "Fixing the culture is the most critical—and the most difficult—part of a corporate transformation."[11]

Structural and cultural inertia are powerful determinants of short-term success, yet can hold the organization hostage to its past. Whereas structural inertia is more easily recognized, discussed, and changed by managers, cultural inertia seems to be much more difficult for managers to deal with. Indeed, because it is so ephemeral and difficult to attack directly, cultural inertia is a key reason for managers' failure to successfully introduce revolutionary change—even when they know it is called for.

## THE CHALLENGE OF CULTURE AND SUSTAINED GROWTH

The paradox of culture in helping or hindering companies as they compete can be seen in many ways. Consider, for example, the list of companies shown in Table 2.3. In these firms, featured in the business press over the past few years, culture was seen as a significant driver of the organization's success or failure. What is notable about this list is its diversity. The importance of

**TABLE 2.3**

### CULTURE AS A FACTOR IN ORGANIZATIONAL SUCCESS OR FAILURE

| | | |
|---|---|---|
| Hewlett-Packard | British Airways | Federal Express |
| Oki Electric | Kodak | Sears |
| Johnson & Johnson | AlliedSignal | Deutsche Bank |
| General Electric | The Home Depot | PepsiCo |
| Silicon Graphics | McKinsey | Philips |
| Motorola | Royal Dutch/Shell | Bausch & Lomb |
| Levi Strauss | Southwest Airlines | Applied Materials |
| Microsoft | PPG | General Motors |
| Samsung | Nike | Wal-Mart |
| Siemens | Saturn | Boeing |
| Nordstrom | IBM | Nissan |
| Procter & Gamble | Tenneco | Rover |
| Coca Cola | Broken Hill Proprietary | Ford |
| Lucky-Goldstar | Goldman, Sachs | NUMMI |
| SBC Warburg | Westinghouse | United Airlines |
| Apple | Bear Stearns | British Petroleum |
| Swiss Bank Corp | Rubbermaid | Unilever |
| Nokia | Matsushita | Salomon |
| Intel | Chrysler | Rubbermaid |
| Aetna | Medtronics | Kao |

organizational culture transcends country, industry, and firm size. Whether an electronics giant like Samsung, a Hong Kong bank, a U.S. conglomerate like AlliedSignal, a high-tech firm like Applied Materials, a low-tech company such as Nordstrom, or a car manufacturer like Nissan, Rover, or General Motors, culture appears to be a critical factor in the performance of the company. Moreover, people use similar language in describing the importance of culture. Listen to Yukata Kume, former president of Nissan: "The most challenging task I faced when I became president five years ago was to reform the corporate culture . . . I decided that the major reason for our suffering or business predicament lay within Nissan itself."[12] Or Jack Welch at GE commenting on the future demands on organizations: "In the nineties the heroes, the winners, will be entire companies that have developed cultures that instead of fearing the pace of change, relish it."[13]

While news articles about success and failure do not constitute proof of anything, they offer an interesting window on the concerns of practicing managers and savvy journalists. Whether the issue is can Nike successfully export its "Just do it" culture to help drive global growth, or can Nokia, a Finnish maker of mobile phones, shed its stodgy culture in time to compete in the fast-moving telecommunications market, the managerial challenges are similar: How can managers diagnose and actively shape organizational cultures to both execute today's strategies and create streams of innovation that shape tomorrow's competitive advantage? To help focus on the crucial issue of organizational cultures, reflect on the following examples, one in which organizational culture helped a firm succeed, the other in which culture provided a significant part of the problem in adapting to new circumstances.

## The Good News: Culture Can Provide Competitive Advantage

First, consider the remarkable transformation of British Airways. In 1981, British Airways lost almost $1 billion. Their customers often referred to the airline by its initials, BA, as Bloody Awful. Ask frequent flyers about their experiences on BA then, and they'll tell you horror stories. Even the employees were embarrassed. One employee acknowledges, "I remember going to parties in the late 1970s, and if you wanted to have a civilized conversation, you didn't actually say that you worked for British Airways, because it got you talking about people's last travel experience, which was usually an unpleasant one." When the British government announced that the firm was to be privatized, the *Financial Times* sniffed that some investors might buy the stock, but only because "every market has a few masochists."

Yet a scant five years later, BA's profits were the highest in the industry: 94 percent of its employees bought stock in 1987 when the firm went public, and passengers were making statements like, "I can't tell you how my memory of British Airways as a company and the experience I had 10 years ago contrasts with today. The improvement in service is truly remarkable." What accounted for this turnaround? The answer is largely to be found in the cultural revolution engineered by the firm's top management, Lord King and Sir Colin Marshall.

After deciding that it was in the service business rather than the transportation business, British Airways sent virtually its entire 37,000-person work force through a two-day culture change program entitled "Putting People First." Almost all the 1,400 managers went through a five-day version entitled "Managing People First" (MPF). On the surface this program is not conceptually unique. What separates MPF from most management training sessions is its magnitude, the consistency with which it is applied, and the support of top management. Chairman Colin Marshall called it the "single most important program now in operation" at BA and he has addressed almost all the 64 MPF classes.[14]

British Airway's culture change effort emphasized instilling the new culture, establishing an evaluation scheme that measured not only what managers did but also how they did it, and designing a compensation program with bonuses up to 20 percent based on managerial behavior. Managers at BA appreciate that any airline can load passengers on a plane and fly them across the Atlantic. BA understands that any competitive advantage has to be in the service it offers customers. As Rob Nelson, head of the program notes, "The issue with customer service is that you can train monkeys to smile and make eye contact, but what the hell do you do when you get a nonstandard requirement?"

Retaining essentially the same work force, flying largely the same routes, and using the same technology, British Airways has become one of the world's leading airlines. Its competitive advantage is not in strategy or technology but in a culture shared throughout the organization. British Airways' cultural revolution permitted major process innovations in the way it handled its passengers. These process innovations helped redefine passenger expectations about service quality, which competitors have found difficult to imitate.

## The Bad News: Culture Can Stifle Innovation and Change

The very culture associated with a firm's earlier success often becomes part of its downfall. Think briefly about two icons of American business success and the difficulties they have faced: IBM and Sears.

Certainly the computer business is a complex one. IBM was, and is, a very large firm, which complicates any decision-making process. Nevertheless, numerous presumably smart people were employed specifically to anticipate changes and ensure that the firm was prepared to meet them. How, then, can we account for a failure that has cost almost 200,000 people their jobs and shareholders a loss of billions of dollars?

In part, the answer includes aspects of strategy, organizational design, technology, and staffing. However, perhaps the most important piece, and certainly a part of the solution, lies in the culture of IBM—a culture characterized by an inward focus, extensive procedures for resolving issues through consensus and "push back," an arrogance bred by previous success, and a sense of entitlement on the part of some employees that guaranteed jobs without a quid pro quo. This culture, masquerading as the old IBM's basic beliefs in excellence, customer satisfaction, and respect for the individual led to a preoccupation with internal procedures rather than an understanding of the changing market. In his letter to the shareholders in the 1993 annual report, CEO Lou Gerstner states, "We have been too bureaucratic and too preoccupied with our own view of the world." He sees as one of his toughest and most critical tasks changing this entrenched and patriarchal culture into one characterized by a sense of urgency. Without this shift, he believes IBM will continue to squander its talent and technology.[15]

In a very different industrial context, a similar drama is playing out at Sears, the great American retailer. Again, the picture is a complicated one and it would be wrong to oversimplify it. The broad outlines of the problem are, however, quite visible. Until 1991, Sears was the largest retailer in the United States with more than 800 stores and 500,000 employees, including more than 6,000 at headquarters in the Sears Tower in Chicago. For decades it was America's family department store, a place where one could buy everything from clothes to tools to kitchen appliances. However, by the mid-1980s, trouble had begun to surface. Market share had fallen 15 percent from its high in the 1970s, the stock price had dropped by 40 percent since Edward Brennan became CEO in 1985, and chronic high costs hindered Sears from matching the prices of competitors such as Wal-Mart, Kmart, Circuit City, The Home Depot, and other low-cost specialty stores.

Under Brennan's leadership, Sears made a number of strategic changes in attempts to halt the slide. Yet the execution of the strategy was dismal. Observers and analysts attributed the failure to Brennan's inability to revamp the old Sears culture that, as one respected analyst noted, was a "culture rooted in a long tradition of dominating the retailing industry. But this success bred in Sears executives an arrogance and an internal focus that was almost xenophobic." Another observed that "The main problem with Sears is that its managers and executives are 'Sears-ized,'—so indoctrinated in the lore of past glories and so entrenched in an overwhelming bureaucracy that they cannot change easily."[16] The old Sears culture, like the old IBM culture, was a product of its success: proud, inward-looking, and resistant to change.

The lesson is simple: Organizational culture is key both to short-term success and, unless managed correctly, to long-term failure. Culture can provide competitive advantage, but it can also create obstacles to the innovation and change necessary to be successful. In the face of significant changes in technology, regulation, or competition, great managers understand this dynamic and effectively manage the short-term demands for increasing congruence and bolstering today's culture and the periodic need to transform their organization and re-create their unit's culture. These organizational transformations involve simultaneous shifts in the firm's structure and systems as well as in its culture and competencies. Making changes in structure and systems is relatively easy; making changes in culture is not. Actively managing organizational cultures that can handle both incremental and discontinuous change is perhaps the most demanding aspect of the management of strategic innovation and change.

## AMBIDEXTROUS ORGANIZATIONS: LEADING EVOLUTIONARY AND REVOLUTIONARY CHANGE

How can managers break the tyranny of today's success? As we discuss in Chapter 7, ambidextrous organizations—organizations with internally inconsistent competencies, structures, and cultures, yet with a single vision—provide the range of capabilities for excelling both today and tomorrow. They give managers options from which they can proactively shape evolving innovation streams. But when a management team decides either to shape a dominant design or to initiate a product or process discontinuity, it must also launch discontinuous organizational change.

For managers this means operating part of the time in a world of relative stability and incremental change, and part of the time in a world of revolutionary change. Innovation streams and technology cycles require that managers periodically destroy their existing products and organizational alignments as innovation streams evolve. As Hewlett-Packard CEO Lou Platt notes, "We have to be willing to cannibalize what we're doing today in order to ensure our leadership in the future. It's counter to human nature but you have to kill your business while it is still working."[17]

Yet building ambidextrous organizations and initiating revolutionary change is difficult. Four hundred years ago Niccolo Machiavelli noted, "There is no more delicate matter to take in hand, nor more dangerous to conduct, nor more doubtful in its success, than to be a leader in the introduction of changes. For he who innovates will have for enemies all those who are well off under the old order of things, and only lukewarm supporters in those who might be better off under the new."[18]

While there are clear benefits to proactive change, only a small minority of farsighted firms initiate discontinuous change before a performance decline. Doing so entails risk. One reason for RCA's failure to compete in the solid-state market and for SSIH's inability to compete in quartz movements was the firms' reluctance to sacrifice a certain revenue stream from vacuum tubes and mechanical watches for as yet uncertain profits from transistors and quartz watches. Yet great managers are willing to take this step. In Andy Grove's words, "There is at least one point in the history of any company when you have to change dramatically to rise to the next performance level. Miss the moment and you start to decline."[19]

The real test of leadership, then, is to be able to compete successfully in both the short term through increasing the alignment or fit among strategy, structure, individual competencies, culture, and processes while simultaneously preparing for the inevitable organization revolutions required by shifting innovation streams. The ability to shape innovation streams hinges on an organization's ability to simultaneously engage in multiple types of innovation. Managing an organization that can succeed at both incremental and radical innovation is like juggling. A juggler who is very good at manipulating just a couple of balls is not interesting. It is only when the juggler can handle multiple balls at one time that his or her skill is respected. For organizations, success for both today and tomorrow requires managers who can simultaneously juggle several inconsistent organizational architectures and cultures and who can build and manage ambidextrous organizations.

Building ambidextrous organizations and managing innovation streams and revolutionary change are all anchored in today's success. If an organization is not successful today, there can be no tomorrow. Chapter 3 introduces the fundamental building blocks of winning through innovation—setting a unit's strategy, objectives, and vision and, in turn, clarifying crucial performance or opportunity gaps. By managing more successfully for today, managers provide the leverage for shaping innovation streams for tomorrow.

# C H A P T E R 3

## DEFINING PROBLEMS AND
## OPPORTUNITIES:
## A FOUNDATION FOR SUCCESS

FOR MORE THAN A CENTURY, THE INDUSTRIAL GASES
Division of BOC, a large British conglomerate, had joined the
march of industrial progress serving the British Empire. Its
35,000 people worked in 15 countries to produce and deliver
oxygen, nitrogen, helium, and other natural gases to a variety of
users, ranging from food to steel to semiconductors.

BOC Gases maintained a steady course until 1993. Then, in
a sharp break with its traditions, C. K. Chow, an aggressive, Hong
Kong–based entrepreneur and head of BOC's North Pacific
region, was promoted to CEO. Chow knew that BOC Gases faced
a set of emerging problems. Several of its key global customers
were complaining about getting mixed messages and confusing
reports about prices, products, and technologies from the various
regions. Those customers were demanding global solutions
while BOC was intent on providing independent, local responses.
Chow also believed that BOC was beginning to fall behind
technologically. With competitors forging ahead with bold new
products and processes, BOC seemed to be introducing only local

innovations. In his view, the firm's ability to shape technology and develop global innovations was poor. While Chow saw a set of opportunities for BOC, he faced a set of powerful regional managers who were quite content with BOC's current performance. Chow knew that without the regional managers' energy, there would be no change.

## MANAGERIAL PROBLEM SOLVING: PROBLEM OR OPPORTUNITY DEFINITION

Whether at BOC or in the U.S. Navy, if an organization faces no threat, inertia and the status quo will undermine needed innovation. In contrast, organizational crises often trigger substantial innovation and change. All too frequently, the necessity to change is born of crisis conditions (for example, at IBM and the Swiss watchmakers). The most successful firms, however, do not wait for crises to occur; rather, their managers say, "If we don't move now, we will be in trouble in the near future." They proactively generate crises and opportunities by creating, and solving, problems.

We now focus on the initial step in managerial problem solving—problem and opportunity identification. Just as physicians first focus on their patients' presenting symptoms, managers must identify their organization's critical problems. This done, they can then diagnose the causes of these problems and, in turn, take action to address them—while avoiding unexpected side effects. Similarly, once opportunities are identified, managers can analyze those aspects of the current organization that will get in the way of achieving the unit's aspirations.[1]

How can managers determine what are their most important problems or opportunities? First, a manager (and his or her team) needs to be clear about the strategy, objectives, and vision of the unit. Such clarity is the bedrock of managing innovation and change. Only when strategy, objectives, and vision are defined can managers move on to an honest appraisal of the current performance of their organization. The comparison between expected performance (based on strategy, objectives, and vision) and actual performance requires managers to see the performance of their organization as it really is—not how they hope, imagine, or wish it to be. The difference between expectations and actual performance constitutes the performance gap that a manager and his or her team must diagnose and resolve.

Strategy is not reserved for senior levels. It is a critical part of every manager's job. Knowing clearly how an organization or a unit intends to compete and what its objectives and aspirations are is the first step in disciplined problem definition and problem solving. If there is any ambiguity or lack of clarity in this process, managers will find it difficult to manage effectively for either today or tomorrow. It is the old cliché that unless you are clear about where you are going, any direction is fine.

In our experience, managers have a great deal of difficulty understanding critical problems and opportunities. Confronted by the relentless pressures and complexities of day-to-day business, operating managers frequently lack the time and distance necessary to define objectively the problems they face. Yet, without attaining clarity in problem definition, managers may take seemingly effective short-term actions that, in fact, fail to address the larger, more critical long-term problems or opportunities. At BOC, for example, until Chow and his team clarify and agree on the importance of global customers and technology development, managerial attention will continue to focus on local issues.

While performance problems are real and immediate issues, opportunities are potential future problems if the organization does not act today. Excellent managers are those whose units have no performance gaps today but are able to define future opportunities to energize the organization now. Contrary to "If it's not broken, don't fix it," we suggest that if the organization is not broken, consider breaking it by creating opportunity gaps. Lt. Sims's difficulty arose in part because the navy had no performance gap—it was already the most accurate navy in the world. It took Teddy Roosevelt to perceive that if the navy did not implement continuous aim gunfire before its competitors did, it would be in trouble in the future. Defining opportunity gaps in the face of today's success is a hard sell.

The way a problem or an opportunity is defined determines the solutions considered. Every manager confronts similar issues every day—deciding which of the many problems or opportunities facing the organization need to be addressed, even if doing so may affect short-term performance. Unless the manager is clear about the difference between expectations and outcomes, problems or opportunities are likely to be seen as ambiguous or political, and innovation and change are, in turn, stifled.

## UNDERSTANDING STRATEGIC CONTEXT

But how are decisions made about what strategy to adopt, which objectives to shoot for, and what will be a unit's guiding vision? Although there are no easy answers, three key factors set the context in which a manager and his or her team determine their strategy, objectives, and vision: (1) the environment in which the unit operates, (2) the resources available to the manager, and (3) the history of the organization or unit (see Figure 3.1). Understanding these opportunities and constraints helps a manager formulate realistic aspirations and directions for his or her unit.[2]

### Environment

**COMPETITIVE.** In deciding on strategy, objectives, and vision, managers must first assess the competitive opportunities and threats facing their unit. These include entries into and exits from the unit's product class (who are the current and likely competitors?) and the nature of the competitive rivalry (cost, service, new products). Chow and his team, for instance, identified key competitive rivalry both from existing industrial gas suppliers

FIGURE 3.1

## FROM STRATEGIC CONTEXT TO STRATEGIC CHOICES

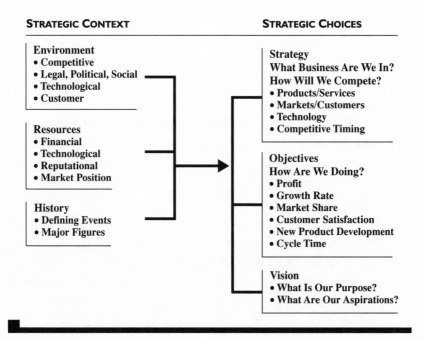

STRATEGIC CONTEXT      STRATEGIC CHOICES

**Environment**
- Competitive
- Legal, Political, Social
- Technological
- Customer

**Resources**
- Financial
- Technological
- Reputational
- Market Position

**History**
- Defining Events
- Major Figures

**Strategy**
What Business Are We In?
How Will We Compete?
- Products/Services
- Markets/Customers
- Technology
- Competitive Timing

**Objectives**
How Are We Doing?
- Profit
- Growth Rate
- Market Share
- Customer Satisfaction
- New Product Development
- Cycle Time

**Vision**
- What Is Our Purpose?
- What Are Our Aspirations?

(L'Air Liquide and Praxar) as well as from new suppliers of industrial gases. These global players were competing on service, product quality, and innovation.

**LEGAL, POLITICAL, SOCIAL.** Managers also need to consider how legal, political, and social factors affect their ability to compete. This requires that they understand the competitive consequences of regulation, deregulation, and privatization as well as ecological issues and changing customer demographics. Depending on the unit or organization, this assessment may include such factors as the opening up of Europe in 1992, the passage of the North American Free Trade Agreement, the abolishment of apartheid in South Africa, the reunification of Germany, or the shift in government in Hong Kong in 1997. At

BOC, for example, the opening of the EC had direct implications on the nature of competition in Europe, even as the end of apartheid fundamentally changed their organization in South Africa.

**TECHNOLOGICAL.** Across industries, from high to low technology, for services and products, technological change can pose a profound competitive opportunity or threat. Technological shifts and the evolution of industry standards can rapidly change a product class (recall the industries listed in Table 1.1). Whether in information services, banking, aluminum, or automobile manufacturing, shifts in technology increase competition or open up periods of ferment that are often threatening to veteran firms and offer opportunities for new entrants. Given the expense and complexity of technologies and the nature of technological change, no one firm can control the pace and direction of technological change. Yet managers must track technological opportunities and threats as they make strategic decisions. For example, at BOC, Chow and his team had to consider the impact of noncryogenic gas supplies. The industrial gases business is currently dominated by cryogenic air-separation processes, but if noncryogenic technology were perfected, it could transform the industry.

**CUSTOMER DEMAND.** Finally, in an era of total quality management, managers need to understand their internal and external customers' evolving requirements. For example, Chow's team at BOC observed that more and more of their customers were global and wanted integrated gas supply solutions, as opposed to BOC's traditional country-by-country solutions.

## Resources

Every manager must also appreciate the full range of resources—financial, technological, reputational, and personnel—available to the organization, and realistically assess their strengths and weaknesses compared to those of competitors. Managers with substantial financial, technological, and human resources have greater strategic flexibility than managers with limited resources. A dean at a wealthy, private college, for example, is likely to have more strategic options than a dean of a publicly supported university.

## History

The final contextual factor a manager must be sensitive to is his or her unit's unique history. The behavior of any organization today is, at least in part, a reflection of past events and precedents. Organizational history can have powerful, unnoticed effects on present behavior.[3] Managers need to understand their unit's past, how it was founded or formed, the key events or crises that shaped its evolution, and how the unit has been managed. This history is often reflected in current culture, processes, structure, and competencies. At BOC, Chow and his team quickly realized that they would be unable to deal with customer requirements for integrated gas solutions unless they were able to get beyond BOC's historical legacy of independent regions. The older and more distinguished the organization, the more its history needs to be considered. In terms of innovation and change, organizational history often holds a firm hostage to its past.

Managers must also understand who their predecessor was and what his or her legacy is, what their predecessors did and did not do. These prior actions shape today's opportunities and constraints. If these precedents are ignored, managers run the risk of falling victim to ghosts of leaders past. For example, at BOC, Chow understood that his predecessors took a laissez-faire approach to managing BOC as a federation of autonomous business units. The regional directors had operated as autonomous entrepreneurs for decades. With this knowledge Chow could assess the aspects of BOC's history that would impede needed change.

## FROM STRATEGIC CONTEXT TO STRATEGIC CHOICES

Understanding the context of environment, resources, and history, managers can make better decisions about a unit's strategy, objectives, and vision. A unit's strategy defines what business it is in, how it intends to compete, and who its target customers are. Objectives are a set of measurable expectations against which actual performance can be compared. While strategy and objectives define what business a unit is in, its customers, and its standards of performance, vision expresses a unit's broader aspiration.

### Business Unit Strategy

Strategy is embodied in the choices made by managers about how a unit wants to compete. Given the opportunities and threats faced and the unit's strengths and weaknesses, strategy is defined by choices that include:

1. *Products or services offered.* The first strategic decision is the choice of what product or service will be produced and the range of offerings. Anaquest was a specialty pharmaceutical company that traditionally focused on a narrow range of anesthetic agents. In 1991, Martin McGlynn, Anaquest's new president, reassessed the firm's strategy. Faced with increased competition from Baxter and Abbot, and increasingly frequent requests from anesthesiologists for full-service suppliers, McGlynn and his team moved Anaquest from a single-product anesthetics producer to a broad supplier of anesthetic agents.

2. *Target markets or customers.* The second strategic decision is the choice of target market or customer. Whether the customer is internal or external, whether the unit produces a product or a service, managers need to determine who their customers are. Any change in customers also reflects a change

in business unit strategy. McGlynn and his team felt that Anaquest held a strong position in the mature U.S. market, yet had no real presence in Europe or the Far East. They decided not only to compete in the North American market, but also to move aggressively into relatively underserved markets in Europe and Japan. Whereas McGlynn moved Anaquest into new markets, a competitive assessment by Chow and his team led them to conclude that BOC must be strong in both regional and industrial markets. They moved to bolster BOC's historical geographic strengths with market sector strength in electronic gases, food, and steel.

3. *Technology choices.* Whether in high- or low-technology industries, whether producing a product or service, managers need to be clear about their technological choices in the service of their unit's business strategy. Since no organization or business unit can afford to invest in all relevant technologies, managers must inevitably choose which technologies to invest in and how much to invest.[4] Having clarified their business strategy, McGlynn and his team had to make a choice. Because Anaquest could not afford to invest in the three inhalant and transdermal technologies simultaneously, it decided to focus its limited technology investment on a single inhalant and a single transdermal technology.

4. *Competitive timing.* A final aspect of business unit strategy is that of competitive timing, or when to move in a product class. Should the product or service be the first in the market and attempt to gain brand awareness and market position, or should managers wait until the market has been developed and consumer tastes are known? For example, McGlynn and his team at Anaquest had to decide whether the firm wanted to be a first mover in the anesthetics market or should wait to be a quick second. The timing decision can have significant consequences for resource allocation and the design of organizations.

## Business Unit Objectives

While strategy defines how the business will compete, objectives are a measurable set of shorter term standards and targets used to assess performance. Thus, managers must not only be clear about products, markets, technology, and timing, but must also define objectives or standards to assess performance. These objectives may include profit and growth rates, market share, customer satisfaction, new product development, and cycle time.

Scott Kisting is a regional vice president at Norwest Bank who was recruited to help reinvigorate branch banking. Prior to his arrival, Norwest branches had sales volumes objectives and a host of sales measurement systems, which often led local managers to focus on selling whatever would help them meet their daily sales goals. Predictably, these were often the easiest products to move. So, for instance, rather than rolling over a $50,000 CD, an enterprising bank manager would encourage the customer to purchase five $10,000 CDs. Needless to say, Norwest was not developing long-term relationships with its customers. As a part of his strategy to improve sales through building better relationships and providing improved service, Kisting developed measures to track the process of relationship building: how many calls were made, how many households were profiled, and teller-customer satisfaction surveys. The results were remarkable: Customer satisfaction increased dramatically. What Kisting did was clarify his strategy and then establish objectives and, in turn, develop measures appropriate for assessing the success of his strategy. Business unit strategy, then, reflects the way in which an organization competes, and objectives reflect measurable standards to which the management team holds their unit accountable.

## Business Unit Vision

Vision defines an organization's overarching purpose and captures the reason for its existence in a way that allows members to feel good about their efforts. Vision reflects the aspirations of a manager's unit. It offers a reason why members of the organization should feel some passion about successfully executing the strategy. Where a good strategy and objectives engage people intellectually, a vision engages people emotionally.[5]

In a 1992 interview, John Young, then CEO of Hewlett-Packard, commented, "Maximizing shareholder wealth has always been way down the list. Yes, profit is a cornerstone of what we do—it is a measure of our contribution and a means of self-financed growth—but it has never been the *point* in and of itself."[6] He went on to explain that the real point is to do something that you can be proud of. HP's vision, expressed in the "HP Way" and continually reinforced by management, is one that engages people's emotions. The HP Way expresses the principles the company represents and how it is managed, including a belief in people, participation, recognition, security, and a chance to learn. These principles are continually reinforced by management. They form an important basis for a relationship between people and the firm; a relationship that engages people emotionally as well as economically.

There are important practical benefits to a well-articulated vision. When a vision is clear, consistently articulated, and widely shared, decisions throughout the organization can be made in a more consistent, directed way. However, if the vision is not clear, or if senior managers do not practice what they preach, these inconsistencies trigger cynicism, frustration, and increased organizational politics. The lack of a clear vision and clear core values forces managers to rely on formal controls to guide behavior, which is an ineffective way to harness human assets. Of all the concepts in this book, vision is the most vague and ephemeral, and yet perhaps one of the most crucial.

In drafting a competitive vision, the following guidelines are useful. First, the vision statement should be short and to the point. Second, it should be engaging and challenging; it must be a stretch. Third, it must be realistic, not the Boy Scout code. Finally, it should not be confounded with strategy or measurable objectives. Vision can be communicated through statements like, "We will be . . . ," or "We aspire to be . . . ," or "We intend to be . . ." Management formulates these statements and, more important, owns and behaves consistently with every word in them.

One of the first actions Paul O'Neill took upon becoming CEO of Alcoa in 1989 was to draft, with his top team, a vision for the firm. After several days of work, reflection, and debate, they decided on the following: Alcoa "will be the best aluminum company in the world, and a leader in other businesses in which we choose to compete. Alcoa will be a growing worldwide company dedicated to excellence through quality, . . ."[7] While some of Alcoa's strategies, objectives, and structures have changed since then, its fundamental vision has not. Indeed, were you to meet O'Neill on an airplane, you would see that his passion and energy still focus on this vision. He speaks with conviction about the details of his strategy, objectives, earnings, and technology, but his real fervor is to infuse the corporation with the passion for Alcoa's vision. He wants Alcoa's 56,000 employees all to feel passionately that they can, and will, be the highest quality, lowest cost producer of aluminum in the world.

Skip LeFauve, CEO of Saturn, engaged his employees in a similar exercise. Feeling that aspiring to customer "satisfaction" was too ordinary, they determined to aspire to customer "enthusiasm." At General Electric, Welch and his team have espoused a clear, simple vision: "GE will be the world's most aggressive, innovative actor in any business sector in which it operates. GE will be the fastest, most simple and self-confident organization in the world." This vision guides BOC: "BOC Gases will be recognized as the most customer-focused industrial gases business world-wide. We will achieve this vision through innovation and service created by working together around the globe."

By themselves, these visions are just words unless management convinces employees that they are important enough to live by. Whether they are referred to as mission statements, mottoes, creeds, pledges, aspirations, or philosophies is unimportant. What is important is that people take them seriously. The danger is that the effort to draft a vision becomes simply another exercise, a waste of time. A vision that people believe in can add passion and enthusiasm to an organization. A vision that people either do not understand or believe in undermines management's credibility and is a source of great cynicism.

People want to believe that they are part of an effort to do something beyond making a profit but sometimes feel vaguely embarrassed by the hype often associated with vision statements. However, there are sound reasons why visions can be extraordinarily valuable. A widely shared, strongly held vision can provide a sense of psychological attachment and motivation that cannot be duplicated with formal incentives. When a vision helps create the core values of an organization, it can provide the foundation for the culture or social control system that is essential in rapidly changing situations. When communicated in a way that people believe, a vision becomes a part of the organization's motivational foundation. Well-implemented organizational visions help coordinate action without formal rules and systems.

Just as articulating a vision is crucial at the corporate level, it is also vital for divisions, business units, and functional areas—from the chairman to the first-level supervisor. The watch division of Hattori-Seiko, a diversified Japanese organization, has had a single overarching vision since the early 1960s. Before the Tokyo Olympic Games, the general manager espoused a vision for Hattori-Seiko's watch business: "We will dominate world-wide watch production." Note that in the 1960s, it was not possible to know whether this was a vision or a hallucination! At the time, Seiko was a minor player in the watch industry. Yet, anchored by this vision, Seiko was able to adapt its strategy and objectives and, brick by brick, build an enormous presence in the watch industry.

While corporate visions tend to be broad and abstract, lower-level visions are more specific and concrete. Managers throughout Alcoa, for instance, are encouraged to articulate their own units' specific aspirations. Thus a mine manager in Australia says, "We will be the most customer-oriented, quality focused mine in Australia." If O'Neill can attain such clarity of vision throughout Alcoa, his firm's abstract vision can become reality.

Visions at every level of the firm must be internally consistent, short, simple, understandable, and emotionally engaging. Great corporations and business units have relatively stable visions, even as strategy and objectives change as a product class evolves. These visions can serve as an organizational anchor when other aspects of the business shift. As James Collins and Jerry Porras conclude in their study of visionary organizations, "The essence of a visionary company comes in the translation of its core ideology and its own unique drive for progress into the very fabric of the organization—into goals, strategies, tactics, policies, processes, cultural practices, management behaviors, building layouts, pay systems, accounting systems, job design—into everything that the company does."[8] Collins and Porras are absolutely clear in asserting that a vision statement does not make for a visionary company. That requires relentless attention to living the values. This means that if subordinate managers receive mixed messages from above, they must still articulate a vision for their own unit and attempt to manage upward in a way that minimizes conflicting signals.

When we ask executives from firms around the world to describe their company's visions, we get similar answers. Most organizations aspire to be the world's best, want to delight customers, or aim to be the most innovative in their industry. Indeed, Pêchney and Aluswiss, European aluminum firms, have very similar visions to Alcoa's. Such similarity is not necessarily bad. Most people respond to certain universal values such as striving to be the best, respecting others, and contributing to the social good. While there is little variability in visions, there is great variability in their execution. Because execution separates winners from losers, we spend the bulk of our book on executing strategy, objectives, and vision more swiftly than the competition.

In summary, managers operate in complex and uncertain circumstances. Often there is no way to know whether a particular strategy or vision is correct, yet the consequences of strategic error can be substantial. To cope with this unpleasant reality, managers need to be able to do two things. First, they must be accurate and realistic in assessing competitive opportunities and threats as well as their own strengths and weaknesses. Second, should these assessments prove incorrect, managers must take their only recourse—being strategically flexible, thus allowing for rapid adjustment to changing circumstances. In this regard, the capacity to make swift organizational changes, and to learn from one's actions, offers some insurance in a rapidly shifting world.

## IDENTIFYING GAPS

Having established a clear strategy, objectives, and vision, managers must then look at the hard, cold reality of the organization's current performance to determine how it is doing in reaching those goals. That examination will reveal performance gaps or opportunity gaps—where the organization might be in the future if it proactively initiates change today.

### Performance Gaps

The desired organizational performance expressed in strategy, objectives, and vision must be assessed against actual performance. Organizational performance gaps are the differences between desired and real performance (see Figure 3.2).[9] For example, in 1995 Ed Fox was the captain of New York City's 75th Precinct. When William Bratton was appointed police commissioner, he mandated a 10-point across-the-board decrease in crime rates. As a manager, Ed Fox clearly saw the performance gap his precinct faced: a target of a 10 percent reduction while crime rates in his district were up, on some measures, 24 percent.

In identifying performance gaps, it is crucial to recognize who is the manager doing the diagnosis: where is that manager

**FIGURE 3.2**

**PERFORMANCE AND OPPORTUNITY GAPS**

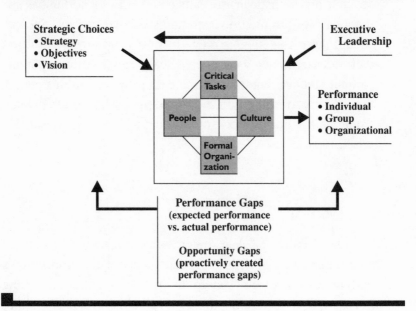

positioned in the larger system, who is his or her supervisor, and who are his or her direct reports. What constitutes a problem will depend critically on those variables. Performance gaps are defined from a particular manager's perspective. For Captain Fox, his performance problem concerns the 75th Precinct, not the larger issues in the Bronx. His solutions will depend on the unique circumstances he and his officers face, not on the larger issues faced by Bratton.

The specific outputs to examine are contingent on the unit's strategy, objectives, and vision. For example, in 1982, when People Express Airline was targeting the "sofa trade" (people who would otherwise sit on the sofa in front of the TV instead of traveling), complaints from business travelers about the lack of an interline reservation system were not important outcomes. In 1984, after a decision was made to target business customers, however, their complaints became critical organizational outcomes. Similarly, as soon as Chow and his team at BOC Gases identified global customer satisfaction and market leadership as key objectives, their lack of effectiveness in meeting global customer requirements became strategic problems.

Managers will likely uncover many performance gaps. Rather than taking on too many issues simultaneously, they should take the next step and prioritize the top two or three critical ones. Prioritizing performance gaps is fundamentally a political issue. Managers must make clear, or help their subordinates make clear, today's most critical problems. At GE, Welch and his senior team drove systemwide change by ensuring that all managers participated in GE's Work-Out Program. Welch communicated forcefully that to live up to GE's vision of speed, simplicity, and self-confidence, and to be number one or two, required the full participation of all managers in the program. It was a nonnegotiable issue. Once today's critical problems are solved, managers can then move on to the next set of critical performance gaps.

## Opportunity Gaps

Highly effective organizations may not have any pressing problems at a given point in time. In such cases, managers must look outside the firm and ask what will or might happen in the product class in the future. Based on these predictions, the manager can create an opportunity for the future to which the organization must respond today.[10] When O'Neill arrived at Alcoa in 1989, it was already the world's most profitable aluminum company. O'Neill and his team, however, believed that possible changes in the world aluminum market (e.g., the dumping of low-cost Russian ingots) would confront Alcoa with serious cost and quality problems in the future. Given these predicted competitive shifts, O'Neill and his team initiated sweeping changes throughout the firm, including a set of cultural, structural, and reward system changes based on the quality of Alcoa's products and services. Alcoa moved before it was forced to.

Alternatively, managers can create opportunity gaps by raising performance standards. In 1990 PepsiCo's sales were more
than $7 billion and earnings were up 10 percent, but Craig
Weatherup, president of the Pepsi-Cola division, feared that the
soda market would turn flat. In anticipation, he created a crisis,
declaring that only a 15 percent growth in earnings would be
satisfactory in the future. By changing the division's strategy and
objectives, Weatherup defined an opportunity gap that mandated
the efforts of his 30,000 employees. Three years later, the division
met its 15% earnings objective.

A senior executive at Chrysler is quoted as saying, "Living
with success is always a challenge." He recognized that success
is often associated with a tendency to become conservative, to
avoid risk, and to rely on proven ways of doing things. These
inertial forces hold organizations hostage to their distinguished
pasts and stunt innovation and change. Without the creative
tensions associated with clear performance or opportunity gaps,
organizations become stagnant. They reinforce the status quo,
becoming better and better at competing in the short term and
consequently becoming highly vulnerable in the face of long-
term change. The recent histories of IBM, General Motors,
Philips, DEC, and Jaguar are too striking and similar to ignore.
Indeed, both Microsoft and Intel live by the adage coined by
Andy Grove, CEO of Intel: "Only the paranoid survive."

Winning through innovation starts with managers and their
teams identifying performance and opportunity gaps clearly.
While this assertion may sound obvious, it is remarkable how
many managers engage in change efforts without a clear understanding of their unit's critical performance or opportunity gaps.
Having clearly defined these gaps, we now move on to diagnose
and solve these performance or opportunity gaps. We describe a
proven tool for helping managers initiate systematic diagnoses
of the causes of their current performance gaps or those aspects
of their current organization that will hinder the firm's ability to
achieve its opportunities.

## CHAPTER 4

# MANAGERIAL PROBLEM SOLVING: A CONGRUENCE APPROACH

KURT HUBER IS A LEAN, INTENSE MANAGER WITH
a doctorate in chemistry and 18 years of experience managing
within Ciba-Geigy. In 1993, he was transferred as head of Ciba's
U.K. chemical plant to general manager of its plant in Grenzach,
Germany. The Grenzach plant was a large facility located on the
Rhine River bordering Switzerland. Originally established in
1898, it was one of Ciba's oldest plants, a traditional chemical
manufacturing site with a long-service, highly skilled work
force; formal union-management relations; a seven-level formal
hierarchy; a functional structure; and rigid work rules. The
facility had four separate production lines and manufactured a
variety of chemical compounds for Ciba's industrial divisions.
It was also one of the Chemical Division's least competitive
plants, with labor costs 20 percent above comparable European
facilities and four times more costly than wages paid by emerging
competitors in Mexico, China, and India. Reflecting these cost
problems were a loss in market share, as well as a lack of new
products. Worse, since chemical production facilities are expen-

sive, they need to run at full volume. Yet, as volume dropped, the already costly facility became even less competitive. Huber's assignment was to either fix the plant or close it.

Huber had spearheaded other successful turnarounds but had serious doubts about Grenzach. "There were too many problems and too many possible causes. I knew that addressing one or two of them wouldn't work. I didn't think a standard turnaround effort would succeed." The sheer magnitude of the problems was almost overwhelming. Huber knew that he had only one shot at fixing Grenzach. The head of the Chemicals Division made it clear that he had 24 months or 1,500 people would lose their jobs, including Huber.

To solve this problem, Huber needed a method that would quickly and accurately identify the root causes of Grenzach's problems. Once critical performance or opportunity gaps are identified, managers like Kurt Huber can rapidly diagnose the causes of these gaps and, in turn, take action to close them. To help managers like Huber perform this diagnosis, we introduce a congruence-based problem-solving approach that is straightforward, easy to use, and supported by an extensive body of research and practice.[1] Our approach does not require outside consultants or sophisticated technology. This method has been used by managers, from CEOs to first-level managers, around the world. It suggests that the alignment, or congruence, between strategy and four organizational building blocks—critical tasks and work flows, formal organizational arrangements, people, and culture—drives today's success. Incongruence, a lack of alignment, or inconsistencies among these elements is almost always at the root of today's performance gaps (see Figure 4.1).[2]

The reason this systematic approach is important is simple: Unless managers and their teams clearly understand the roots of today's performance gaps or those barriers to achieving strategic opportunities, their attempts to solve these problems or realize the opportunities are likely to be incomplete or cause other unanticipated problems. We illustrate this problem-solving approach with the cases of three managers in three different coun-

FIGURE 4.1

## ORGANIZATIONAL ARCHITECTURE: A CONGRUENCE MODEL OF ORGANIZATIONS

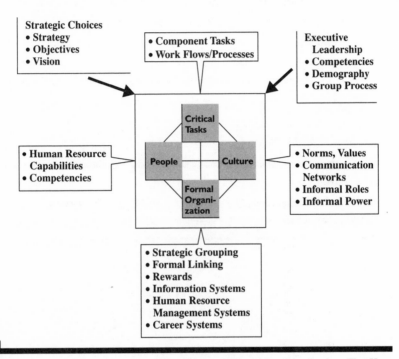

SOURCE: Adapted from D. Nadler and M. Tushman, "Designing Organizations That Have Good Fit," in *Organizational Architecture,* edited by D. Nadler. (San Francisco: Jossey-Bass, 1992.)

tries and in three different industries: Kurt Huber, head of the Grenzach plant of Ciba-Geigy, C.K. Chow, CEO of BOC's Industrial Gases business headquartered outside of London, and John Torrance, vice president of R&D at Medtek, a clinical diagnostic instrument firm located in New York.

## A PROCESS FOR ORGANIZATIONAL PROBLEM SOLVING

First we outline the five steps needed to use the model and complete a congruence analysis. Each step is simple and straightforward. Although we focus on managers who have used this approach, we encourage readers to apply it to their own performance or opportunity gaps. At the end of this chapter there is a practical guide that shows in greater detail how a congruence analysis may be done. This will be useful for gaining a greater understanding of organizational data gathering and in doing a careful diagnosis of your own issues. Here we offer a quick overview of this problem-solving process to illustrate the power of this five-step approach (see Figure 4.2).

**FIGURE 4.2**

**A PROCESS FOR ORGANIZATIONAL PROBLEM SOLVING AND LEARNING**

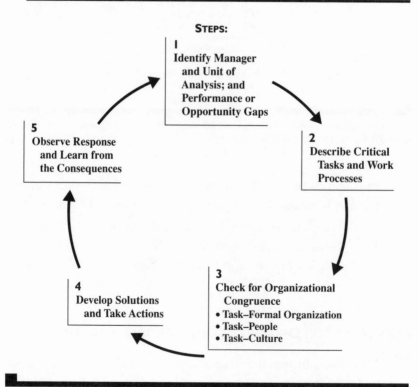

**STEPS:**

**1** Identify Manager and Unit of Analysis; and Performance or Opportunity Gaps

**2** Describe Critical Tasks and Work Processes

**3** Check for Organizational Congruence
- Task–Formal Organization
- Task–People
- Task–Culture

**4** Develop Solutions and Take Actions

**5** Observe Response and Learn from the Consequences

## Step 1: Identify the Unit's Crucial Performance or Opportunity Gaps

A diagnosis begins with a manager and his or her team defining the performance gaps facing their unit or organization. It is important in doing this to identify those problems or opportunities that lie at least potentially within control of the unit and avoid defining gaps too broadly or in a way that cedes responsibility to a higher level manager. The person doing the diagnosis needs to "own" the gap. At BOC Gases, for example, Chow and his team identified lack of innovation and customer responsiveness as the key performance gaps. For John Torrance at Medtek, the gap centered on a failure to produce new products and turnover among key scientists.

Kurt Huber, faced with the challenge of fixing or closing Grenzach, gathered his senior team at an off-site meeting to reach consensus on the critical performance gaps they needed to address. To help focus its efforts, Huber began by asking each member of the team to prepare an obituary (*Nachruf*) describing how and when they believed Grenzach would fail. The results were sobering. All the managers predicted that if left unchecked, the plant would fail within the next several years. One common cause of death was identified as "a lack of agreement and focus among management about problems." Motivated by this insight, the team identified a list of problems, including:

- Loss of market share and shrinking margins

- Lack of new products

- Slow introduction of new products

- Loss of sales

- Cost of goods sold too high

After discussion, Huber and his team decided that the most critical issue to be resolved was "Loss of market share and shrinking margins." Having taken this first step, they turned to diagnosing the root causes of the gap.

## Step 2: Describe Critical Tasks and Work Processes

With clarity about vision and strategy, managers can then describe the critical tasks necessary to implement the strategy. What are the concrete tasks necessary to accomplish the objectives and add value from the customer's perspective? In describing these, also consider how much interdependence or integration is needed among the critical tasks. The amount of required integration is a critical determinant of the skills, structure, and culture required for successful execution of strategy. (Again, the section on critical tasks in "A Practical Guide to Using the Congruence Model" at the end of this chapter provides a full explanation.) For instance, at Medtek, Torrance realized that if he were to be successful at developing innovative new products, his laboratory would have to be world-class in chemical and hydraulic technologies and be able to link these technologies to manufacturing and marketing requirements. For Chow at BOC, a critical task identified for delivering customized service to global customers was close integration across geographically dispersed organizations. With the Grenzach team's goal of reducing costs, the critical tasks were to maintain the functional excellence within the plant as well as to increase integration across the functional areas.

## Step 3: Check for Organizational Congruence

Once the critical tasks and work processes have been defined, the alignment or congruence of the three other major organizational building blocks (formal organization structure and systems, people, and the culture or informal organization) can be examined to ensure that these elements are supporting the attainment of the critical tasks. The key diagnostic questions for assessing congruence are: Given the critical tasks and work flows that must be accomplished, how aligned or congruent are the current formal organizational arrangements (e.g., structure, systems, rewards), culture (e.g., norms, values, informal communication networks), and people (e.g., individual competencies, motives)? Do these organizational building blocks fit with task requirements? Do they fit with each other?

This diagnosis requires only that a manager or team carefully and systematically describe each component of the model and consider its alignment with the critical tasks and work processes. The goal is to describe these, preferably on paper or flip chart, to see whether the current organization is aligned with the critical tasks required to meet the strategic challenges. To the extent that these components fit with each other, the organization is likely to be successful in the short run. On the other hand, if the components are incongruent with the critical tasks or with each other, these inconsistencies are likely to be at the root of today's performance gaps. (The guide at the chapter's end provides a more detailed explanation.) To briefly illustrate this process, consider the diagnoses that Chow and Huber completed at BOC and Grenzach shown in Figures 4.3a and 4.3b and 4.4. (Solid lines indicate congruent relationships; dotted lines indicate incongruent relationships.)

**ALIGNING THE FORMAL ORGANIZATION.** To ensure that the formal organization and critical tasks are aligned, ask the following diagnostic question: Given the critical tasks and processes needed to execute the strategy, does the current structure facilitate the accomplishment of both the component tasks and their required integration? For example, as shown in Figure 4.3b, Chow and his team identified as a key inconsistency the misfit of their current geographic structure with the critical task of global integration. While BOC's strategic goal was to provide service to global customers, its structure promoted fierce geographic loyalties and offered no way to link these geographic units together. At Grenzach (Figure 4.4), Huber and his team noted that the seven-level hierarchy and formal structure were inconsistent with speed and were associated with higher costs of coordination and supervision. Further, the rigid job specifications resulted in overstaffing and slow response times.

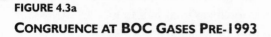

**FIGURE 4.3a**

**CONGRUENCE AT BOC GASES PRE-1993**

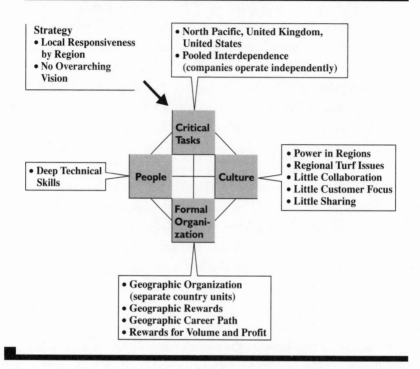

Several related questions to ask when checking the alignment of the formal organization are: Do the formal linking mechanisms facilitate task integration? Do the existing measurement, control, and career systems track the outcomes important for the execution of the critical tasks and work flows? and Given task demands, are the right things being rewarded (e.g., compensation, recognition, and promotion)? At BOC, the financial reporting system was geographically based and did not permit worldwide reporting by customer. At Grenzach, promotions historically had been based on rigid compliance with procedures. Risk taking and boundary spanning were frowned on. In both instances, it was clear that the formal organization was not aligned with critical tasks.

**FIGURE 4.3b**

## LACK OF CONGRUENCE IN 1993 AT BOC IS CAUSED BY NEW STRATEGY, VISION, AND CRITICAL TASKS

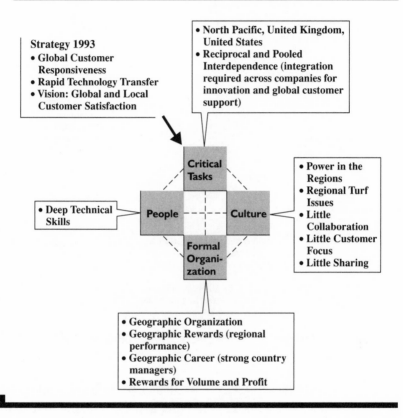

**Strategy 1993**
- Global Customer Responsiveness
- Rapid Technology Transfer
- Vision: Global and Local Customer Satisfaction

- North Pacific, United Kingdom, United States
- Reciprocal and Pooled Interdependence (integration required across companies for innovation and global customer support)

- Deep Technical Skills

**Critical Tasks**

**People**

**Culture**

**Formal Organization**

- Power in the Regions
- Regional Turf Issues
- Little Collaboration
- Little Customer Focus
- Little Sharing

- Geographic Organization
- Geographic Rewards (regional performance)
- Geographic Career (strong country managers)
- Rewards for Volume and Profit

ALIGNING HUMAN RESOURCES. In addition to checking for the congruence of the formal organization and critical tasks, managers also need to verify that their human resources are aligned with the critical tasks; that is, to ensure that people have the right skill sets and are motivated and committed to accomplish critical tasks. Here several diagnostic questions can be asked: Given the critical tasks, do people have the required competencies to perform them? Are there additional skills or incentives that are needed? Can employees be trained in these new skills or do we need to bring in new people?

**FIGURE 4.4**

**GRENZACH'S INTERNAL CONGRUENCE BEFORE HUBER**

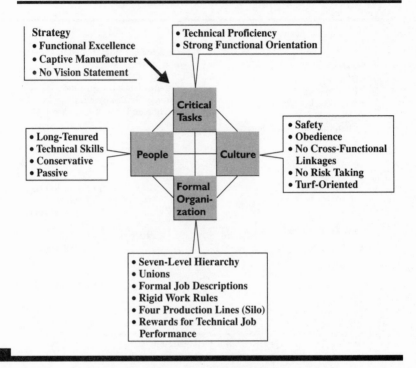

For example, at BOC middle managers had deep engineering skills but were weak in marketing and the collaborative skills needed to operate a global matrix. A similar incongruency was discovered at Grenzach. With the firm's emphasis on narrow technical skills, it was apparent to the Grenzach team that people throughout the plant would need help in working across boundaries. Further, Huber's team observed that the greatest danger resided among managers who lacked the skills needed to manage in a flatter, less top-down organization. Both teams also realized that there was a further inconsistency between the reward system and the new skills required. Unless the formal and informal reward systems were changed, they realized that there would be little incentive for people to acquire the needed new competencies or to excel at them.

**ALIGNING THE CULTURE.** Finally, there is the difficult issue of ensuring congruence between the unit's or organization's culture and the required critical tasks. Does the existing culture energize the accomplishment of the critical tasks? Do the informal communication network and informal distribution of power help get the work done? Are there existing aspects of the current culture that may hinder the execution of these tasks? As we shall see in Chapter 5, this is a critical and much overlooked factor in the management of innovation.

For instance, at Grenzach the culture diagnosis identified as central norms a reluctance to take ownership and a reliance on being told what to do rather than a willingness to take action. Huber and his team knew immediately that these norms would never encourage the initiative and responsiveness required by a flatter and cross-functional organization. Unless these norms were changed, neither the cost savings from a leaner organization nor the bottom-up innovation required would occur. At BOC, the current culture of noncooperation across geographies was misaligned with the critical tasks and the new formal organizational arrangements.

This short overview illustrates how the alignment of strategy, critical tasks, and the basic organizational building blocks of the formal organization (structure, systems, and rewards), people (competencies and motivation), and the culture (norms, values, informal communication, and power) is associated with short-term success. A lack of fit among these elements is the cause of performance gaps (assuming the strategy chosen is appropriate) and may require managers and their teams to realign their formal structures, people, and culture with their new critical tasks. Ironically, it is usually the case that the misalignments result from past organizational strengths that, if not modified, can become a future liability.

## Step 4: Develop Solutions and Take Corrective Actions

Once core inconsistencies are identified, managers can then take targeted action to bring the system back into alignment. The greater the number of inconsistencies among the organizational building blocks, the more substantial the interventions must be. For instance, a change in only one or two components, such as a new reward system or a shift in culture to reflect a new competitive demand, can usually be managed as incremental change. Systemwide lack of congruence, requiring changes in three or more of the organizational building blocks, demands discontinuous organizational change.

For instance, at Grenzach, Huber and his team determined that to survive they would have to change their critical tasks (technical proficiency and increased integration). Chow and his team at BOC came to a similar conclusion. To help them focus their efforts, both managers and their teams developed revised congruence models that reflected the needed realignment (see Figures 4.5 and 4.6). Realigning Grenzach required simultaneous changes in human resources (new skills, gradual downsizing), formal organizational arrangements (from seven levels to three with new structures, systems, and rewards), and a radically different culture (from security, stability, technology, and tradition to teamwork, initiative, flexibility, openness, and customer orientation). The discontinuous change effort took a year and a massive amount of energy and involvement of Huber and his team. After the initial resistance, the results are gratifying. Today, a new Grenzach plant has emerged with a competitive cost structure, new products, lower accident and absenteeism rates, and the ability to compete in global markets.

A similar discontinuous change has occurred at BOC Gases. Based on their diagnosis, Chow and his team have implemented a new global matrix structure supported by a new measurement and control system; changed the culture to promote collabora-

**FIGURE 4.5**

## CONGRUENCIES REQUIRED BY GRENZACH'S NEW STRATEGY AND VISION

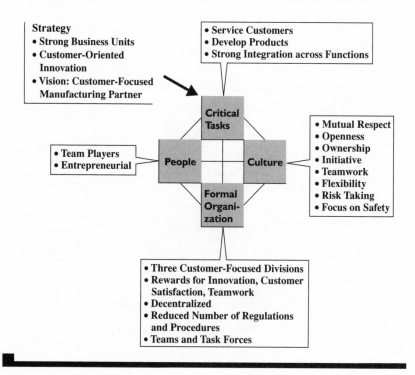

tion, cross-boundary communication, and a customer focus; and brought in new marketing skills. These systemwide changes are bearing fruit. By 1996, BOC Gases was winning new gas supply contracts, leading innovation, and running more efficiently. For managers in both organizations, the process was the same: Identify the performance gaps; determine the critical tasks needed to achieve strategic objectives; assess the congruence among tasks, people, the formal organization, and culture; and, depending on the diagnosis, take actions targeted to bring these inconsistencies into alignment with the critical tasks.

FIGURE 4.6

## ESTABLISHING NEW CONGRUENCIES AT BOC GASES POST-1993

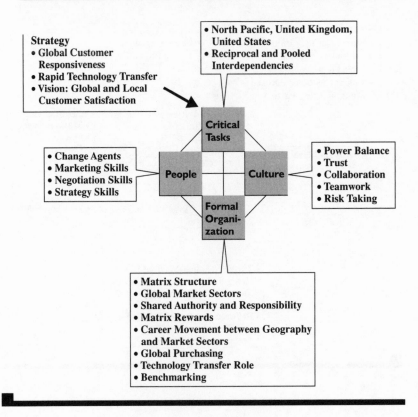

Strategy
- Global Customer Responsiveness
- Rapid Technology Transfer
- Vision: Global and Local Customer Satisfaction

- North Pacific, United Kingdom, United States
- Reciprocal and Pooled Interdependencies

Critical Tasks

- Change Agents
- Marketing Skills
- Negotiation Skills
- Strategy Skills

People

Culture

- Power Balance
- Trust
- Collaboration
- Teamwork
- Risk Taking

Formal Organization

- Matrix Structure
- Global Market Sectors
- Shared Authority and Responsibility
- Matrix Rewards
- Career Movement between Geography and Market Sectors
- Global Purchasing
- Technology Transfer Role
- Benchmarking

## Step 5: Observe the Response and Learn from the Consequences

Since any action is likely to be incomplete, it is improbable that all performance gaps will be reduced. The diagnosis and actions will typically reveal other problems. But managers and their teams can learn from these situations and reinitiate the process. The idea is to continually refine and readjust the internal congruence of the unit, not to determine the optimal solution for all

problems. At Grenzach, for instance, Huber has recently reiniti-
ated the culture change process and changed the structure and
rewards systems to make the plant even more entrepreneurial.
At BOC, the inevitable difficulties in operating in a matrix
organization have caused Chow and his team to iterate their
diagnosis and to refine their operations further. Unlike the old
Peters and Waterman exhortation, "Ready, fire, aim," managers
at Grenzach and BOC have used a rapid, diagnostically driven
process to continuously aim and fire.

## ASSESSING CONGRUENCE

Organizational diagnoses are made to understand the causes of
today's performance gaps or to anticipate what might cause
problems in the future. Managers begin by first gathering data
and describing the four organizational building blocks. Once this
is done, the fit among them can be evaluated by determining the
degree to which the needs, demands, goals, and structure of each
component are aligned with the others. For example, is the
reward system congruent with the culture? Are the skills of the
people consistent with the career paths offered? Does the structure of the unit facilitate accomplishment of the critical tasks?
See Table 4.1 for a full set of congruence relationships.

Internal fit is associated with short-term organizational performance. A lack of congruence between components, drives
performance shortfalls and is a root cause of today's problems.
Since these root causes can be anywhere in the system, managers
need to be systematic in their diagnosis. Rather than solving the
problem, an incomplete diagnosis or partial fix may lead to
further problems. While each congruence relationship is important (see the guide at the end of this chapter for more detail), the
three relating to aligning (or realigning) organizational components to get the unit's critical tasks accomplished are particularly
crucial. These three alignments are:

**TABLE 4.1**

**CONGRUENCE AMONG ORGANIZATIONAL BUILDING BLOCKS**

| Fit | Issues |
| --- | --- |
| People/Formal Organization | How are individual needs met by the organizational arrangements? Are individuals motivated to accomplish critical tasks? Do individuals have clear perceptions of organizational structures? |
| People/Critical Tasks | Do individuals have the skills and abilities to meet task demands? How are individual needs met by the task? |
| People/Culture | How are individual needs met by the informal organization? |
| Critical Tasks/ Formal Organization | Are formal organizational arrangements adequate to meet the demands of the task? Do they motivate behavior that is consistent with task demands? |
| Critical Tasks/ Culture | Does the culture facilitate task performance? Does it help meet the demands of the task? |
| Formal Organization/ Culture | Are the goals, rewards, and structures of the culture consistent with those of the formal organization? |

1. Task-People. To what extent do the skills, abilities, and motives of today's human resources fit with task requirements? For example, at BOC, Chow's new strategy and tasks demanded deep marketing competencies. Yet an audit of Chow's current marketing skills indicated real weaknesses not only within Chow's team but also within the larger organization. If this task-human resource inconsistency is not addressed, BOC's ability to execute its new strategy will be stunted.

2. Task-Formal Organization. To what extent do organizational arrangements fit with task requirements? For example, at Medtek, Torrance's laboratory was functionally organized but

the new tasks emphasized developing new products, which required strong integration across functions. Unless formal linking mechanisms are developed, this task-structure inconsistency will impede the innovation critical to Medtek's survival.

3. Task-Culture. To what extent does the unit's culture fit with task requirements? At Grenzach, almost a hundred years of tradition emphasized technical excellence and formal authority. But the new task requirements demand speed, teamwork, and initiative. If left unaddressed, the old culture would drag down Huber's efforts to save the plant, regardless of how the organization is structured. This culture-task inconsistency was a major cause of the performance gap at Grenzach.

Organizational diagnoses pivot on the critical tasks and work processes. Once these are specified, managers can use the congruence model to diagnose the current degree of fit between their current organization and that needed to successfully execute their strategy. The basic principle of our approach is: Today's effectiveness is enhanced the greater the total degree of congruence among different organizational components. The lack of congruence among organizational buildings blocks are the causes of today's performance or opportunity gaps.

Once critical problems or opportunities and their root causes are identified, the focus is not on searching for the single "right" answer, but on a process by which managers can determine which of several possibly correct answers might work for them. For a particular manager with a particular context and performance gaps, there are almost always a number of right answers. The correct ones are those that deal with the specific inconsistencies identified in the diagnoses. For example, at BOC Gases, Chow and his team discovered that the current structures, systems, cultures, and marketing capabilities were inconsistent with their aspirations for effective technology transfer and satisfied global customers. This diagnosis led, in turn, to several possible systemwide changes at BOC. Chow and his team evaluated the relative costs and benefits of the various options and decided on a global matrix as their structural intervention.

While our method does not provide optimal answers, it does offer a rigorous process for initiating targeted actions based on systematic analysis. No intervention will ever be perfect. Our approach simply asks managers to quickly gather data, take targeted action, and learn from their actions. As Percy Barnevik of ABB is fond of saying, "Nothing is worse than procrastination. . . . It's better to make decisions quickly and be right seven out of ten times than to waste time trying to achieve the perfect solution."[3] In articulating the management principles for ABB, Barnevik notes that to stick one's neck out and do the right thing is obviously best. But he says that second best is to take action, make a mistake, and learn from your actions. To take no action is the only unacceptable behavior for ABB managers. We agree. It is better to get an approximately correct solution quickly than an optimal solution slowly. Organizational learning is about finding good-enough solutions to important problems or opportunities and making error-correcting adjustments to get better and better; learning, especially in a rapidly changing world, is not about always finding the precise answer.

## USING THE CONGRUENCE MODEL

We have helped and observed hundreds of managers using the congruence model. The guide at the end of this chapter reflects our experience and provides greater detail on doing a diagnosis. Based on the experiences of these managers, a number of suggestions for using the congruence model as a tool for managerial problem solving have been offered. They reflect common problems that managers have encountered and their suggestions for how to avoid these difficulties. The following rules of thumb are designed to alert managers to possible pitfalls before using the congruence model and ensure greater success from its use.

1. Be clear about the unit of analysis; that is, who owns the problem. What is controllable and what isn't? Managers in different positions may have different problems and develop different diagnoses to the same performance gaps. The first step in organizational diagnosis is to clarify who the manager is and to identify performance or opportunity gaps from that perspective. This sounds trivial but it is easy for a manager to define a problem from the boss's or CEO's perspective with the result that many solutions are not implementable because they exceed the specific manager's control.

2. To the extent that the strategy or vision is wrong, no amount of diagnosis and root cause analysis will help. Organizations exist to accomplish strategic goals. If the strategy emphasizes the wrong product or service, to the wrong market, with the wrong technology and bad timing, no amount of organizational problem solving can help. Tight alignment with the wrong strategy ensures quick failure.

3. Comprehensive diagnoses are necessary. Since success depends on the alignment of the four organizational building blocks, it is critical that any diagnosis consider all of them. Focusing on one or two, as is customary in reengineering or TQM efforts, may miss the need to align other components. For instance, a common failure in reengineering efforts is that managers ignore the informal organization with the result that cultural inertia and political resistance wreck the process.

4. The type of change required depends on the number of inconsistencies discovered. If a diagnosis reveals incongruencies between only one or two organizational building blocks, incremental change is possible. If, however, the diagnosis shows inconsistencies among three or more building blocks (e.g., new critical tasks require changes in people, formal arrangements, and culture), discontinuous change is needed. As we will see in Chapter 8, this has important

ramifications for how a manager thinks about and initiates change.

5. For any diagnosis, there may be many possible interventions. As such, there is no single best solution. Rather, the question is what set or combination of components needs to be changed to achieve congruence? Different managers may choose to intervene in different ways. What is important is that any intervention deal with the inconsistencies identified in the diagnosis and drive greater congruence among the building blocks.

6. Our approach focuses on problem definition and root cause analyses from a particular manager's position. Sometimes, a diagnosis shows that the root causes of the performance gap are beyond the control of the focal manager. In these circumstances, the manager needs the skills to manage his or her boss, peers, customers, or others outside the unit. If the manager lacks these influence skills outside his or her area or has no leverage, all the diagnostic work will yield is an insightful but frustrated manager.

7. The congruence approach emphasizes gathering data prior to taking action. Although logical, our experience suggests that this is often an unnatural act for many managers. In the press of day-to-day business, managers often lack the time to be systematic. There is a bias toward immediate, decisive action. We urge managers to step back and gather data prior to intervening—to be systematic in their diagnoses.[4] This is not paralysis through analysis but data-driven problem solving. Both Chow and Huber completed their initial diagnoses over two-day periods, not months of analysis. Their diagnoses led, in turn, to systematic interventions over 12–18 month periods.

8. Successful problem solving is a function of both what managers do (i.e., the actions they take) and how they do it (i.e., their execution). Effective managers do the right thing and do it well. Knowing what to do is half the solution. Being

able to implement the needed changes is equally as important. Great ideas executed poorly are as bad as poor ideas executed flawlessly. To help avoid these problems, we discuss specific tools for the management of change in Chapters 8 and 9.

9. This disciplined problem-solving approach and learning from one's actions is associated with greater effectiveness over time. Different managers may develop different diagnoses for the same problem. Further, the same diagnosis can spawn multiple possible interventions. Rather than focusing on the correct intervention to solve a particular problem, our approach asks managers to focus on the process by which they attack the problem. All managers will make mistakes in both diagnoses and action. Excellent managers are not paralyzed by studying problems, or by making mistakes, rather, they are able to learn by doing.[5]

Although managers may know that organizational hardware and software must fit task requirements, they are often most familiar and comfortable with the vertical axis of our model—the organization's technical systems. Given the difficulty of both diagnosing and changing the organization's software, we move in Chapter 5 to a detailed discussion of culture and social control.

# A PRACTICAL GUIDE TO USING THE CONGRUENCE MODEL

Our congruence model is rooted in gathering systematic organizational data and assessing to what extent the firm's current people, formal organization arrangements, and culture help (or hinder) accomplishing critical tasks. We now describe each organizational component and the different congruence relations in more detail.

## CRITICAL TASKS AND WORK FLOWS

The reason an organization, or a unit within an organization, exists is to accomplish the tasks necessary to achieving its strategic goals and vision. Whether the structure, systems, rewards, people, and culture of the organization or the unit are appropriate can be evaluated only in terms of how these elements help or hinder the execution of the critical tasks. Organizational diagnoses, then, begins by systematically describing the critical tasks, always posing the question: Do these tasks and task processes help achieve our strategic goals?[6]

The critical task data need to be gathered *within* a manager's unit (What tasks does the unit perform?) and between this unit and other interdependent areas (Are our tasks critically interdependent with areas within and outside our organization?). For example, if BOC's vision is to compete by serving customers globally as well as locally, the tasks that must be performed include those that satisfy the current requirements of manufacturing and distributing locally as well as those new tasks required to integrate the entire system around a set of global customers.

In analyzing tasks and work flows, managers need to understand their unit's component tasks and how work flows among these tasks and with other interdependent areas.

## Component Tasks

What are the pieces of work that a particular manager must get accomplished to meet the strategic goals? For Chow, the component tasks were managing the industrial gases business in each country. In Torrance's laboratory, the critical tasks were research and development in hydraulics, advanced development in clinical chemistry, and other technical service work.

A key consideration in examining component tasks is the amount of uncertainty each one entails. Highly uncertain tasks are difficult to preplan and cannot be executed by standard routines. Tasks that have fundamentally different levels of uncertainty may need to be separated from one another and organized and managed differently. Where component tasks differ in terms of uncertainty, so too must the structures, competencies, and cultures, and leadership styles associated with them.[7] For example, even though each country that BOC was involved with was in the same business, the competitive uncertainties were much higher in the Pacific Rim than in the more predictable and mature British market. Thus the strategy, structure, people, and processes in Great Britain may need to be different from those in the Pacific Rim.

---

Within your unit, what are the key component tasks to be accomplished? Do these tasks differ in terms of task uncertainty? Are some routine, others nonroutine?

## Work Flows

Who has to do what to and with whom to get the product made or the service performed? Asking this question gets at the work flows or interdependencies among component tasks within and among units. For Chow, this means understanding the work flows between geographic regions in the development of new products and in meeting the needs of global customers. For Torrance, this means understanding the work flows between units within his lab and among his lab and marketing, sales, and production.

Three types of interdependence affect congruence with other organizational building blocks: pooled, sequential, and reciprocal interdependence (see Figure 4.7). Each type of interdependence requires different formal organizations, cultures, and human resource capabilities.[8]

**FIGURE 4.7**

**TYPES OF INTERDEPENDENCIES**

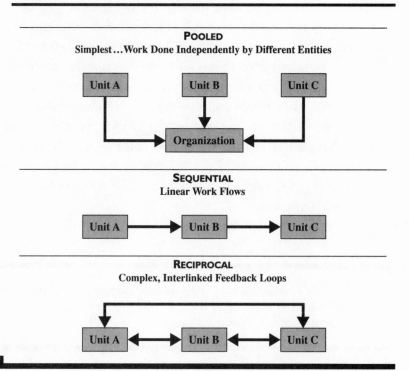

**POOLED**
Simplest...Work Done Independently by Different Entities

Unit A      Unit B      Unit C

Organization

**SEQUENTIAL**
Linear Work Flows

Unit A ⟶ Unit B ⟶ Unit C

**RECIPROCAL**
Complex, Interlinked Feedback Loops

Unit A ⟷ Unit B ⟷ Unit C

Pooled interdependence exists when component tasks have no linkage with one another; that is, each subunit does its own work, and the larger system's performance is simply the sum of each subunit's output. While units with pooled interdependence may share common resources, such as access to corporate capital or human resources, no work flows between these independent entities. Pooled interdependence is the simplest form of interdependence to manage—with no cross-unit interdependence there is little need for the systems and structures necessary to coordinate actions.

Sequential interdependence exists when component tasks are linked in a linear sequence. In a sequential work process, early component tasks must be completed before later tasks are accomplished, making each unit dependent only on the immediately preceding one. The structures and systems of sequential interdependence are more complex than those in pooled processes because more planning and coordination are required to accommodate work flows. Similarly, people in sequential situations require more interpersonal skills to facilitate negotiation and coordination with those involved in the sequential work flows. Under the old Grenzach organization, work flowed from one process to the next in a typical linear manufacturing process.

Reciprocal interdependence exists when each component task is inherently linked to other tasks; that is, the completion of one component task is dependent not only on the preceding task but also those that follow. Reciprocal interdependence is the most complex form of interdependence. Diagrams of reciprocal task processes are filled with double-headed arrows and complex feedback loops. So intrinsic is reciprocity to such work flows that complexity remains even after these processes have been reengineered. These complex interdependencies require collaboration, teamwork, and trust because their work processes demand mutual adjustment.

While pooled, sequential, and reciprocal processes are distinct forms of interdependence, managers typically have to deal with several types of interdependencies simultaneously. Most of the work at Chow's gas companies is done through pooled interdependencies, but addressing both innovation and global customer requirements also involves reciprocal processes. At Medtek, Torrance's R&D managers had to deal with both pooled and reciprocal interdependence situations to develop new products.

Managers must diagnose work flows across multiple boundaries. Not only do they have to diagnose work flows laterally and vertically within their organization, but managers must also describe them externally with suppliers, vendors, and alliance partners. These extra-organizational linkages are increasingly important as more and more organizations establish joint ventures, alliances, and strategic partnerships.[9] The higher the manager's level in the firm, the more critical the extra-organizational processes become.

Innovation in organizations always involves reciprocal interdependence. One reason managing innovation is so difficult is that the work requirements are necessarily highly interdependent and complex.[10] Managing innovation demands linkages among customer requirements, technological possibilities, and manufacturing capabilities. Furthermore, these linkages often take place across functional areas separated by both organizational and geographic boundaries.[11] Inevitably, these complex work processes must often be accomplished along with the more routine work.

Because critical tasks and work processes are driven by strategy, they can change as the unit's strategy changes. At BOC Gases, to the extent that Chow and his team want to operate their business as a worldwide federation of distinct national organizations, there is little interdependence between countries. If, however, Chow and his team decided to compete as a global solutions provider, the country organizations and the members of Chow's team would need to establish and manage reciprocal work flows even as they continued to manage their local businesses independently.

> What work flows exist within your unit, among your unit and other areas of your organization, and with areas outside of your organization? To what extent do these work flows differ? For example, does your unit have reciprocal interdependence with other areas? What about pooled or sequential interdependence?

## PEOPLE: DIAGNOSING HUMAN RESOURCES

Managers must also ensure that their people are aligned with critical tasks and work processes.[12] This requires assessing four aspects of the companies' human resources: competencies (What are they good or bad at?), motives (What rewards are most effective in motivating them?), demographics (How long have people worked together?), and country differences (What is the cultural mix?).

### Human Resource Competencies

Do people have the knowledge, skills, and abilities to perform the critical tasks and work flows? Managers must gather these data not only about their direct reports but also about themselves and their supervisors, critical peers, and external colleagues. What are each player's strengths and weaknesses with respect to task requirements? To what extent does the management team have both content and interpersonal skills?

At Southwest Airlines great care is taken during staff selection to ensure that people have a positive attitude and a willingness to be team players. These qualities are important since the critical tasks at Southwest emphasize keeping costs low through high employee productivity and having fun. Without these characteristics, Southwest would have a difficult time executing its strategy of low cost and superlative customer service. At ABB, Percy Barnevik says that to be an effective global executive, "You need the ability to understand other people's ways of doing things." For ABB to succeed at operating in 230 countries, Barnevik asserts that his global managers must be open-minded, patient, and incisive. He believes that without these competencies, it would be difficult to think globally and act locally. Managers need to be clear about how well the competencies of their human resources fit critical tasks and work flow demands.

## Motives

Beyond competencies, managers can gather data on individual differences in motivation so that they can design reward systems that are aligned with both individual needs and critical tasks. In his Pulitzer Prize–winning book, *The Soul of a New Machine,* Tracy Kidder details the heroics involved in the development of a new computer by Data General engineers.[13] He describes how project leader Tom West based his human resource strategy on hiring only young, newly graduated engineers with high achievement needs. Older, more experienced engineers might have said that the time frame for the project was impossible, but the inexperienced youngsters, unequipped to anticipate the daunting demands of the task ahead, responded enthusiastically to West's extraordinarily challenging jobs and outrageous deadlines. The project burned out many of the team members and some left Data General. West simply hired the next wave of young, technology-driven high achievers.

This unconventional human resource strategy succeeded because West knew enough not to choose more experienced people and because he motivated his team masterfully. Similarly, Chow knew he had to hire more entrepreneurial managers to run his market-sensitive Far East businesses, while he needed more focused, technically oriented managers to run his mature, cost-oriented U.K. businesses. Choosing the right people and motivating them to get the job done does not mean that managers must be psychologists; it does ask them to be sensitive to individual differences and motivate people accordingly.[14]

## Demographics

How long has the team worked together (i.e., How old is the group?), and what is its functional mix? Are there important differences in ages and backgrounds that may affect group dynamics? The challenges of managing young, heterogeneous teams are different from those of managing older, more homogeneous teams.[15] While young, heterogeneous teams may be better able to deal with complexity and uncertainty, older teams may be better able to execute in stable, more certain contexts. Further, how different is the manager from the rest of the team? The greater the demographic differences, the greater the potential for team conflict. When Chow was promoted to CEO, he had 20 years' experience with BOC and knew all his direct reports. Contrast his challenges with those of Paul O'Neill, who stepped into the CEO position at Alcoa having no aluminum industry experience and inheriting a team of executives, all of whom had grown up in the aluminum industry and had worked with each other for, on average, more than 15 years.

## National Cultures

How do people from different national cultures deal with interpersonal differences, resolve conflicts, and relate to the organization? Managers need to be sensitive to these differences not only in managing individuals from different countries, but also in managing the consequences of the diversity in their management teams. For example, Kurt Huber's British engineers at Grenzach may need to be managed differently than his Japanese engineers, who, in turn, may need to be managed differently than the mostly German work force. Huber will have to be sensitive to these country differences not only in managing these individuals, but also in managing the consequences of the diversity in his management team.

Human resource practices may have a greater impact on a unit's employee characteristics and competencies than do country effects.[16] While there are important differences in national cultures, these are often attenuated by the systematic effects of training, education, socialization, rewards, and career systems. Percy Barnevik observes that ABB is a company without a home—it is, however, at home around the world.[17] While its managers speak English, ABB is not American; while it is headquartered in Zurich, ABB is not Swiss; while Barnevik and several members of the board are Swedish, ABB is not a Swedish company. Rather, ABB is a company of the world—it thinks globally (with globally oriented managers) but acts locally (with locally focused country organizations). The commonality of managerial practices and ABB's ability to leverage competencies and skills worldwide come from its ability to mold managers from hundreds of countries into a network of collaborative teams that speak a common ABB managerial language. These shared skills and competencies are driven by ABB's comprehensively designed human resource practices.

---

- Describe the human resource characteristics within your unit as well as within your team and your manager's team. What are the skills, abilities, demography, and key individual and country differences within your unit? What motivates your boss and members of your team?

- To what extent do your human resources have the skills, motivation, and abilities to accomplish critical tasks and work processes?

---

## THE FORMAL ORGANIZATION

The third step of the diagnosis is an examination of the congruence between critical tasks and the formal organization. The formal arrangements include the stated structures, roles, procedures, measures, and systems that managers use to direct, control, and motivate individuals and groups to perform the unit's critical tasks.[18] These arrangements have an enormous impact on a firm's performance. Typically senior management has the most control over formal organizational arrangements. But middle managers can also control a range of formal procedures such as promotion, job design, and subunit organizational design and can tailor training and rewards to best fit their subordinates' needs. In making a diagnosis to understand roots of today's performance gaps, managers need to consider several dimensions of the formal organization: strategic grouping; linking mechanisms; and formal reward, measurement, and control systems.

## Strategic Grouping

Strategic grouping refers to the unit's formal structure. There are only a limited number of strategic grouping options—by function, market, geography, product, or some combination of these options (e.g., function and product). For example, while Chow's gases business was organized by country, some of his team were pushing a country by market matrix structure.

While structures that combine grouping options are designed to be responsive to several strategically important dimensions simultaneously, they are also characterized by conflict and role overlaps. For example, in the early 1990s, Percy Barnevik chose a three-dimensional structure for ABB, organizing the company by products, geography, and function. Such a structure guaranteed tension as managers are pushed to balance country, product, and functional demands. In Barnevik's opinion, this complex organization structure was required if ABB was to execute its vision to "Think globally, act locally, with world-class technology."

The strategic grouping decision is the most fundamental choice managers make after strategy, objectives, and vision are established. From that key choice emerges the range of more operational structures, rewards, career, and linkage decisions. There is no optimal organizational structure; each strategic grouping choice has its costs and benefits.[19] So rather than being imposed from without, the choice among possible options is driven from within by the unit's own strategy and vision. The grouping choice, then, will reflect the unit's strategy and facilitate the accomplishment of the critical tasks necessary to execute that strategy. Since strategic grouping decisions affect the larger organization, these decisions must be made in collaboration with the manager's boss and his or her peers.

The strategic grouping decision is one that needs to be revisited as the organization's strategies evolve and develop. Today's organizational form usually reflects yesterday's strategy; it is an artifact of the organization's history. But as strategy changes, the organizational architecture must also shift. Insofar as managers use yesterday's structure to execute today's strategy, the organization may be held hostage to its past.[20] If, for example, BOC Gases, R&D at Medtek, or Grenzach at Ciba are to move on their respective strategies and critical tasks, Chow and Huber, and their teams must revisit their strategic grouping choices. In each case, existing structures were stifling task execution.

Of all the formal organization choices that managers make, strategic grouping is perhaps the most consequential. It affects not only other formal organizational arrangements, but also the unit's human resources and culture. While the choice of strategic grouping is crucial, it is frequently a decision that is either ignored or made in a cavalier fashion.

## Linking Mechanisms

Linking mechanisms are the formal organizational arrangements that knit together various parts of the firm and link it to its suppliers, customers, and partners.[21] Formal linking mechanisms include plans, committees, teams, task forces, brand or project managers, and liaison roles. For a particular unit, linking mechanisms can range from the simple (relying on plans) to the complex (using teams and task forces). After describing critical work processes within their unit and between their unit and external areas, managers can evaluate the extent to which existing linking mechanisms are congruent with work flows.

The choice of linking mechanisms should be driven by work flows inside and outside the unit. If linking requirements are minimal, linking mechanisms can be simple.[22] If task interdependencies are complex, however, linking mechanisms should reflect the complexity. At BOC Gases, for example, if little linkage is required between country organizations, Chow may choose to be the formal linking mechanism himself. If, however, global customers require integrated, worldwide delivery systems, more complicated formal linking mechanisms, such as global product teams and information systems, will be needed to deal with the increased interdependence.

The choice of strategic linking mechanisms between the manager's unit and other units should also be consistent with extra-unit work processes. Each complex, reciprocal interdependency with another area needs to be managed with complex formal linkage mechanisms. For instance, Wal-Mart is Procter & Gamble's single largest customer. Given the volume and complexities of the relationship, the two companies have established a joint organization, staffed by employees from both companies, designed solely to manage their mutual interdependence. At Ciba, Kurt Huber needs to choose linking mechanisms within his production unit as well as a set of complex linking mechanisms to integrate with other functional areas in the Grenzach plant and in the larger Chemical Division. Managers must, then, choose formal linking mechanisms that attend to work processes within their units, across with peer units, up with the manager's boss, and outside with suppliers, customers, and/or alliance partners.

## Formal Reward, Measurement, and Control Systems

Organizations usually get what they measure and reward.[23] For that reason, an organization's formal reward, measurement, and control systems must be consistent with its critical task requirements. Managers must assess existing rewards, measurement, and control systems. Too often, what is measured is not consistent with critical task requirements. When a large group of managers in a major U.S. computer company were asked what it takes to get ahead, there was great consensus that giving good presentations, massaging your boss, and being politically sensitive were critical success factors. This was in an organization where senior management stressed the need for innovation and risk taking! In a similar survey of a large, diversified European firm, managers responded that avoiding risks and being conservative were rewarded. Again, this was what the formal reward system reinforced even though efforts were under way to make the company fast and flexible.

If the component tasks are different, reward systems need to be different. Recall that Chow's booming Far East businesses faced very different tasks than did the same business in the more mature U.K. market. Since the work requirements between regions are so different, the reward and measurement systems must also be different. If, however, cooperation and integration are needed to accomplish critical tasks (for example, the development of a new gas technology), the reward system should monitor and reinforce successful collaboration. BOC's country organizations should also be measured on and rewarded for their joint efforts.

Managers must also ensure that their formal reward and measurement systems are equitable. Both high- and low-performing individuals, groups, and teams must see the consequences of high performance. If rewards are perceived as being allocated equally (without reference to performance), they provide no incentive for high performance.[24] The only reward system worse than an equality-based system is a random one in which no one knows how rewards are allocated! While it may be difficult to assess performance, particularly for complex, highly interdependent tasks, well-designed, equity-based reward systems can be a powerful driver of organizational effectiveness, just as poorly designed reward systems can be a root cause of today's performance gaps.

## Career and Promotion Systems

A final element of the formal organization to be checked for alignment with the critical tasks is the promotion and career system. Promotion ladders are closely watched by employees and should reflect the requirements of critical tasks. For example, if managers at BOC are hired and promoted only within the national organization, the firm will amass great competency and depth within its various geographic areas but few cross-country competencies or informal communication networks. In contrast, the career and promotion systems at ABB emphasize both technical and global competencies through functional career management as well as global integration through cross-business and global job mobility. At Philips, until recently, successful careers meant being promoted to country manager. This led some of their most talented people to become national organization managers. With the reorganization of Philips as a global product organization, however, the previous career system was no longer aligned with the requirements of the critical tasks. Unless this system is changed, it may unwittingly anchor Philips to the past and create barriers to the execution of its new strategy.

- Describe your unit's formal organizational arrangements. What is your unit's formal structure? What are the formal linking mechanisms within your unit, within your larger organization, and with areas outside your firm? What is formally measured and controlled in your organization? How do your formal career and promotion systems operate?

- To what extent does your formal organization help get your critical tasks accomplished? To what extent are your structure, system, rewards, and controls congruent with the task and work flow requirements?

## CULTURE AND THE INFORMAL ORGANIZATION

While organizational arrangements reflect decisions about formal structure, rewards, and roles, the informal organization reflects emergent structures, rewards, and roles. Informal patterns of interaction drive a firm's informal structure, power, and communication networks. Emergent norms and values define the organization's culture and act as a social control system.[25] While culture can facilitate innovation, it can also get in the way. Unless managers are sensitive to the effects of social control and actively shape informal patterns of interaction, culture may act as an inertial force hindering innovation and change. These emergent patterns can be diagnosed and shaped by managers. To what extent is there a fit between critical tasks and the unit's culture and informal organization?

### Norms and Values

An organization or group's culture is defined by its norms and values. Values reflect beliefs about what is really important. Norms are the widely shared and strongly held social expectations about appropriate attitudes and behavior such that compliance with the norm is seen as right and appropriate and noncompliance is punished.[26] Norms and values are the foundations of organizational culture that can help or hinder the execution of a unit's strategy. At Intel, the large semiconductor firm, a widely shared value throughout the organization is speed, so employees all realize the importance of getting things done quickly.

In organizations, norms can affect a variety of outcomes such as work behaviors (e.g., People don't work on weekends or Taking the initiative is expected), attitudes (It's us against them), orientation toward customers (We pay particular attention to customer feedback here), relations with units outside the focal unit (We just don't trust or pay much attention to R&D types), conflict resolution methods (We don't confront conflict openly), and dress codes (We're supposed to wear ties when we interact with management). Since norms reflect shared agreements about what's important, it is common to see variations across an organization and its subunits. Norms in a manufacturing unit, for instance, are likely to be different from those in marketing; norms in one location may be different from those in another.

Managers can gather data on norms by noting the way they and others (particularly newcomers) are treated and by observing what actions and attitudes group members approve or disapprove. For example, in the early 1980s, one of the authors spent a sabbatical year teaching and conducting research with faculty at the Harvard Business School and the Sloan School at MIT. These two business units (note that the unit of analysis here is the business school as opposed to other parts of the university) are in the same business and are located no more than two miles from each other. Yet the two organizations had completely different cultures. New Harvard faculty quickly learned that the school paid attention to teaching—faculty were supposed to get to know the students' names and spend time with the MBAs. At the Sloan School, in contrast, faculty soon learned to pay attention to their own research agendas. Course coordination meetings were sometimes missed, but faculty research colloquia were not. While neither norm was necessarily better than the other, each reflected the school's strategy at the time—Harvard's emphasis on MBA education and Sloan's on research.

Organizations with widely shared norms and values often show great consistency of attitudes and behavior. When people are asked, "What's important around here?" the less the variance in response, the stronger the core values and the stronger the culture. Whenever core values are highly focused, norms are also focused and consistent. On the other hand, when core values are diffuse (15 different people give 15 different answers to the diagnostic question), operating norms are apt to be diffuse.

Managers need to distinguish between vision and their unit's actual norms and values. Vision is an aspiration; norms and values reflect the reality of the shared social expectations within the unit. Vision and the organization's real norms and values may or may not be aligned. For example, at Alcoa, Paul O'Neill espoused a vision of leadership through quality. But if employees at an Alcoa bauxite mine in Australia are asked, "What's important around here?" and they do not answer, "Quality," O'Neill's vision is only a corporate slogan that is not shared in the field. For this reason, managers must not only be clear and consistent in articulating a competitive vision, they must also be able to step back and gather data on their unit's actual shared norms and values.

It is difficult to actively shape core values and culture without a clearly articulated competitive vision.[27] If vision is clearly espoused and modeled by the executive team, then it is easier to shape norms and core values. When that vision is ambiguous or not clearly communicated, norms and core values develop on their own, which can result in different and inconsistent expectations across units. While such variation can be appropriate, agreement on certain fundamental values (e.g., the value of teamwork or personal integrity) is essential for the rapid execution of strategy. Fuzzy core values and inconsistent norms can result in chaos, confusion, and increased organizational politics.

## Communication Networks

Informal patterns of communication, who actually talks to whom within and outside the manager's unit, provide detail about the heart of the informal organization.[28] Figure 4.8 is a sociometric map of who-talks-to-whom in John Torrance's laboratory. Simply by looking at these patterns of interaction it is easy to spot the key individuals. By looking for communication nodes in the network, managers can predict that 59, 19, 74, 40, 80, 39, and 32 are key players. These key individuals and their associated networks have a major impact on innovation and change efforts.

Informal social networks also provide insight into the distribution of informal power within the organization. While formal power is a function of rank or position in the hierarchy, informal power is a reflection of social location. Figure 4.8 shows that 59, 19, 74, 40, 80, and 32 have considerable informal power. One way to assess informal power is by asking questions such as,

FIGURE 4.8

INFORMAL PATTERNS OF COMMUNICATION AT MEDTEK

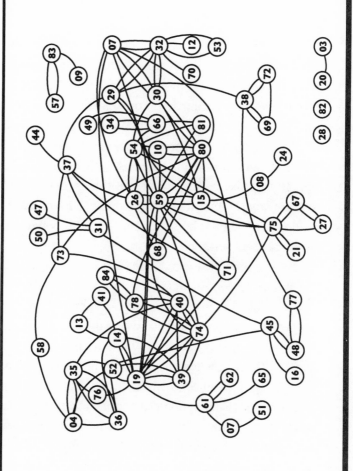

When you need something done, whom do you go to? or How do things work around here? When professionals in the R&D laboratory were asked these questions, they did not nominate Torrance or any member of his top team. Rather, they identified the informal power centers such as numbers 59, 19, and 74. Individuals such as numbers 28, 82, 50, and 47 had very little informal power—they were communication isolates in this system.

Formal power is very different from informal power, and the two do not necessarily overlap. While formal power relies on rank and the ability to monitor and reward, informal power is rooted in social location. In Figure 4.8, Torrance was number 50. Although he may have substantial formal power, he clearly had little informal power. Worse, his team members (47, 73, and 31) were isolated from each other as well as from others in the laboratory. It is not surprising that this group relied on formal authority and systems to manage change. Such reliance on formal systems will seldom be sufficient to get the job done in highly interdependent settings.

It is also possible to predict leadership style from a manager's position in the communication network. Simply based on social location and without any data on personality or background, one can predict that Torrance (50) was a distant, aloof, manage-by-the-numbers type of manager, while number 19 was more participative. Indeed, when asked how he managed change, Torrance replied, "By reengineering work flows and by changing structures and roles." He ignored the crucial impact of the informal organization in his laboratory. Had he been more sensitive to these informal dynamics, he might have known that numbers 19, 59, 80, and 74 were developing a coalition to bring him down. The lesson is clear: Managers need to pay attention to both formal and informal power—and appreciate that these two types of power may not overlap.

Informal power cannot be conferred on a person; it can only be earned or developed by attending to two fundamental individual characteristics—work-related expertise and interpersonal competence.[29] Individuals become informal communication nodes partly because they have information and expertise that others need and partly because they have interpersonal skills. While managers cannot confer informal power, they can create the conditions where an individual can become informally powerful through job assignments, job rotation, committee assignment, travel expenses, and personal coaching. The most influential managers are, of course, those who have both formal and informal power.

But what about number 28? Notice how isolated this person is. Is it possible to predict his or her effectiveness? When asked, most managers suggest that number 28 is either a low-performing individual or a new employee. Yet, if this person were an independent contributor (e.g., a great bench scientist), then he or she could in fact be among the most important members of the network. The point here is that the effectiveness of different social locations or network structures cannot be predicted without information about the nature of the task and associated work processes. In this setting, number 28 was not an independent contributor but a member of a project team (along with 82, 20, and 3) that was supposed to be highly interdependent with other teams in the lab. Given this information, it becomes clear that number 28 was indeed a poor performer, and his team was the lowest performing team in the laboratory. The communication networks were not congruent with the task requirements.

It is more difficult to gather reliable data on organizational culture than on the other organizational building blocks, but necessary nonetheless. Our experience indicates that while a single individual may not be good at gathering reliable data on informal dynamics, when several individuals are brought together to discuss norms, values, networks, informal roles and power, a reliable picture of an organization's informal organization quickly emerges. Note that the diagnosis of the informal organization need not be 100 percent accurate—it only needs to be more informed than a particular manager's existing understanding of the informal organization. Over time, through action and learning from the unit's response to those actions, managers can update their understanding of their unit's informal organization.

- Describe the culture of your organization. What are your unit's norms and values? What are the informal communication networks like in your unit and between your unit and outside areas? Who are the informally powerful individuals in your unit and in the larger organization? Where are you located in your unit's informal communication network?

- To what extent does your culture and informal organization facilitate task accomplishment? To what extent are your unit's norms, values, informal communication networks, and informal power consistent with task demands?

Critical tasks and work flows, people, the formal organization, and culture are the four building blocks whose interactions drive organizational performance. While each is important in shaping performance, there are significant differences in how most managers approach them. In the model shown in Figure 4.1, the vertical axis, defined by critical tasks and work flows and the formal organization, represents the formal control system, the organization's hardware. The horizontal axis, consisting of people and culture, represents the social control system, the organization's software. Almost all managers learn to use the formal control axis effectively. They understand and can apply the techniques of reengineering, restructuring, and performance-based compensation. Most managers are, however, far less comfortable and adept at using the social control system, perceiving issues of psychology and culture as less precise and harder to manage. Yet, largely because of this lack of attention, it is the social control system that may hold the key to the effective management of innovation and change. We now turn to diagnosing and shaping culture and social control.

# Leveraging Culture for Innovation and Competitive Advantage

WHAT IS FEDERAL EXPRESS'S COMPETITIVE ADVANTAGE in the air package industry? Not price. Rather, there is a widely shared perception by its customers that it will, in the words of an old advertisement, "Absolutely, positively get it there overnight." A belief in this reliability is what differentiates FedEx from the competition. One large firm has a corporate contract with a competitor. But managers told us that for really critical deliveries, they relied on FedEx—even if they had to pay for it themselves.

If reliability is a key to competitive advantage at FedEx, what critical tasks ensure it? Undoubtedly, there are many, including the need to invest in the latest technology, the importance of precise scheduling, speed, and efficiency in sorting. Employees believe in the absolute importance of customer service and fulfill the task of "making the plane." And what culture is needed to accomplish these critical tasks? Analysis shows norms and values like speed, a sense of urgency, teamwork, doing whatever it takes to please the customer, listening, initiative, flexibility, and risk taking—all are directly related to "making the plane" and satisfying the customer. At FedEx, organizational culture is an integral part of their competitive advantage.

## LINKING STRATEGY TO CULTURE

Finding the right strategy, vision, and purpose are essential for long-term success, but they also have important motivational properties. They provide organizational members with a sense that the work matters for more than instrumental ends. Motivation and sustainable commitment come from individuals' beliefs that their efforts are contributing to something worthwhile. In the short term, each of us may be motivated by the prospect of a promotion, a raise, or meeting a deadline. But in the longer term, commitment requires that people genuinely believe their efforts contribute to some higher good and make a difference. A shared vision helps infuse the organization with meaning and purpose beyond institutional ends.[1]

Many firms emphasize values such as quality, customer service, teamwork, respect for the individual, and innovation—themes with universal appeal that help people feel they are aspiring to higher goals. In some fortunate organizations, these values begin to take on a life of their own, guiding how people act and think and relate to one another. While market share, return on investment, and performance against budget are useful and important measures for assessing short-term performance, the values and norms that drive behavior, which combined form an organization's culture, are among the most critical factors in determining long-term strategic success. Profit is important, but only if it signals something larger to employees.

Thus, FedEx emphasizes People, Service, and Profit, which sends a small but telling signal to its employees that they are more important than more profits. Ford talks about the 3Ps, referring to People, Products, and Profit. Mary Kay Ash says that her company adage is God, Family, Job, and notes that in that order they work, and out of that order nothing works.[2] She talks not about selling cosmetics but about developing leadership potential in women. Bob Haas at Levi Strauss talks about Levi's corporate aspirations, which include being ethical. He recognizes the link between aspirations and strategy. Without a credible strategy, and profit, people won't pay much attention to any so-called noble purpose. On the other hand, simply having a strategy will not fully engage people's hearts unless they feel there is a larger purpose to their work. David Packard, in a speech to HP managers, observed that "I think many people assume, wrongly, that a company exists solely to make money. While this is an important result of a company's existence, we have to go deeper and find the real reasons for our being."[3] Thus, when a company credibly stands for something of universal value to its employees, the level of commitment or identification is deeper and more enduring.

It is easy to talk about sentiments like having a "noble purpose" or "respecting diversity," but the skeptics (who ought to include all managers in firms that have downsized) are right to think that these are simply words that senior management mouths as long as things are going well. Talk is cheap. Yet there are important psychological reasons to take these sentiments seriously. To the extent that a manager can motivate enthusiastic and committed employees, this human energy can be an invaluable resource.

To manage organizational culture effectively, managers must be clear in their own minds about the type of culture and the specific norms and values that will help the organization reach its strategic goals; next they must decide how to promote the needed norms and to diminish the importance of those that may hinder the attainment of critical tasks. For a practical guide to diagnosing your own organization's culture and identifying potential cultural inconsistencies, see the guide for diagnosing culture at the end of this chapter.

## ORGANIZATIONAL CULTURE: THE NORMS AND VALUES THAT GOVERN BEHAVIOR

Culture can be seen in the norms and values that characterize a group or organization; that is, organizational culture is a system of shared values and norms that define appropriate attitudes and behaviors for its members.[4]

Norms are socially created expectations about acceptable organizational attitudes and behavior. So, for example, sexism and racism are not acceptable. Jokes are appropriate in some settings but not others. Norms obviously vary across national cultures. For instance, dealing with conflict directly in North America is generally considered a good thing while in Japan or Great Britain the same behavior may be seen as impolite or overly aggressive. What it means to be "on time" is different in Indonesia than it is in Switzerland. At this level, most people are aware of the importance of norms.[5]

What we are less appreciative of is how powerful norms can be in shaping our own behavior, especially in organizational settings. Not only do we, as members of a particular group, unconsciously accept norms and use them to guide our behavior and interpret that of others, but each of us constructs our own version of reality, negotiating, as it were, the significance of events and behaviors as we interact with our environments and with one another. Much of what we know, what we accept as true or important arises from these social agreements or norms, which vary from unit to unit and across organizations. In order to know what is important we may rely on our own experience (e.g., activities in which we have invested time and effort), information from other group members (e.g., the approval or disapproval attached to certain attitudes and behaviors), and clear signals from management (e.g., what is consistently rewarded or punished).

Our natural tendency is to see a person and their actions more vividly than the environment he or she is responding to, and thus we often attribute to people certain motives and characteristics and fail to recognize the importance of context in determining behavior. Interestingly, we tend not to do this when explaining our own behavior. Instead, we are acutely aware of the signals and pressures on us to behave in certain ways. Widely shared norms can be powerful determinants of attitudes and behavior, even if we are often unaware of their effects. In this sense, our attitudes and behavior are influenced more by a process of "social learning" than by our underlying needs or personality.[6]

## USING CULTURE AS A SOCIAL CONTROL SYSTEM

While both the academic and business press are filled with references to culture, the concept itself often seems abstract and difficult for managers to get a handle on, especially those who favor a more detached, rational approach to management. To address this critical topic, let's think not about culture, but about a subject most managers are more comfortable with: control. Much of management is really about control; about getting people to do what is necessary to accomplish the work, preferably in a way that uses their full potential and makes them feel motivated and engaged.

At its essence, control comes from the knowledge that someone who matters to us is paying close attention to what we are doing and will tell us how we are doing. Formal control systems, whether financial planning systems, budgets, inventory control, or safety programs, are effective when those being monitored are aware that others who matter to them, such as a boss or staff department, know how they're doing and will provide rewards or punishments for compliance or noncompliance.

In the same way that these formal control processes guide behavior, culture serves as a social control system. If we care about others, for instance, we like them and we want them to like us, and if we have some agreement about what is important, we are under their control. That is, if I care about you and we agree about what is important and how to act, whenever we are together, we effectively control each other.

In organizations, there are numerous agreements about what's right or wrong and what's important and unimportant. For example, in the early 1980s, both Roger Smith, then CEO of GM, and Don Petersen, CEO of Ford, announced quality efforts at their respective organizations. At the time, Ford's quality levels were the worst in Detroit and three times worse than those of the Japanese. Half a dozen years later, Ford's quality was the highest among U.S. automakers, an achievement reached without reorganization or an infusion of outsiders. Ford underwent a cultural revolution driven by Don Petersen and his senior team. More than 80 percent of these improvements came from the human side, not from automation.[7] During this same period, GM—with the exception of NUMMI, its joint venture with Toyota—largely failed in its quality effort. Rather than truly focus on quality, it relied on technology and financial numbers.

Whatever senior managers claim is important, most people in organizations soon figure out what really counts and how to behave. These shared agreements and social expectations constitute a powerful and pervasive social control system within groups and organizations—a system that we show can be more powerful and effective than some formal control systems.

But culture should not be equated with the vision or values espoused by senior management. Simply having a formal statement of the company values or laminated cards that employees carry in their wallets is no guarantee that these values are shared. In a perfect world, of course, the culture of the business should reflect these values. Unfortunately, it seldom does, at least not without substantial effort by management to inculcate the values over extended periods of time. When thinking about culture managers should focus on the norms and values that are really shared, the unofficial customs, rituals, and language that guide people in their actions.

## Using Norms for Social Control

In order to diagnose and manage culture, we need to appreciate that norms vary in two important ways. First, they can vary in the extent of their consensus, or in how widely shared they are. Before a social control system can operate, there needs to be shared agreement that certain values, attitudes, and behaviors are important. Simple consensus, however, is not sufficient. With enough publicity, espoused values like quality or customer service may become widely known, but not necessarily practiced. Therefore, in order to have a strong culture, the norm must also be characterized by intensity; that is, people who share the norm must feel strongly enough about it that they are willing to tell others when the normal is violated. An example will help illustrate the importance of having consensus and intensity.

DuPont is, by most standards, considered a strong culture company. When we have asked DuPont managers to identify the central norms that characterize the firm, we've always gotten the same response: safety. This makes sense, given that the company began by manufacturing explosives and maintains a safety record almost twice as good as the industry average. The power of this norm was brought home by an MBA who worked for DuPont: The first day on the job, walking downstairs in his office building and minding his own business, he was met by a person coming up the stairs who noted that he was not holding onto the banister and said in no uncertain terms, "You don't have your hand on the banister. Get your hand on the banister." The MBA was nonplused but complied, and even though he never saw the person again, he notes that he now always uses the banister, tells his kids to use it, and even admonishes perfect strangers to do the same. This is what is we mean by intensity—the willingness of employees to tell each other when they're not living up to the shared expectations about what is right and wrong. This is social control in operation.

From a managerial perspective, the relevant question is whether the organization's social control system supports or hinders managers in accomplishing their critical tasks. A manager is a signal generator: He or she reduces uncertainty and ambiguity about what is important and how to act. In this role, managers at all organizational levels may have significant control over the informational context in which their subordinates operate. By providing clear and consistent signals about what is important and should be attended to and what is inappropriate and should not be tolerated, managers help people focus and interpret events in strategically appropriate ways.

For example, as Intel moved from a semiconductor memory company to a seller of microprocessors and systems, norms associated with customer orientation became more central. The extent to which this new value has become an integral part of Intel's culture is evident from the current put-down used with technologists who still have not gotten the message, "C'mon, stop being a chip-head."[8] Employees now share an expectation that customers are important, and they convey this message to each other when individual attitudes and behaviors don't meet Intel's new norms of behavior and strategic values.

## The Downside of Managing with Formal Control

Given that control is at the heart of organizations, it is not surprising that both managers and academics should be preoccupied with it.[9] Without a means to coordinate or control collective action, organizations would provide no advantage over individual efforts. When most of us think about designing control systems, we typically try to measure either outcomes or behavior or both (see the simplified model in Figure 5.1). If we can measure factors like sales per hour, margins, number of defects, or customer satisfaction, we feel we are in control. In cases where assessing outcomes is difficult or impossible, we settle for measures of behavior. When measures of both outcomes and behavior are available, we can know with precision whether the

**FIGURE 5.1**

## CONTROL IN ORGANIZATIONS

ABILITY TO MEASURE BEHAVIOR

|  | | High | Low |
|---|---|---|---|
| **ABILITY TO MEASURE OUTCOMES** | **High** | Measure Both Outcomes and Behavior | Measure Outcomes Only |
| | **Low** | Measure Behavior Only | ? |

work is being done in the prescribed way. Our uncertainty and dependence on others are reduced because we can quickly identify deviations. We can also be more confident that we are rewarding the high performers and punishing those who fail to measure up.

But is this the most efficient approach to control? Think for a minute about the types of jobs associated with extensive formal control systems, especially those that rely on monitoring both outcomes and behavior. These jobs include traditional assembly line work and many retail sales positions. Anyone who has held such a job can tell you quickly how incumbents feel about their work: not trusted, overcontrolled, a cog in a machine. As a result, they are often unmotivated.

But at organizations like NUMMI, employees' experiences are quite different. Instead of feeling unmotivated, the workers have a sense of autonomy and responsibility; rather than relying on a formal control system, team members control each other. For instance, there are no industrial engineers at the NUMMI auto plant, and work teams assume responsibility for work design and efficiency. New workers are trained in industrial engineering techniques, and the team itself does the redesign and improvements. One of the authors was walking through the NUMMI plant with a team member who proudly pointed out how he and his team had figured out that by repositioning some soda pop machines they were able to reduce the time for the just-in-time inventory run by two seconds.

NUMMI work teams routinely take responsibility for improving their own work and rely on group problem solving to achieve their goals. At NUMMI, social control supplants or supplements formal control. By contrast, in a typical Detroit plant industrial engineers would perform time and motion studies and instruct the workers in how and when to act. Under this extensive control, the workers would, in turn, likely be unmotivated and, where possible, expend effort and ingenuity in figuring out ways to beat the system rather than improve it.

The importance of social control can be seen most vividly in Figure 5.1, in the cell where it is difficult to assess either outcomes or behaviors reliably and accurately. The jobs in this cell include those that have large, unprogrammed demands, such as R&D, consulting, and technical specialties like information systems, and almost all service jobs, which are characterized by frequent change and unpredictability. With work requirements becoming more complex, uncertain, and changing, control systems cannot be static and formal. Rather, control must come in the form of social control systems that allow directed autonomy and rely on the judgment of employees informed by clarity about the vision and objectives of the business.

The flaws in formal control systems become apparent when their underlying assumptions are revealed. First, formal control relies on the idea that almost everything of importance can be anticipated in advance, a reasonable assumption only in a stable or slowly changing environment. The second assumption is that top-down authority is legitimate and worthy of compliance, based on the belief that workers will comply with directives in exchange for a fair day's pay. While most people continue to accept authority in organizational hierarchies as legitimate, there has been a growing acknowledgment that people want more from work, including an opportunity to contribute and use their talents. The third assumption implicit in the use of formal control is that extrinsic rewards are largely sufficient to direct job-relevant behavior and that these can be based on the measurement of outcomes. But this assumption is, at best, incomplete. Not only do we understand that what gets measured often overwhelms what doesn't, we also know that nonmonetary rewards can sometimes provide more powerful motivation than money or promotions.

A close examination of successful firms and managers suggests the need for both formal and social control systems, with the latter sometimes viewed as a powerful alternative to the former. Indeed, the more organizations are downsized and made leaner, the more these firms must rely on social control both to motivate and monitor behaviors. In *What America Does Right*, Bob Waterman explores the success of FedEx, a company that relies on extensive formal and social control systems. Waterman notes that, "everyone I talked to at FedEx—from couriers to middle managers to people at the top—say the thing they like most about the company is the freedom to do things their way. Managing this delicate balance—between potentially oppressive systems and the cheerful attitudes of a clearly enthusiastic work force—turns out to be the key to FedEx's success."[10] In his view, FedEx has it both ways—formal systems that serve its strategic ends and social controls that motivate and empower employees. The irony is that social control systems can be more powerful and less intrusive than formal controls.

## Integrating National and Organizational Culture

Until now we have concentrated on culture as it operates within organizations, but how does organizational culture relate to national culture? Is it meaningful to talk about organizational culture independent of national culture? Managers of global firms confront such questions daily. Is Hewlett-Packard in Germany still HP, or is it uniquely German? Any discussion of organizational culture needs to be placed in the context of national culture because both cultures operate simultaneously, sometimes complementing each other and sometimes working in opposition.

Organizational cultures can differ as much within countries as they do across countries. A visit to Japan shows that Honda, Nissan, and Toyota are as different from one another as GM, Chrysler, and Ford. Ciba-Geigy is as different from Hoffman-LaRoche as Pfizer is from Merck. We asked Dr. Krauer, former chairman of Ciba-Geigy and the new chairman of Novartis (the company formed by the merger of Ciba and Sandoz), if he saw any problems with his effort to implement a worldwide culture change with 90,000 employees operating in more than 40 countries. His answer, reflecting his long international experience, was unequivocal: "It isn't a major issue. Of course, you need to take into account local conditions. You have to do it in a way that is compatible. There are countries in which the role of the manager is perceived differently. But the basic values are the same. Only the practices are different." This view is echoed by Ciba-Geigy Japan President Paul Dudler, who when asked if Ciba didn't need to adapt itself to the Japanese culture, said, "Of course, we must. We are in Japan, so we have to do many things the way they are being done here. . . . But we should never lose our own identity. We are not imitating, we are adapting."[11]

What companies and managers like these point to is the importance of adjusting the practices used for social control to the local culture. They do not question the importance of shared norms and values as a critical way to integrate the company. Thus, many of the truly global corporations like Shell, Unilever, and ABB are noted for their distinctive organizational cultures. Excellent managers develop social control systems that work in conjunction with national cultures. This requires them to be clear about the norms needed to successfully accomplish the organization's critical tasks while appreciating the basic norms of the national culture.

## PROMOTING INNOVATION THROUGH SOCIAL CONTROL

Because innovation involves unpredictability, risk taking, and nonstandard solutions—factors not easily managed by formal control systems—the effective management of culture lies at the heart of organizational innovation.[12] To understand how managers and organizations enhance innovation, six years ago we systematically began to ask participants in executive programs on strategic innovation and change to suggest norms that helped promote innovation in their organizations. We challenged participants to identify those expectations that, if they were widely shared and strongly held in their business, would significantly enhance both creativity and implementation. More than 2,000 managers from Asia, Europe, Africa, and the United States have participated in these discussions. Managers from industries as diverse as mining, financial services, health care, heavy manufacturing, consumer products, and high technology have responded. The consistency of their responses across disparate geographies and industries is remarkable.

Table 5.1 shows norms associated with innovation identified by managers from five very different firms. All recognize the fundamental importance of designing workplaces that stimulate creativity and the implementation of new ideas.

After hearing similar suggestions from many sources, we decided to validate our findings by conducting a study of more than 200 managers from 29 groups in high-technology firms in Silicon Valley.[13] The results confirmed the idea that innovation is reflected in norms that promote the two component processes of creativity and implementation. Groups that had comparatively strong norms for both were rated as the most innovative. Simply promoting creativity or focusing on speed to implement it did not guarantee innovation. Both are needed.

**TABLE 5.1**

## NORMS FOR INNOVATION

| South African Natural Resources Company | European Pharmaceutical Company | U.S. Financial Services Firm | International R&D Managers | Japanese Beer Company |
|---|---|---|---|---|
| Mistakes OK | Rewards | Acceptance of failure | Freedom to fail | Cooperation |
| Recognition | Acceptance of failure | Freedom to try things | Risk taking | Mistakes OK |
| Rewards | — careful | — time | — fast | Openness |
| Mutual respect | — learn | — support | — prudent | Flexibility |
| Open communication | — calculated | — resources | — cheap | Clear direction |
| Freedom to | Clear objectives | Clear goals | Rewards | Ideas are valued |
| experiment | Sharing of information | Celebration of success | Involvement | Rewards for |
| Expectation of change | Teamwork | Removal of barriers | Toleration of dissent | innovation |
| Challenge the | Commitment from | to change | Listening | |
| status quo | the top | Setting an example | Positive role models | |
| Equal partners | Empowerment | Resources | Resources | |

## Norms to Promote Creativity

Two main ingredients stimulate creativity: (1) support for risk taking and change and (2) tolerance of mistakes. In our study, managers invariably identified these elements as critical for innovation. When pushed about how to apply these ideas, they had some very practical advice.

SUPPORT FOR RISK TAKING AND CHANGE. Clearly, one important way of signaling that something is important is by rewarding it. Most managers we spoke to, however, were not convinced that monetary rewards were very effective at promoting creativity. They felt that recognition from management, colleagues, and others was more powerful. Thus, at companies like 3M, Dow, and the French petrochemical company, Elf Acquitane, managers rely on nonmonetary rewards like recognition to signal their support of innovation. At BOC, winners of innovation awards receive team trophies, individual plaques, and trips to London for meetings with senior management. Recognizing that innovation often requires extensive teamwork means that individual-based awards may be less effective in promoting innovation than team-based recognition and rewards.

In addition to suggesting the need to recognize creativity, managers were also quick to note that to stimulate creativity, one had to be prepared to encourage risk taking and accept failures. For these managers, designing mechanisms to encourage these factors seemed more important than providing a formal monetary reward system, no matter how cleverly designed. One manager at DuPont recalled how a group in his department had tried an innovative approach to a problem that had failed miserably. Rather than ignore the failure, he decided to have a recognition celebration and label the failure as a good try. At Hershey Foods, a manager instituted the "Exalted Order of the Extended Neck" for employees who exhibited entrepreneurship. At Nordstrom and FedEx, heroes often include people who tried to satisfy customers and failed, as well as those who succeeded.[14]

Aligning culture sometimes involves modifying the formal reward system. More often, however, it requires that managers simply use foresight and imagination to provide small rewards and informal recognition for creative attempts. It also requires that managers genuinely understand the values and needs of their employees. What motivates Ph.D. chemists in Switzerland is likely to be different from what motivates retail clerks in San Francisco or managers in a Japanese manufacturing firm. Once the rewards are adapted to the particular environment, rewards and recognition can stimulate creativity. The managerial challenge is to design these rewards in a manner consistent with the underlying values of the employees.

Another important means for encouraging support for creativity and risk taking is to promote a positive attitude toward change. When Fred Smith, CEO of FedEx, tells employees to be mavericks, he also tells them when he proposed the original idea for the company in a college term paper, he received a C, with the admonition that the idea would never work. One FedEx worker is quoted as saying, "I don't have any fear that if I try something that doesn't work, there will be repercussions. There have been a few things that didn't work. We just didn't do them the next day."[15] At Alagasco, a natural gas distributor in Alabama, the president passed out a variety of business cards to his employees encouraging them to try to do things differently. He told them each card was like the get-out-of-jail-free card in Monopoly. If employees try something and it fails, they can turn in their card and be forgiven.

Underneath this seemingly silly behavior is a serious message: It's OK to think out of the box. Managers who want to inspire employees to be creative must convey a consistent message that challenging the status quo is expected. At Odetics, a small aerospace company, for instance, management has an explicit policy of "structured spontaneity," which refers to a policy of deliberately not institutionalizing things. Procter & Gamble also drives this message home using a performance appraisal process. When subordinates set their annual goals, they are expected to show how they will change their job during the coming year. At Rubbermaid, responsibility for each of the 4,700 products is assigned to a team. Team compensation is tied in part to new product introductions, including a corporate goal of 33 percent of corporate revenues from products introduced in the past five years.

**TOLERANCE OF MISTAKES.** Another major ingredient in the development of organizational creativity is a tolerance for mistakes, both personal and organizational. This is easy to say and hard to do, and most of us are justifiably cynical when bosses say that it's OK to make mistakes; we have also seen careers that have been damaged when people took this exhortation at face value. Managers can get past this resistance in part by being very clear about what types of risk taking and mistakes are OK. At Johnson & Johnson, R.W. Johnson's maxim, "Failure is our most important product," lives on, but J&J managers are careful to communicate what constitutes a reasonable mistake. Mistakes are permitted if they are based on analysis, foster learning, and are modest in impact. There must be continual support for those who try and do not succeed. As a Delta Airlines supervisor observed, "One thing that helps us to admit that we have made a mistake is that people who are above us don't hold it against us. In this company, if you make a mistake and you recognize it and something positive comes out of that, that's a positive for the company."[16]

Under these circumstances, creativity cannot help but be increased as employees see innovation modeled by managers, watch co-workers get rewarded, hear it talked about by their peers, and observe that good-faith mistakes are not only tolerated but may even be approved of. Little creativity occurs when management emphasizes not making mistakes and always punishes those who made them. As Jack Welch says, "The trick is not to punish those who fall short. If they improve, you reward them—even if they haven't reached the goal."[17]

## Norms to Promote Implementation

The second set of norms that are critical in enhancing innovation are those that are actionable. Once creative ideas and approaches are identified, will they be enacted? There are two important types of norms that ensure action: (1) those that emphasize effective teamwork and group functioning, and (2) those that emphasize speed and urgency.

TEAMWORK. In complex organizations, innovation almost always involves getting people to alter the way they operate. As we noted in Chapter 4, when tasks are characterized by sequential or reciprocal interdependence, any change in work flow requires adjustment by those doing the work. Introducing a new product, process, or technology disrupts the old way of doing things. Implementation of the required changes is enhanced when groups operate effectively, when they hold common goals, and openly share information.

Effective group functioning is enhanced when members like and respect each other, understand others' perspectives and operating styles, can resolve disagreements, and can communicate effectively. Such effectiveness is based partly on skills and abilities that can be learned (e.g., problem solving) and partly on shared expectations within the group (e.g., norms about mutual respect and how to resolve differences). Hewitt Associates and J.P. Morgan believe that their competitive advantage rests in part on their ability to act as a team to meet their clients' needs. At Goldman, Sachs, where teamwork has long been a core value, a primary consideration for promotion is the ability to be a team player. "If you can't sublimate your ego or work with others, you have a problem," said a top partner.[18]

At Odetics, a software engineer said, "Everyone works very hard and everyone is very team-oriented. They do their own part, but they support everyone else. If we're working on a deadline or a program, as soon as one person gets their work done, they will go and help the next person to get theirs done." The explicit expectation in these organizations is that people will be helpful to one another rather than competitive.

Implementation is also enhanced when groups share values and common goals. A common vision, whether corporate or lower level, can be a powerful way to coordinate people and involve them emotionally. At Motorola, for instance, people often say "I am a Motorolan," not "I work at Motorola." In organizations and groups in which no such commonality exists, the implementation of new approaches must proceed more slowly, as members negotiate disparate perspectives and beliefs.

Implementation also depends on sharing information openly, including good news and bad. If groups are to function effectively, they must deal with the way the world is, not the way they would like it to be. At Springfield ReManufacturing, the CEO, Jack Stack, believes that unless all employees know and understand the firm's financial data, they won't understand how their jobs contribute to the whole. All employees are, therefore, educated in how to read a financial statement and interpret accounting data. Each week the company shuts down the machines for half an hour so that every employee can study the latest financial statements. This wide dissemination of information not only enhances understanding and motivation, it also signals to all employees that they are trusted and that there is a reciprocal obligation between the firm and the worker.

**SPEED AND URGENCY.** Another group of norms that promotes the implementation of innovation and change involves speed and urgency: (1) the idea that decisions should be made quickly, (2) expectations that promote flexibility and adaptability, and (3) a sense of personal autonomy that encourages action. Each factor supports getting things done and is distinct from the norms that enhance creativity.

The first relates to the speed with which decisions are taken. In some places, norms may include expectations that speed is important, the pace of work is rapid, and people are expected to work long hours. In other situations, the pace is leisurely, working hard is not valued, and someone who works hard is considered a "rate buster." At Microsoft, for instance, people work all hours of the day and night. There is also a sense of insecurity that drives people to excel. At Intel, Andy Grove refers to this attitude as "competitive paranoia" and notes, "The pace of work these days isn't easy to live with, but welcome to the Nineties."[19] Compare this attitude with that of a government worker who said, "I can't think of a day when I haven't done nothing. I do nothing three-fourths of the time, not including sleeping."

At Goldman, Sachs, 60–80 hour weeks are the norm, and the expectation is that people are prepared to sacrifice their personal lives to ensure the work gets done. FedEx's policy is that every employee or customer query is answered that day, even if the answer is only that the issue is being worked on. At other firms, norms sometimes convey an expectation that inaction is the preferred alternative and initiative is not expected or desired. At Preston Trucking, a worker (now called an "associate") described how under the old system employees never did anything without authorization, including something as simple as changing a light bulb. People were expected to come to work and do what they were told. Since the early 1990s, however, there has been a cultural revolution emphasizing initiative and innovation. Norms now emphasize the expectation that workers will be flexible and use their initiative. In 1991, the 5,000 plus associates generated more than 7,500 suggestions for improvement. For its part, management now shares performance and financial information, actively encourages innovation, and emphasizes trust and team-work. Meanwhile, since the deregulation of the trucking industry in 1980, more than 75 percent of Preston's direct competitors have failed.

The second element in promoting implementation through social control is flexibility and adaptability. At Avis, the em-ployee-owned rental car company, there is an emphasis on EPGs (Employee Participation Groups), which allow teams of em-ployee-owners to develop locally responsive actions to help the company. In New York, they developed a job-swap program in which employees at local airports swapped jobs for short periods with others at corporate headquarters to learn more about each other's work. In Hawaii, the local EPG designed its own Avis outfits to fit the tropical environment (in Avis red). At BE&K, a large construction company, there is a deliberate policy of not having rigid job descriptions in order to encourage responsibility. At Chaparral Steel, employees are given encouragement and opportunities to learn every job in their department. From the employee's perspective, this approach provides growth and challenge. From the firm's viewpoint, it enhances flexibility. In these and other firms, the ability to adapt to changing circumstances, take initiative and responsibility, and modify the way work gets done is an integral part of the job.

The third element in promoting speed and urgency are norms associated with a sense of autonomy. Not only do individual employees have the latitude to take action but also the obligation to do so. A core value at Johnson & Johnson is decentralization, which stresses the autonomy of the group companies. Managers are expected to run their own companies and undertake their own strategic planning without interference from corporate headquarters. Early on, HP adopted as a core part of its philosophy the idea that managers should give subordinates a well-defined objective, allow as much freedom as possible in working toward that objective, and see that their contributors were recognized throughout the company.

At a more microlevel, many firms emphasize employee autonomy in the way they minimize rules and design jobs. At Chaparral Steel, one employee said, "The main thing that makes me happy about getting up in the morning and coming to work is the fact that I like what I do and have freedom."[20] At TDIndustries, an employee-owned plumbing and air-conditioning company, senior management highlights freedom as a core value, which translates into continual efforts to free up employees so they can do their jobs in the way they best see fit. Gary Brackett, a service technician, said, "Around here you're basically your own boss. I do big jobs for my boss. He sends me out, I go look at the job, I bid on it, and I put it in. Half the time he doesn't even see the job or know what's involved unless I tell him." A Nordstrom salesman said, "Where else could I get paid so well and have so much autonomy?. . . No one tells me what to do, and I feel I can go as far as my dedication will take me. I feel like an entrepreneur." While Nordstrom demands strong conformity around such norms as dress, positive attitudes, and treating customers in a particular way, its workers feel free.

Developing shared expectations among employees to promote innovation takes time and requires absolute consistency by managers at all levels and constant repetition of the message. To help see how norms can be used by managers, we turn our attention in the next chapter to mechanisms or levers that can be used to shape organizational culture.

# A Practical Guide to Diagnosing Culture

If one of the keys to the successful execution of strategy is culture, how does a manager diagnose the norms and values that characterize an organization? Think about how new members of an organization learn what is really important and expected of them. First, there are the official expectations expressed in job descriptions, company policies, personnel manuals, and instructions from the boss. People are told about work hours, performance evaluation schemes, ethical codes, safety requirements, and company benefits. Most employees understand that these prescriptions are only an introduction to the organization's culture. Official policy and actual practice often diverge. Therefore, while new employees pay attention to the formalities, they also want to learn how things actually work. To learn that, new people pay close attention to the verbal and nonverbal cues from other colleagues and supervisors. Either explicitly or implicitly the following questions need to be answered before a newcomer is able to understand the culture.

- What do I have to do to fit in?

- What is really important around here?

- What do my new colleagues think is important?

- What do I have to say and do to feel like I'm one of the group?

- What do I have to do to get my boss's attention (good and bad)?

- How do things really get done around here?

- What does it take to get ahead?

Knowing the answers to these questions helps us fit in and be accepted. Fitting in is an integral part of our self-esteem. We often know when we are doing well only by comparing ourselves with others. When we are accepted and valued by others, our self-image is enhanced. But first we need to know what others think is important in terms of values, attitudes, and behavior. Their words and actions help us answer the questions posed above. We watch carefully to see what behaviors are rewarded, both formally by the organization and, more immediately, what is approved or disapproved of informally by our co-workers and immediate supervisor.

Colleagues often provide us with more frequent rewards and punishments than does the organization's formal reward system. On a daily basis we get feedback from colleagues indicating whether we are liked and respected, whether we are seen as contributing to the group, and whether we are doing the right or wrong thing. Our attitudes and behavior are significantly affected by those around us, especially if we care about them. The esteem of our fellow workers may be more motivating than an annual pay raise, especially when our job performance is dependent to some degree on the cooperation and goodwill of colleagues.

This is not to say that we do not listen to the pronouncements of senior managers. Of course, we do. We also watch their behaviors to see if what they say matches what they do. The combination of signals from those above us, the formal measurement and reward systems, and our colleagues' interpretations of events all help us decide what is really important.

## CONDUCTING A CULTURE DIAGNOSIS

The process outlined in the box helps explain how a manager can diagnose group or organizational culture. This six-step ap-

**Step 1:** Identify critical strategic challenges.

**Step 2:** Link the strategy for meeting these challenges to the critical tasks needed to implement it.

**Step 3:** Identify the norms and values that will help accomplish critical tasks.

**Step 4:** Diagnose the norms that characterize the current culture.

**Step 5:** Identify gaps between the norms needed and existing ones.

**Step 6:** Decide on actions needed to reduce these gaps.

proach can be used to diagnose culture at the group, unit division, or corporate level. While the diagnosis will differ depending on the level of analysis, the process remains the same.

*Step 1*. As described in Chapter 3, the first step in diagnosing congruence is to identify the strategic challenges facing the unit. To define the competitive advantage of the business, answer the following diagnostic questions:

- Who are your customers and what are their needs?

- Which market segments are you targeting?

- How broad or narrow is your product or service offering?

- Why should customers prefer your product or service to a competitor's?

- What are the competencies you possess that others can't easily imitate?

- How do you make money in these segments?

Regardless of his or her level in the organization's hierarchy, the person (or group) making the diagnosis needs to begin by turning these answers into clear, specific objectives.

*Step 2*. Once the group or individual has listed the strategic challenges, identify the critical tasks required to accomplish each objective. Be as clear as possible in identifying these tasks by answering the following questions:

- What are the half-dozen specific tasks that absolutely must be accomplished if you are to successfully execute your strategy?

- How much interdependence is required among units in order to coordinate these tasks?

- Do I understand the work flow?

- Is this list complete and internally consistent?

*Step 3*. After listing the critical tasks, identify what norms are needed in the future to ensure that the tasks are accomplished effectively. These are the specific attitudes and behaviors that, if widely shared and strongly felt among employees, would directly help the execution of the critical tasks. For example, while general norms needed for some tasks may include customer service, quality, and flexibility, these terms are too vague to help employees understand exactly how to behave. Those norms must be defined in terms of the specific attitudes and behaviors needed. This step requires managers to think through what their expectations really are and express them clearly, avoiding trendy buzz words as examples of what the norm means in the context of the workplace.

- What value, if widely shared and strongly held throughout the unit, would further the accomplishment of the critical tasks? (Answer this question for each of the half-dozen tasks listed.)

- What are the specific attitudes and behaviors that would be consistent with values and ensure that the critical tasks are accomplished?

- Is it reasonable to expect these attitudes and behaviors from people given the existing reward system?

The importance of understanding the norms needed to execute the critical tasks was demonstrated in a successful high-technology company in Silicon Valley. Historically, its strategy had been to be a first-mover, always developing innovative products with a clear technological edge. But, as senior managers looked into the future, they realized that their technological lead was slipping. While their products were successful because of their technology, they were not viewed as reliable. Moreover, customers saw the company as arrogant and unresponsive. Senior management recognized that the company's future success would rest jointly on its ability to be creative in developing new technology and its ability to improve substantially the reliability of the product line and customer service.

The problem, management recognized, was that the current emphasis on technology needed to be modified if the company was to compete successfully in the next few years. Quality, reliability, and customer service, as well as creativity, needed to be shared throughout the firm. Rather than simply communicate that creativity, for example, needed to become a part of the culture, top management offered a concrete definition of creativity as, "an emphasis on identifying new ways of doing things. There is a continuous effort to seek out new products and processes. We always encourage new ideas." Concrete definitions of other needed norms such as customer service and quality were also developed.

Though these definitions were widely known, people throughout the organization were unclear about what the new norms meant and what behaviors were expected in their day-to-day activities. Quality meant that people were expected to do whatever was necessary, even if it meant disrupting production and cost schedules. Similarly, employees understood that creativity was not limited to the technologists. Managers were expected to seek out new ways of doing things and to encourage their subordinates to do the same. This, in turn, permitted senior management to reward and recognize those who behaved appropriately. Less well articulated definitions would not have been effective in energizing the whole organization.

*Step 4.* After identifying the norms required for future success, assess the current culture. The intent here is to identify those norms, positive and negative, that accurately describe the shared expectations within the unit. Particular attention should be placed on identifying norms that can help or hinder the accomplishment of the critical tasks listed in Step 2. Managers and their teams should generate a list of the current norms by reflecting on the diagnostic questions posed earlier:

- Imagine that a close friend joins your organization. If she asked you about what to do to be seen as an excellent performer, what advice would you give her?

- If she asked what she should avoid do to ensure that she didn't fail, what would you say?

- What is really rewarded in the organization (versus what management says is rewarded)?

- What does it actually take to get ahead?

A slightly more structured approach can also be used by asking a small focus group of five to eight people familiar with the current culture to identify the norms and values that characterize the unit. Table 5.2 is a worksheet for this exercise. After a series of representative groups has participated, the norms and values that define the culture can be assessed by noting which norms are shared across groups (consensus) and which are seen as most important (intensity).

*Step 5.* Once the norms needed for future success and the norms that characterize the unit are known, they can then be compared, and any gaps or inconsistencies can be identified.

- Do the norms that define the current culture hinder, if unchanged, the execution of the critical tasks?

- Are there norms that are important for the accomplishment of the critical tasks that are currently not valued?

- Are there inconsistencies between what we say is important and the current culture?

**TABLE 5.2**

## ORGANIZATIONAL CULTURE DIAGNOSIS WORKSHEET

As you know, the norms and values that define an organization's culture can vary substantially across hierarchical levels and subunits. These variations may help or hinder innovation within the organization. To assess the current culture, we would like each group to identify those norms and values that, *in your experience,* characterize the culture in your organization. These should be those norms and values that you feel are widely shared. So please take 60 minutes and address the following three questions.

1. First, take 40 minutes and, as a group, identify the central norms and values you feel characterize the culture in your organization. These should be the half-dozen or so core values or beliefs that, *in your experience,* characterize the way the culture operates. They are not necessarily what senior management professes, but are accurate descriptions of the way things really are. Please list them in order of importance.

2. Now take 10 minutes and identify those norms and values you believe should characterize the organization's culture but at present do not. These should be those norms or beliefs that you feel are important for achieving the organization's critical strategic objectives in the next two to three years but are not widely shared or strongly held. They could be, for example, values that people talk about but do not practice.

3. Now take 10 minutes and list those things that you feel are really rewarded within the organization. In your experience, what does it really take to be successful within the company? What are those things that management really pays attention to? If you were to advise a friend who had just joined the company, what would you advise him or her to do to be successful?

Norms that will help accomplish the critical tasks need to be preserved while those that will hinder attainment need to be attenuated.

*Step 6.* The final step in the culture diagnosis process is to identify the causes of each important gap between what exists today and what is required for future success.

- Is the current reward system aligned with the norms needed?

- Do the existing structure and systems support the adoption of the norms needed?

- Are the right outcomes and processes being measured?

- Are the needed norms consistent with the values and expectations of the work force?

- Do the people have the requisite skills and motivation necessary to adopt new attitudes and behaviors?

- Is senior management consistently modeling and reinforcing the desired norms?

The congruence model can be used to get at the roots of these cultural gaps and can be used to systematically examine the alignment between the norms needed for the successful accomplishment of the critical tasks and people (motivation and skills), the formal organization (rewards, careers, structures, systems), and the demands of the critical tasks (interdependence, work flow). The overarching search is either for needed norms that are not aligned or for norms that are currently valued which need to be eliminated or downplayed in the future.

There will often be multiple causes for the presence or absence of a norm. Often, gaps occur simply because of a time lag between an espoused set of values and gradually coming to believe that a new regime is necessary. Many times what managers say is not matched by their actions, leaving employees confused and suspicious. While it may take time and coordinated effort, we will show in the next chapter how managers, armed with data on the cultural gaps, can manage cultural change.

# C  H  A  P  T  E  R  6

## SHAPING ORGANIZATIONAL CULTURE

WHILE RETAIL FIRMS LIKE FEDERATED, MACY'S, AND Carter-Hawley-Hale have wrestled with bankruptcy, Nordstrom has grown from 36 stores and 9,000 employees in 1983 to 76 stores and more than 35,000 employees by 1995, with average sales per square foot double the industry average. What accounts for Nordstrom's competitive advantage? A close reading of the strategy literature quickly suggests that it is not the usual factors such as barriers to entry, power over suppliers and customers, or lack of industry rivalry. The retail industry is quite competitive and buyers and suppliers move easily from one firm to another. It isn't location, merchandise, store appearance, or even the piano in the lobby. Each of these factors is easily imitated. Rather, as anyone who has shopped Nordstrom knows, it is the remarkable service that Nordstrom provides that differentiates it from its competitors. How remarkable? Consider just two anecdotes told by customers.

At an executive program several years ago, we asked the managers if they had any experience with Nordstrom. Because most of the participants were from outside the United States, we didn't expect any would. However, one enthusiastic participant, Danny Halperin, a manager of a service business in South Africa, announced he had just spent two full days shopping at Nordstrom. (Indeed, he went on to say that his real reason for attending the program was not for the wisdom and insights of the course but to visit the local Nordstrom store to see if its service was as incredible as people claimed.) First, he had heard about the Nordstrom return policy and decided to test it. He brought with him a pair of trousers that he had purchased in South Africa. He marched into the men's wear department and informed the salesman that he was attending an executive program and had brought the trousers with him to the United States, only to learn that they were the wrong size. Would the salesman accept them as a return? As someone in the service business himself, he was prepared for the usual run around. He was, therefore, surprised when the salesman asked him how much he had paid, reached into the cash register, and gave him that amount. There were no supervisors summoned to initial the transaction and no visits to the cashier.

But that was not the real test. After getting over his shock, Danny asked the salesman if he could help him buy some pantyhose for his wife. Without a word, the salesman led Danny to the women's department and stopped in front of the pantyhose counter. He then asked Danny the logical question, "What size is your wife?" Danny's response was, "I don't know." In most stores this would be the end of the story. In this case, however, the salesman simply located three saleswomen of varying sizes, lined them up, and asked Danny to identify the one most similar in size to his wife.

How does Nordstrom elicit acts of initiative like these? How does an organization design and operate systems that deliver service levels that differentiate it from its competitors? A piece of the answer is surprising and contained in the Nordstrom employee handbook, which all new employees are given. Its single page reads:

WELCOME TO NORDSTROM.
We're glad to have you with our company.
Our number one goal is to provide outstanding
customer service.
Set both your personal and professional goals high.
We have great confidence in your ability to achieve them.
Nordstrom Rules:
Rule #1: Use your good judgment in all situations.
There will be no additional rules.
Please feel free to ask your department manager,
store manager, or division general manager
any question at any time.

Nordstrom relies not on extensive policies and procedures but the judgment of its employees; that is, the norms that characterize the culture provide the control. Skeptics might reasonably ask, "What happens if employees lack good judgment or customers try to abuse the system?" A similar concern could be raised about how a firm like FedEx can succeed while encouraging its 40,000 employees to be mavericks and constantly take risks. On the face of it, this approach seems like a recipe for chaos, but it isn't. Nordstrom and FedEx use culture to coordinate activities in the face of the need for change. Nonstandard requirements are the true test of service. Employees need to give the help the customer wants, not the help a policy or procedure dictates.

As we discussed in Chapter 5, in order to manage organizational culture effectively, managers need to be clear about the specific norms and values that will help the organization execute its strategy. Managers must then decide how to promote the needed norms and reduce those that get in the way.

There are three important levers managers can use to influence the social control system of their units: shaping culture through participation or systems of involvement that lead people to feel responsible, using management behavior to convey vivid messages about what attitudes and behaviors are important, and designing comprehensive systems of reward and recognition that are targeted at those attitudes and behaviors critical for success.

## SHAPING CULTURE THROUGH PARTICIPATION AND COMMITMENT

To illustrate how managers in strong culture organizations use participation to build commitment and shape interpretations and culture, consider the results of an unlikely experiment in which participants were asked to voluntarily eat an earthworm. Intuition tells us that most people would not eat earthworms; therefore, only a small group of people who were unnaturally adventurous or trying to impress others would voluntarily do it. Yet the surprising results of the study showed that close to 50 percent of the participants ate them.[1]

Why? The answer lies in the way the experiment was structured. Subjects became incrementally involved through making a series of public commitments. Once a series of small commitments is made, it becomes progressively more difficult to back out. Behavior leads to attitudes. Doing is believing. Former CEO of Ford, Don Petersen, noted that when you get behavior, you get commitment.

More precisely, three characteristics of the participation process lead people toward increasing commitment: choice, or the opportunity to participate; visibility, or making choices that are public and can be witnessed by others who matter; and irrevocability, or a sense that some line has been crossed. Note that here participation is not democracy, not permissiveness. People are encouraged to make choices within certain guidelines. At NUMMI, team members have a great deal of choice in how best to design their work, not in whether the plant will build cars or pick-up trucks.

Each characteristic makes a decision more binding. Decisions made without strong external pressure increase feelings of personal responsibility, reduce the ability to justify our actions by pointing to another motive (such as money), or external pressure (such as a manager), and enhance positive feelings (if I chose to do this, it must be worthwhile; otherwise, why would I do it?). Visibility makes it difficult to excuse nonperformance and motivates one to do what one promised. Finally, irrevocability discourages individuals from considering alternative choices and focuses energy on the chosen course.[2]

## Commitment through Choice

Managers or firms use the psychology of choice to promote commitment by

- designing systems and procedures that encourage people to continually make choices;

- emphasizing the intrinsic rewards for tasks, not just the instrumental ones;

- obtaining incremental or step-by-step choices;

- ensuring that people have a realistic picture before choosing and inoculating them against future surprises.

Consider what happens when managers design and use systems that encourage people to continually be involved and make choices. At NUMMI, team members are responsible for selecting new members, which makes good sense because the team is responsible for the work. Psychologically, however, it makes even better sense. New members understand that they are being evaluated and need to fit in to be chosen. This increases the importance of co-workers as a group of others who matter to us. Old members immediately feel a sense of responsibility for making the right choice and living with the consequences.

In the old GM Fremont plant there were 80 industrial engineers. NUMMI has none. If the team opts to do the work design, it is its responsibility to make the design work, not to blame the industrial engineers. For example, team members decided not to spend the $120,000 needed to repair the escalator. A sign prominently points out the fact that the team members made the decision. NUMMI, like many other strong culture firms, also makes extensive use of choice and incremental commitment in the hiring process. Candidates must participate, without compensation, for three days in an assessment center where their ability to fit in is diagnosed. The entire process is one of requiring the prospective applicant to make continual choices in the presence of clear signals about expected attitudes and behaviors.[3]

Other strong culture firms also use choice and incremental commitment in the selection and orientation process. At Marriott, one manager reported that the company rejected 90 percent of would-be guest associates. Under its old hiring practices, Marriott lost more than 40 percent of its new hires in the first three months. Now both the selection and orientation processes emphasize the emotional content of the work and the norms and values needed to do that work.[4] At Disney, the director of training said, "The real secret is modeling [employees'] behavior and perpetuating the Disney culture with stories." In doing so, Disney loses only about 15 percent of its front-line employees annually, compared with 60 percent in the hospitality industry. In the service industry, hiring people committed to the organization's values is crucial because front-line employees determine customer satisfaction.

These stressful, prolonged screening and selection processes do serve a purpose. The applicant's escalating time investment, the clear signals about expected attitudes and behavior, the emotional stress of the interviews, the public commitments of interest and enthusiasm, the decision not to drop out, and the increasing psychological investment all combine to make the applicant's ultimate decision seem a positive one. It would be difficult *not* to have a sense of success for having survived such an arduous process. When the new employee accepts the job, he or she begins with a realistic sense of what is required, finds like-minded colleagues, and is apt to be psychologically committed. As an employee of Cooper Tires said, "This company prides itself on being a real pain in the butt to get in. I think six months had lapsed from the first time I talked to the Industrial Relations people until I was given an offer. The good news is that when people come to Cooper, they hardly ever leave."[5]

While many organizations can modify their hiring processes to encourage choice, most managers don't have the luxury of beginning over with new employees. One mechanism used to shape commitment by firms as diverse as Levi Strauss, McDonnell-Douglas, and PTT, the Dutch telecommunications company, is to have people re-apply for their jobs. While this can be anxiety-producing, under some circumstances it can generate a feeling of crisis and cause people to rethink their commitments. It can shake people out of a status quo mentality and offer managers an opportunity to reframe employees' thinking about work. This is one of the underlying psychological forces at work in many reengineering and downsizing efforts. Psychologically, the process requires people to choose, in a voluntary, public, and irrevocable way, how to do their jobs.

The Work-Out program at GE, or the major change efforts under way at Philips's Operation Centurion, is precisely the sort of effort that also involves people continually. "The only way I see to get more productivity is getting people involved and excited about their jobs. . . . When people see their ideas count, their dignity is raised . . . They feel more important. They are more important!" says Welch. "If you're not thinking all the time about making every person more valuable, you don't have a chance. What's the alternative? Wasted minds? Uninvolved people? A labor force that's angry or bored?"[6] Involvement is directly associated with acceptance, motivation, and productivity. The point is not to argue for a specific technique such as reengineering or TQM but to think about designing systems and processes that permit continuous incremental commitment, and to design them to be consistent with the values and expectations of the work force.

Often this involves a set of incremental or step-by-step choices as people become progressively more involved. A close examination of the selection processes of strong culture firms like Disney, Southwest Airlines, HP, and others shows a progressive involvement with escalating commitment. And, just as with the earthworm experiment, organizations often inoculate potential employees against future doubts by ensuring that they have a realistic picture of the firm before joining. These organizations are honest about what is expected from their members and encourage people to either accept their norms before becoming regular employees (such as during a probationary period) or to help applicants who will not fit in to select out early.

## Commitment through Visibility

Firms also use visibility to enhance commitment by

- publicizing an individual's activities and accomplishments among peers, other employees, clients, and family;

- using appropriate ceremonies and symbols to promote a sense of belonging and identification with the group;

- encouraging public expressions of loyalty with customers and clients, at meetings, and with family and friends;

- encouraging the development of social relations among members; and

- using group evaluation and approval as a part of the feedback process.

The psychological reason for each of these actions, whether deliberate or not, is to capitalize on the commitment that can result from making choices publicly, especially among those who matter, like friends and family.

For example, at Haworth, the office furniture manufacturer, the orientation program for new members includes their families. Similarly, the president of the Honda plant at Marysville introduces the company's philosophy, not only to new employees, but also to their families. Cypress Semiconductor has a tradition of making a home visit to make hiring offers and to recruit the spouses of important professional-level candidates. Other firms routinely attempt to foster social ties among new employees, and enhance the importance of public acts. Their actions can range from the seemingly trivial—such as Quad/Graphics' production of an annual yearbook with every employee's photograph, date of hire, and spouse's name—to encouraging deeper and longer term relationships among employees.

Tandem Computer used to fill most of its positions internally and encourage "Tandemites"—as employees refer to themselves—to recommend friends and family for positions in the company. New entrants were assigned a sponsor who introduced the person and acted as a mentor. Asked why Tandem placed so much emphasis on swimming pools, parties, and the like, former CEO Jimmy Treybig's immediate response was that he wanted people to like each other and socialize together. He wanted their families to use the company facilities on weekends. Through these shared activities, co-workers become friends and family, and their opinions matter.

Many companies, such as consulting and investment banking firms, require a time commitment that effectively isolates their employees from other social groups and thus heightens the profiles of co-workers as people who matter. The formal evaluation process (such as 360-degree evaluations in which an individual is evaluated by his or her supervisors, peers, and subordinates) used at companies such as Goldman, Morgan Stanley, Merck, and 3M makes the fact salient to employees that their actions are visible and being evaluated. Again, while these processes may induce important substantive benefits, they have valuable psychological consequences as well. Making public commitments in front of co-workers who are family and friends requires a different degree of follow-through than promising something to a stranger.

Think about the rather odd ceremony at Mary Kay in which new sales directors take a sacred oath in front of an auditorium filled with their peers. On the one hand, this is a nice way to recognize people. But psychologically, something deeper is going on. People at this ceremony and similar ones in other organizations, are *publicly* committing to maintaining certain standards of behavior and achieving certain goals. Every time a Mary Kay distributor climbs into her pink Cadillac or Buick, she is sending signals to herself and to others.[7] When groups of employees at Tandem are asked to decide how corporate philosophy should operate in their facility, their response makes a public commitment to maintain certain values, attitudes, and behavior.

As managers and researchers attempt to understand why TQM efforts work or don't work, two findings emerge that reflect the psychology of commitment. Quality teams are more likely to succeed if (1) the team members feel that they have chosen to participate (and not been told that they were "volunteering") and (2) these teams and their efforts are highly visible to those who matter. Team members are often encouraged to publicly commit to certain standards, whether by signing pledges that are prominently posted or giving verbal testimonies in public meetings.

Other efforts include signing off on the product. For instance, workers at Cooper Tires and Lincoln Electric sign each product they build. A second commitment lesson has to do with putting people in touch with customers. Holding aside the valuable information such contacts may offer, the fact is that meeting face-to-face with customers means publicly taking responsibility for the product or service. Meeting another person, especially if he or she can make contact later on, increases an individual's sense of ownership and motivation to deliver on promises. If individuals care about their customer as a colleague or friend, their motivation is increased.

There are other ways managers can promote commitment through visibility. For instance, to foster social ties (and improve the power of the social control system), NUMMI provides funds to teams for social activities, but only if the entire team participates. Whether the team goes fishing, has a picnic, or goes to a ball game, social ties among the members are strengthened. Southwest Airlines has a similar policy of providing small social budgets for employees at each airport. Thus, systems or procedures that enhance the visibility of an individual among his or her peers may increase the power of the social control system.

## Commitment through Irrevocability

A third element of participation that can enhance commitment is irrevocability, or involvements that include a sense that, at some point in the decision process, the choice is final. Psychologically this makes sense as a means to reduce any cognitive dissonance that can arise after making a choice. Thus, managers

- make the commitment process a serious one;

- communicate and label those decisions whose consequences are important to the group;

- get people involved in making the decision;

- emphasize "career" choices, "investments," rather than the "job"; and

- make sure that people know that a commitment is for the long term.

By making the commitment process serious and signaling that a decision is important, the person is encouraged to interpret the choice as a consequential one. For example, by involving senior management in the hiring process, an organization can indicate to potential employees that their decision to work for the firm is important. At Cypress Semiconductor, only the top 18 senior managers are empowered to make job offers, and managers are responsible for recruiting their own new employees. Although this policy may be onerous when added to the manager's other responsibilities, the message, however, is that hiring is too important to be left to the human resource function.

Other ways of increasing irrevocability include getting people involved in the hiring decision, emphasizing "career" choices and long-term investment. Home Depot has a cheer that says:

"Where do you go if you want a job? Sears! Where do you go if you want a career? Home Depot!"[8] At one level, an employee cheer is hardly likely to be critical in determining an employee's attitudes or behavior, but, at another level Home Depot management is signaling that it wants employees to think about the long term. They don't have a job; they have a career. This is signaled in other ways as well. For example, all employees attend weekly product knowledge classes. Part-timers aren't used because they don't have sufficient expertise; the firm is telling employees that they are valuable and it is willing to invest in them.

One of the most compelling uses of irrevocability was conveyed to us in the case of a manager in the Bell system who was responsible for setting up an unregulated subsidiary. His job was to convert more than a thousand "Bell-shaped employees" into aggressive, market-oriented entrepreneurs who could successfully compete in an unregulated environment. As a part of this process, he involved them in a variety of ways in the planning and organization for the new configuration. Finally, after months of hard work, he gathered his new work force in an auditorium for a final meeting before the official launch. Just before lunch, and after painting a vivid portrait of the opportunities and risks that awaited them, he told the participants that he wanted them to rethink their commitment. For those who felt that the risks were too great, he said they should not return after lunch. He told them that he would find them jobs back on the regulated side of the company. Anyone who did return after lunch was making a public commitment to the new venture. He lost a few people, but those who returned were irrevocably committing themselves to going forward. Indeed, when some of the new ventures ran into problems, there was far less complaining among the employees. Management simply pointed out that each had "volunteered."

In all these examples, the psychology is the same. Managers design processes that label some decisions as important, get people involved in making choices about how to proceed, and encourage these choices to be made visible to others who matter. The combined effect of these systems of participation is to promote a sense of ownership, responsibility, and positive feelings toward the results of the choices. (In passing, it is interesting to note the Japanese do not use the literal term for participation, *sanka*. Instead the terms *nattokusei*, which means consent, or *kobetsushido*, individual guidance, are used to describe employees' involvement.)

## SHAPING CULTURE THROUGH SYMBOLIC ACTIONS

As shown in Chapter 5, we all use information from our own behavior and that of others to help define situations. Because we are so sensitive to consistent signals, especially from those who matter to us, information from our boss and senior managers can be enormously powerful in shaping our interpretation of what is important and how to behave. For this reason, managers can be seen as signal generators, consciously or unconsciously sending out messages through their words and actions as to what is really important. This role gives managers an opportunity to help subordinates focus on particular aspects of the work environment, to see events in certain ways, and to help shape their interpretation of events.

To appreciate how this approach differs from conventional views of leadership, consider the diagram in Figure 6.1. In 1981, Jeffrey Pfeffer called attention to the important differences between substantive leadership and management as symbolic action.[9] While traditional conceptions of management are based on managers' formal authority, symbolic actions are those that affect how people understand their own behavior and how they feel about it. So, for example, when a senior manager decides to reallocate financial resources or change the assignments of subordinates or reengineer the work, the action is likely to occur. Whether the decision is right or wrong; it is important to understand how people feel about it. Time may reveal whether the decision was successful or not, but the interpretation of the decision may have important effects on its acceptance. These

**FIGURE 6.1**

**SUBSTANTIVE AND SYMBOLIC LEADERSHIP**

| | | TYPE OF IMPACT | |
|---|---|---|---|
| | | Substantive | Attitudinal |
| BASIS OF AUTHORITY | Formal | Large Effect | Uncertain |
| | Symbolic | Small Effect | Large Effect |

interpretations may also affect how well the decision itself is implemented.

As Pfeffer is fond of saying, in real time it is impossible to know whether a decision is correct or not. What is certain is that we spend far more time dealing with the consequences of our decisions than we do making them. His point is that *how* we deal with the decision can be far more important than the decision itself. In organizations, what is important is that managers of change help their subordinates come to a common interpretation of the meaning of managerial actions. Without a consensus on meaning, implementation will be difficult. In this sense, a primary leadership role for managers is to help people interpret decisions and events in ways that maximize the probability of success. Managers need to be sensitive to both the substantive and symbolic aspects of their leadership to ensure common interpretations.

Managers don't necessarily need to be charismatic, although eloquence and forcefulness are undoubtedly useful. But there is evidence that, over time, the consistency and credibility with which a message is communicated are more important than the wording. Research has also shown that with contradictory messages, such as often occur in organizations simply through misinterpretations, people pay the most attention to nonverbal cues. Disney understands the power of nonverbal actions. One of the first instructions in the *Disney Courtesy Policies* used for training cast members in the theme parks is, "Your posture, gestures, facial expression, manner, and general attitude combine to amplify the positive, warm, and friendly non-verbal communication required." The manual instructs new hires to communicate nonverbally in a variety of ways. Managing symbolically requires that a manager pay close attention to his or her own words and behavior and how they convey meaning to others.

The symbolic side of management includes such activities as providing a clear vision of the unit's goals with which employees can identify emotionally as well as intellectually; ensuring absolute consistency of words and actions to minimize contradictory interpretations by using appropriate symbols, language, and ceremonies to reinforce the message; and designing systems to reward and recognize the intrinsic value of the work.

## Management as Mundane Behavior

Managers' actions are a powerful means of shaping organizational culture. Their behaviors signal what values and what attitudes and behavior are appropriate. Whether or not managers are conscious of the signals they are sending or not, their behaviors are always being observed and define for others what is valued and important. To ensure that actions are not misinterpreted, managers must be unrelentingly consistent in words and actions so that over time they clearly signal which norms are crucial. Managers need to ask themselves a number of questions about their own mundane behaviors that signal what is or is not important.

- Where do I spend time? What gets on the calendar?

- What questions are frequently asked? What questions are never asked?

- What gets followed up? What is forgotten?

- What is referred to in public statements? What are the themes in speeches?

- What is important enough to call a meeting for? What isn't?

- What gets on the agenda? What's on the top? What's last?

- What is emphasized in the summary of meetings?

- What gets celebrated? What are the symbols used? What language is used?

- How are social events used? Who gets invited? Where are they held?

- What signals are conveyed by the physical setting?

When Paul O'Neill became CEO at Alcoa, he immediately began emphasizing quality, cost, and safety. But the people at Alcoa had seen CEOs come and go. So, O'Neill had to convince Alcoa employees that he really meant what he was saying. In addition to making some changes to the compensation plan to put managers and workers on more common ground and freezing the pay of senior executives, O'Neill did away with his company car and driver, opting to drive himself to work. His first day on the job included an appointment with Alcoa's safety director, Charles DiMascio, with instructions that he wanted an "injury-free workplace." This was in a company that already had one of the best safety records in the industry.[10]

To emphasize quality, he ordered top executives to leave their desks and attend 28 days of quality training, which included visits to other companies. Then he began spreading the word to employees, logging more than 175,000 miles and 137 days away from corporate headquarters in his first year on the job. During these visits, he incessantly asked managers questions like How many hours out of 24 are you running your process in control and within capability? He also asked them to benchmark safety, quality, and costs. Echoing Jack Welch, O'Neill said of these efforts, "If you can't convince people that they're more important than the volume of products they get out the door, you haven't got a chance." O'Neill relentlessly matches his behavior to his actions in ways that Alcoa employees cannot fail to see that he is consistent and serious about re-creating the company.

## Managing Language and Symbolic Actions

Like O'Neill, managers use their own actions to shape the informational context in which people work. Whether they appreciate it or not, they are using the psychology we described earlier. They are managing symbolically. For example, consider the symbolism conveyed by managers' use of language. At Mary Kay, there are no salespeople, only "beauty consultants." Direct sales organizations like Mary Kay don't have a hierarchical language of status, but rely on kinship terms such as "family groups" or "family reunions" and "sister groups." Even at Xerox, the smallest work units are also called "family groups." Disney has an entire vocabulary to describe employees and attitudes, including "cast" (employees), "guests" (paying customers), "on stage" (areas where the cast mixes with guests), and "pixie dust" (enthusiasm). McKinsey partners talk about "the Firm" and "engagements," never the "company" or "jobs."

By themselves, the labels applied to positions may seem silly or trivial, but in conjunction with numerous other policies and managerial actions, they bolster the consistency of the message that people are important. As Robert Chapman, editor of the *New Dictionary of American Slang,* notes about language, "It has the double purpose of bonding the user to the group and separating the user from general society."[11] When used appropriately, language can promote a sense of belonging and equality. When not used carefully, it can separate groups and subtly distance people from one another.

Other actions by management can convey the same message. At Intel, NUMMI, TDIndustries, Mars, and HP *all* offices are cubicles. When Jerry Benefield, president of Nissan in Smyrna, Tennessee, was asked about why he dressed the same way as his employees, he said, "If I go out to the plant in a $400 suit and tie, people don't talk to me so freely."[12] He realizes the importance of the symbolism of dress and how it can impede communication.

The point here is not that all employees from the CEO on down should be treated as equals or that employees aren't aware of hierarchy. Everyone at Intel understands that Andy Grove is the boss, regardless of the fact that his office is a cubicle. More important is the symbolism attached to the message and the consistency or inconsistency with which it is sent. At FedEx and Southwest Airlines, both Smith and Herbert Kelleher and their top teams voluntarily took cuts in pay when the airline industry was suffering. Smith said, "The top people should bleed first."[13] The message is that when belt tightening is necessary, everyone should suffer, not just the workers. And that the top should lead the way. Contrast this with the furor that erupted when senior managers at GM received handsome bonuses while laying off thousands of employees. The managers' response was that they had earned their bonuses. While this may have been true, it completely ignored the important symbolic content of the signal.

There are several important lessons here. First, the goal of the message is for the manager to signal through his or her visible actions what is important. Given the norms and values needed for social control, actions convey a graphic sense that people who matter (in this case, management) genuinely care about the values. Conveying something important requires a vivid and consistent set of messages. When CEOs like Smith at FedEx and Barnevik at ABB make an outrageous or striking effort to convey their seriousness, people notice. The impact of the message is visceral.

A second lesson is the critical importance of consistency and repetition in signaling. The senior management at Southwest Airlines believes that every member of the company is equally important in providing memorable service to its customers. A customer's trip may be spoiled as easily by a reservation agent as a pilot. This message is conveyed in numerous written documents. But the written word, no matter how clearly expressed, is easily forgotten. Therefore, senior management engages again and again in actions that signal its beliefs. For instance, once every quarter, the top managers spend a day actually working in a front-line job. The symbolism of this is clear.

The psychology by which we make sense of conflicting signals is well known. We look for and value consistency. In the face of inconsistent behavior, people have a natural tendency to attribute outcomes to luck or some other external cause. Consistent actions on the part of leaders are a prerequisite to having their words taken seriously. In the examples we have cited, vivid, consistent actions reinforce the message. Consistency reduces uncertainty. The moment we notice inconsistency, we begin to wonder if the person is serious. Mixed messages are an excuse to do nothing while waiting to understand what managers really mean.

## SHAPING CULTURE THROUGH REWARDS AND RECOGNITION

The third lever for shaping norms is the use of comprehensive systems of reward and recognition. On occasion, each of us may do the right thing, even if it isn't rewarded or may be even punished. But in the long term, we know that rewards shape behavior. In designing reward systems, we need to recognize the variety of rewards in organizations and understand how they affect behavior. Managers often overestimate the importance of financial rewards and fail to see the more immediate reinforcements that shape behavior in the short term. John Reed, CEO of Citibank, after a $100 million experiment with stock options failed to produce any perceptible change in behavior among the top 100 corporate officers, believes "that money is not a good motivator." Compensation, in its many forms, is not a very effective shaper of specific attitudes and behavior. Although few of us would work for no pay or be motivated if we felt that we were paid inequitably, monetary compensation alone is a crude way to motivate people; the schedule of reinforcement is too long and too predictable.

It is remarkable how often managers do not reward what they say they want rewarded. We routinely deplore the fact that employees are reluctant to pass on bad news to senior managers, or will not share labor-saving ideas. One baby food company had a conventional sales force compensation plan in which sales targets were negotiated annually. Higher level targets then became the base for the following year's negotiations. The national sales manager noticed that sales people in Florida routinely made their targets. It was clear to him that they had figured out a way to increase sales. They denied this and refused to say what their secret was. With much effort, the sales manager finally uncovered their secret: Baby food could be sold to nursing homes. This insight proved valuable for the entire company. Unfortunately, the Florida sales force was punished for its innovation—the new, higher sales targets became the base. In keeping their discovery secret, they had behaved rationally. The failure was that management had not carefully analyzed the reward system it had designed. Instead, it claimed that it wanted one thing (innovation, new ideas, shared learning), and rewarded the opposite (secrecy, protecting your turf).

To shape culture effectively, managers must align their reward systems with their strategic goals and the social control system they want to develop by considering five key factors.

## Think Comprehensively about Rewards

First, understand what is valued by subordinates. The model Mary Kay employee has been a homemaker in the Southwest with a high school education and several children. Mary Kay appreciates that many of these women value family and religion. Many have not received much recognition for their achievements. Therefore, she designs systems that promote the common values shared by her beauty consultants and emphasizes them through continuous recognition. As Gloria Mayfield, a Harvard MBA who works for Mary Kay, puts it, "I didn't see much recognition at IBM. At Mary Kay, if you do well, you know *for a fact,* you'll get recognition. It's not influenced by politics."[14]

At 3M, employees have a different set of values. Technologists aren't motivated by bumble bee pins and flowers. But they do want recognition from their peers. Therefore, 3M offers awards such as the Golden Step Award, the Pathfinder Award, and elevation to the Carlton Society. Former CEO Lou Lehr described how "the spotlight focuses, bells rings, and the video cameras roll on the publicly approved team's success."[15] Bob Swanson, founder of Genentech, a biotechnology company, understood what motivated his scientists: He let them publish their findings right away in leading journals, as if they were at a major university. In Switzerland, Japan, or other collectivistic national cultures, singling out an individual for group recognition may be inappropriate. But this does not mean that recognition is less motivational. Rather, the rewards and recognition need to be provided in a manner consistent with national norms.

### Emphasize Intrinsic Rewards

Managers can also emphasize the intrinsic rewards associated with the work, not only instrumental outcomes such as pay or production. Intrinsic rewards include giving credit for a job well done, personal attention, and small symbolic rewards. Intrinsic rewards are available to all managers, unlike extrinsic ones that may be available only to higher level managers. In direct sales organizations, managers convert what is essentially an economic function (selling) into more of a social function, which includes helping others. The message conveyed is that distributors are spearheading a mission to serve others in some important way.

Because these firms have very flat hierarchies and managers have little formal authority, a critical leadership role is in helping employees focus on the intrinsic value of their efforts.

For example, at Levi Strauss, employees can reward others in the company who have done an exemplary job in living up to their aspirations. Each year every employee gets a small number of coupons that they can give out to other people. Each coupon can be exchanged for $25 or a gift certificate. Dona Goya, Levi's senior vice president of human resources, marvels, "It's amazing how hard people work for recognition."[16] Compensation is a right, recognition is a gift. Formal rewards are expected. The only question is whether they are seen as equitable. Recognition, unless it is seen as routine or insincere, is unexpected and can be given at the appropriate time.

### Ensure Tight Linkages between Rewards and Outcomes

The third lesson has to do with the timing and frequency of rewards. When reinforcement is delayed, learning is reduced—both for the individual receiving the reward and, as important, for those observing it. Recognition and smaller, more frequent rewards are powerful shapers of short-term behavior.

### Capitalize on Social Learning

Much of the power of a strong culture is transmitted as employees learn what is valued by watching or hearing about the successes of others. This learning is tied to concrete, observable attitudes and behaviors, not abstract slogans and values. For instance, service at Nordstrom is not a nebulous concept but a set of specific attitudes and behaviors that people have seen or heard about being rewarded.[17]

The same logic applies to punishment; failure to use an appropriate negative sanction is equivalent, in the eyes of those watching, to reinforcing the undesired behavior.[18] At NUMMI, there are strong norms about absenteeism, whereas under the old GM system, daily absenteeism was above 18 percent. When NUMMI opened, more than 85 percent of its work force came from the old GM plant. To break the cycle, a system was designed such that any worker who is absent, for any reason, more than three times in a 90-day period is charged with an "offense." Four offenses in a year and the employee is discharged. This system, plus the use of teams and the visibility of any team absenteeism, supports the norms about attendance. Effective managers understand that the majority of learning that takes place in organizations comes from people watching others.

## Avoid Routine

Any reward or recognition, no matter how appropriate or deserved, can be devalued if the spirit with which it is given is false or if the reward is expected and not tied to specific norms and outcomes (like another dental program). Novelty and sincerity are crucial; recipients and those watching need to feel that whatever the reward, it is both deserved and given sincerely. The moment the recognition becomes artificial or routine, the signal changes from one of reward to one of manipulation. When recipients believe that they are being manipulated, the credibility of the leader is impugned. Once lost, trust is very difficult to regain.

Consider something as small as a letter of appreciation. In one small communications company, the CEO sends a letter to each employee on the anniversary of his or her joining the company. While in principle this seems like a nice thing to do, it could also be so routinized (everyone gets a letter) as to have no meaning at all. But in this particular company, it does mean something. Two workers with the same anniversary expected to receive a form letter. But when they compared them, they discovered that each letter was genuinely personal. The CEO actually took time to think about each person. The social construction was not another attempt to convince workers that the top manager cared, but a signal that he really did.

The findings of research on reward systems and the experience of strong culture firms are straightforward. First, managers need to be systematic in analyzing the reward systems in their organizations. Second, rewards need to be viewed broadly so as to include not only the conventional ones such as money, promotion, and status, but also the less obvious ones such as personal attention from those who matter, public acknowledgment of a job well done, time off, and extra resources. Recognition, a sense of belonging, achievement, and self-esteem are universal reinforcers, and are often under the control of managers at all levels of the organization.

## BUILDING A COMPREHENSIVE SYSTEM FOR SOCIAL CONTROL

Organizations that successfully rely on social control systems—those with strong cultures—share three characteristics: a rigorous selection system, intensive socialization, and a comprehensive reward and recognition system.

### A Rigorous Selection System

First, these organizations begin with a rigorous employee selection system, one that involves multiple steps, an emphasis on core values, and clear expectations of appropriate attitudes and behaviors. Strong culture firms typically begin by identifying candidates who are likely to value the organization's norms or whose recent experience is likely to make them amenable to a new approach. The recruitment process requires that the potential new employee incrementally involve him- or herself in the organization, often at some personal psychological cost. First impressions are often lasting so in this period recruiters continually emphasize the core values of the organization and intrinsic benefits of belonging, and convey the message that only a particular type of person will fit in.[19]

## Intensive Period of Socialization

Once a new employee has joined the firm, a period of intensive socialization begins, during which he or she is exposed to the core values, beliefs, behaviors, and attitudes of the organization. This orientation typically includes:

- Top management attention and role modeling to signal that the norms and values are important and should be taken seriously;

- Clear, consistent statements, measurement systems, and models all emphasizing the specific attitudes and behaviors desired and rewarded;

- Development of a cohort or set of organizational members who share the goals and values and can act as role models and social support;

- Continual reinforcement and celebration of living according to the beliefs; and

- Opportunities for continuous socialization through training, meetings, and celebrations.

Initiation or boot camp experiences such as these are experienced by new recruits at the Arthur Andersen training school in St. Cloud, Kwik Kopy University (a three-week boot camp outside of Houston), Hamburger U. (McDonald's training center), or the U.S. Marine Corps at Parris Island. Developing a strong cohort and intense interpersonal bonds among new members can reinforce the acceptance of the new norms. Most strong culture firms recognize that these experiences can decay or have a half-life so they include multiple reinforcements. They design occasions that provide refresher experiences, often by having older employees train newer ones. Identification with the firm is promoted and rewarded, providing an opportunity for increased public commitment.

## Comprehensive Rewards and Recognition

The third mechanism common across strong culture firms is the use of comprehensive reward and recognition systems that provide rapid feedback for compliance or noncompliance with organizational norms. These systems

- emphasize the attitudes and behaviors consistent with the norms and values, not simply performance output;

- provide rapid feedback from peers, bosses, and top management; and

- provide not only continuous feedback but also signal public approval of walking the talk and clear intolerance for violations of basic values.

With each mechanism, the role of management remains that of a signal generator, constantly providing information about the appropriate norms and values; a vision that engages people emotionally; a management style that encourages employee involvement; clear, credible words and deeds; and, continual reinforcement of the norms and values. Managers also need to shape the context through well-designed socialization and training programs, the use of teams and groups to promote identification, and training and human resource practices that signal that people do matter.

Where diagnosing and shaping organizational culture is crucial for short-term success, managing multiple, often inconsistent, cultures within a business unit is vital for long-term adaptation. Chapter 7 returns to concepts introduced in Chapter 2: innovation streams, ambidextrous organizations, and multiple cultures needed to retain competitive advantage over time.

# C  H  A  P  T  E  R        7

## MANAGING INNOVATION
## STREAMS IN AMBIDEXTROUS
## ORGANIZATIONS

FROM 1958 TO 1985, OTICON, A DANISH HEARING-
aid company, dominated its market in the United States and
Europe. The firm, under the leadership of Bengt Simonsen,
Torben Nielsen (vice president of technology and production),
and two other senior managers, had a tradition of great technical
and manufacturing excellence. Its behind-the-ear (BTE) hearing
aid was both technologically sophisticated and reasonably
priced.

Oticon's financial and market success were, however, increasingly coupled with a sense of arrogance and insularity
within Oticon's senior team and within its culture. Reflecting the
power of the technologists at Oticon, the emphasis on new
product development focused on technical superiority. Oticon's
managers knew that a technically superior product would sell
itself. Oticon's technologists spent more time talking with each
other than getting to know their diverse, increasingly global,
customers. Its managers were good at improving their products
incrementally, but their increasing cultural arrogance and insu-

larity blinded them to a seemingly minor innovation initiated by Starkey, a much smaller U.S.–based player. Starkey reconfigured the BTE components to produce an in-the-ear (ITE) hearing aid. While the new hearing aid sacrificed sound quality a bit, it was both smaller and less intrusive. The market for Starkey's product was fashion-oriented, rather than hospital- or physician-oriented as was Oticon's.

In 1985, when Starkey introduced ITE products into the marketplace, Simonsen's team and Oticon product managers reacted defensively and actively resisted ITE products. They felt that Starkey's new hearing aids were technically inferior to their product, and, worse yet, could not be mass produced because they had to be custom fitted for each user. Oticon's existing expertise and process improvements had become liabilities; its processes, structure, and culture all prevented it from taking seriously an innovation that violated its ingrained assumptions about the hearing-aid market.

Yet the market for ITE hearing aids boomed. By 1986, 80 percent of the American market shifted to ITE products. As the industry standard moved from the BTE to the ITE configuration, Oticon's historical prosperity evaporated. In the face of dramatic loss in market share (from 15 percent to 9 percent between 1985 and 1986) and in profit, Simonsen and his team left Oticon, to be replaced by Lars Kolind. Kolind and a new team, forced to work in crisis mode, initiated revolutionary change to drive Oticon's transition to the new dominant design in the hearing aid market. Among other things, they replaced the firm's ingrained functional structure and culture with strong cross-functional teams; they substituted mobile work stations for offices; and they encouraged interacting and learning through face-to-face communications with other employees and with customers. The changes soon bore fruit. By 1995, Oticon's profits were up 10 times from their 1990 level and the firm had developed a breakthrough product—digital hearing aids—with the potential for annihilating the market for analog-based hearing products.

What Simonsen's management team failed to recognize is that long-term success depends on the ability to manage different kinds of innovations over time, to lead a range of innovations that must be simultaneously developed within the firm. We call these fundamentally different kinds of innovation *innovation streams,* and we show how managers can build organizations that encourage incremental, architectural (innovation that reconfigures existing technology, as did Starkey's ITE hearing aid), and discontinuous innovation simultaneously. While incremental innovation can be managed within the existing organization, architectural and discontinuous innovation cannot. Rather, architectural and discontinuous innovation must be coupled with more radical organizational change. Although many firms have the technological expertise to implement streams of innovation, their internal forces of stability often hinder the exploitation of this expertise.

Under Simonsen, Oticon was unable to renew itself because it failed to proactively initiate streams of innovation that built on existing technologies; it failed to push those technologies to usher in the next breakthrough. Instead, the firm stuck with its existing products, improving their quality and performance without understanding that the future was contingent on its ability to destroy the very products that it had worked so deliberately to improve. Oticon failed to develop what Lew Platt, CEO of HP, calls "a philosophy of killing off our own products with new technology."[1]

As we described in Chapters 1 and 2, technology- and resource-rich firms often fail to successfully commercialize technologies they helped create. Both the Swiss watch company SSIH and Oticon had once dominated their respective worldwide markets (SSIH through the 1970s and Oticon through the mid-1980s), and both developed new technologies that had the potential to re-create their markets (e.g., quartz movements and in-the-ear volume and tone control). Although SSIH and Oticon had the technology and the resources to innovate, smaller, more aggressive firms were first to market with the new technologies in watches and hearing aids. SSIH's and Oticon's prosperity lasted only until new industry standards destroyed it in a matter of a few short years. Although Oticon returned to prosperity by the early 1990s, it took a financial crisis, a new management team, and a fundamental organizational transformation to break free of its past.

The stultifying, innovation-numbing effects of success are a global phenomenon. Managing by building internal congruence, strong culture, and continuous improvement is not sufficient for sustaining competitive advantage. Worse, under a remarkably common set of conditions, it can trap an organization in its past and lead to catastrophic failure as technologies and markets shift. Erhard Pfeiffer, who has transformed Compaq, succinctly notes that "Nothing is harder than casting aside the thinking, strategies, and biases that propelled a business to its current success. Companies need to learn how to unlearn, to slough off yesterday's wisdom."[2] This is the ultimate irony: Success may be associated with the ability to learn and unlearn.

## MANAGING INNOVATION STREAMS

Whereas Oticon got caught by its prior success and arrogant, insular culture, Ciba-Geigy's Crop Protection Division is a success story. In 1978, Pierre Urech and Peter Nixon were project managers within the division. Collaborating with Janssen Pharmaceuticals, Urech, from R&D, and Nixon, from marketing, developed a chemical compound called propiconazol, which provided a significant improvement in plant protection over the existing market leader made by Bayer. After considerable experimentation with various formulas, Urech and Nixon selected the most promising version of propiconazol, EC250, and pushed the division's senior management to invest in major process improvement to reduce the price of the fungicide, which became known commercially as Tilt. Within two years, Tilt had become the industry standard in fungicides. Profits, sales, and market share soared from 1979 through 1992.

During this period, Ciba initiated numerous incremental innovations in Tilt such as modifying its packaging and dosages; taking it to new regions, including Japan and Brazil; and reformulating it for use on a wider variety of crops such as barley, bananas, and rice. This stream of innovation solidified Tilt's market dominance. More recently, faced with increasing generic competition, senior management in the Crop Protection Division has invested in developing product substitutes for Tilt—products that may at some point replace Tilt in the marketplace. One substitute is a genetically engineered seed that will produce plants that never get sick and so never need Tilt. As Urech and Nixon observed, if Ciba does not substitute for its own product, Bayer or DuPont will. They also observed that this bio-engineered seed has to be developed far away from Ciba's chemical fungicide area in Switzerland, and that if the seed were introduced, it would have to be coupled with discontinuous change in Ciba's Crop Protection organization.

Organizations like Ciba's Crop Protection Division and Microsoft are able to develop incremental innovations (e.g., multiple versions of Tilt or DOS) as well as discontinuous innovation (e.g., genetically engineered seeds or Windows) that alter industry standards or substitute for existing products. Thus Microsoft won the battle for the desktop market by simultaneously supporting generations of DOS and Windows even as it attempts to substitute them with Windows 95. This internal diversity gives Gates and his team options from which they can make bets to shape the operating systems market.

Seiko, in the watch industry, is another organization that has been able to successfully manage innovation streams. Not only has Seiko competed in mechanical watches, the historically dominant technology, but it was also willing to experiment with the quartz and tuning fork movements. In the late 1960s, drawing on their experience from this technological experimentation, Seiko managers made the bold decision to substitute a quartz movement for their existing mechanical movements. This switch led to fundamentally different competitive rules in the watch industry. The cost of buying a watch dropped dramatically and the definition of a watch as a piece of fine jewelry changed to one as a fashion item.

Great firms compete over time by actively shaping innovation streams. These streams include incremental innovation (e.g., thinner mechanical watches), architectural innovation (e.g., continuous aim gunfire, the ITE hearing aid, or SMH's Swatch watch), and discontinuous innovation (e.g., Seiko's quartz movement substituting for mechanical movements). By actively managing streams of innovation, firms take advantage of fundamentally new markets for existing technology and proactively introduce substitute products, which, even as they cannibalize existing products, create new markets and competitive rules.[3]

To understand how managers can cope with the contradictory requirements of these innovations, and shape evolving streams of innovation, we need to understand technology cycles—patterns of technological change where early product variation (e.g., multiple versions of propiconazol) is followed by the emergence of an industry standard (e.g., EC250 in fungicides) and a period of incremental technological change punctuated, in turn, by a subsequent technological breakthrough (e.g., a genetically engineered seed). Understanding technology cycles helps untangle the timing and importance of the various types of innovation and provides insight about windows of opportunity when managerial action can shape innovation streams.

## TECHNOLOGY CYCLES

A technology cycle is triggered by a technological discontinuity, a relatively rare, unpredictable event triggered by scientific or engineering advancement (e.g., batteries substituting for springs in watches). A technological discontinuity ruptures existing in-

cremental innovation patterns and spawns a period of technological ferment, the second stage in the cycle (see Figure 7.1).

During this period of ferment, competing technological variants, each with different operating principles, vie for market
acceptance. The competition occurs between the existing and the
new technology (e.g., the competition between tuning forks,
quartz, and escapement oscillation in the watch industry) as well
as among variants of that new technology. These periods of
ferment are confusing and uncertain, and costly to customers,
suppliers, vendors, and regulatory agencies.

The emergence of a dominant design (or industry standard)
signals the end of the period of ferment and the beginning of the
third stage in a technology cycle. For example, 60-cycle AC
power dominated 120-cycle power (in the United States), the
VHS format dominated Beta in VCR equipment, and the Windows format dominated Mac and OS/2 in operating systems.[4]
Once a dominant design emerges, competing firms switch to the
new standard or risk getting locked out of the market. But how
do dominant designs emerge? Except for the most simple nonassembled products such as cement, closing in on a dominant
design is not a technologically driven event. Rather, dominant
designs arise from competition among alternative technologies
championed by competitors, alliance groups, and government
regulators, each with their own political, social, and economic
agendas. Because no technology can dominate on all possible
criteria, the closing on a dominant design takes place not through
the invisible hand of the market and natural selection, but through
political, organizational, and market-based competition between
the alternative technological variants. Thus, Windows 95 came
to dominate OS/2 and Mac operating systems, and JVC's VHS
format came to dominate Sony's Beta format, not because Windows 95 and VHS were superior technologies, but because they
were good enough and they benefited from successful licensing
and distribution strategies.

The emergence of a dominant design is a watershed event in
a technology cycle. Until that point, competition among alterna-

**FIGURE 7.1**

**TECHNOLOGY CYCLES**

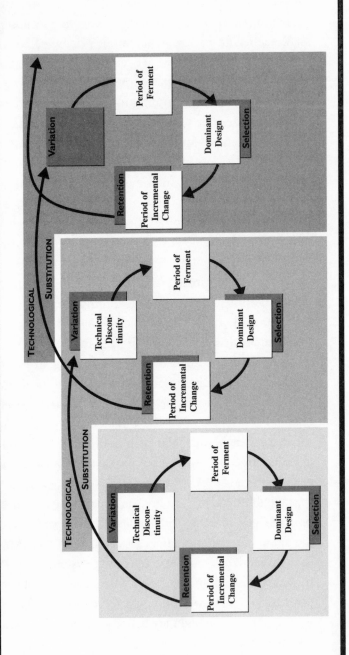

tive technological trajectories drives technological progress; afterward, the technical momentum in the selected technology itself stimulates further technological change. The consequences of betting on the wrong design are devastating—particularly if that subsystem is critical to the overall product (e.g., IBM losing control of the microprocessor and operating system of PCs to Intel and Microsoft, respectively).

In the fourth stage of a technology cycle, innovation shifts from major product variation to major process innovation and, in turn, to incremental innovation—to continuously improving, often significantly advancing, the now standard design. Architectural innovations also emerge during this period of incremental change. Architectural innovations link or combine existing technologies in different ways. Admiral Scott and Lieutenant Sims simply reconfigured existing gun, gear, and sight technology to produce continuous aim gunfire, just as Microsoft simply integrated several of its existing application programs into its Office product. Reconfigured products like these are often brought to different markets, as in Starkey's move into the fashion hearing-aid market. While architectural innovation may be technologically simple and associated with substantial economic returns, these shifts are frequently missed by incumbent firms.

Finally, a subsequent technological discontinuity, a product substitution, triggers yet a new cycle of technological variation, selection, and incremental change. For example, Ciba's Crop Protection Division hosted the development of fundamentally new chemical fungicides as well as biologically engineered seeds. Should one or more of these variants work, it has the potential to substitute for Tilt.

Technology cycles are seen most directly in simple or nonassembled products (e.g., skis, tennis racquets, glass, chemicals). In crop fungicides, Ciba-Geigy's introduction of propiconazol challenged Bayer's and BASF's products. It triggered a period of ferment in which chemical companies developed a large number of alternative formulations of the compound. Once Tilt was recognized as the dominant design, Ciba initiated hundreds of incremental innovations for Tilt and took the original version to different markets. More recently, Ciba began developing several products intended to cannibalize and replace propiconazol. These product substitutes—fundamentally new crop-protection products—will then kick off the next technology cycle in the crop protection market.

In more complex assembled products (e.g., watches) and systems (e.g., radio, voice mail), technology cycles occur at the subsystem level. Watches are assembled products made up of at least five subsystems: energy source, oscillation device, transmission, casing, and display. Each subsystem has its own technology cycle. The pin-lever escapement, for instance, became the dominant design in the oscillation subsystem of watches in the late nineteenth century. Escapements became better and better through incremental changes in the same fundamental design until the late 1960s. But then, between 1968 and 1972, escapement technology was threatened by both tuning fork and quartz oscillation technologies. The period of technological competition between escapements, tuning fork, and quartz movement ended with the emergence of quartz oscillation as the dominant design.[5] Between 1970 and 1985, every subsystem of the watch, from energy source to face, was transformed through its own technology cycle of technical variation, selection of a dominant design, and subsequent period of incremental change.

Furthermore, each subsystem shifts in relative strategic importance as the industry evolves. For example, where oscillation had been the key strategic battlefield through the early 1970s, once the quartz movement became the dominant design, the locus of strategic innovation shifted to the face, energy, and transmission subsystems. One source of strategic advantage, then, is controlling strategically important product subsystems as a market unfolds.

These technology cycles hold across product classes—the only difference between high-technology industries and low is the length of time between the emergence of a dominant design and the subsequent product substitution. Thus, from an innovation perspective, what lies behind the familiar S-shaped product-life-cycle curve are fundamentally different innovation requirements. Periods of ferment are associated with discontinuous product innovation, dominant designs are associated with fundamental process innovation, and periods of incremental change are associated with both incremental and architectural innovation (see Figure 7.2).

## LINKING TECHNOLOGY CYCLES AND INNOVATION STREAMS

The route to sustained competitive advantage is not through succeeding at either incremental, architectural or discontinuous innovation, but through producing streams of innovation (see Figure 7.3). This perspective redirects managerial attention away from a particular innovation or innovation orientation (e.g.,

**FIGURE 7.2**

**INNOVATION PATTERNS AND PRODUCT LIFE CYCLES**

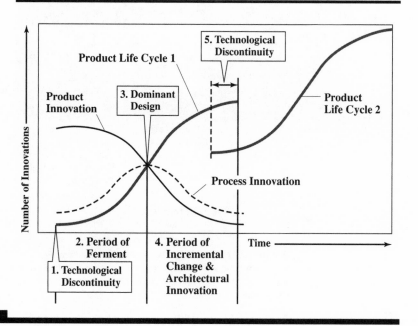

market push versus technology pull; incremental versus discontinuous) and toward series of contrasting innovations that must be produced within a firm over time. Innovation streams highlight the importance of maintaining control over core product subsystems as well as shaping dominant designs and architectural innovation and initiating product substitutes. By proactively shaping dominant designs, undertaking architectural innovations, and initiating product substitutes, managers can capitalize on windows of opportunity to shape technological evolution and, in turn, change the bases of competition.

**FIGURE 7.3**

**TYPES OF INNOVATION AND INNOVATION STREAMS**

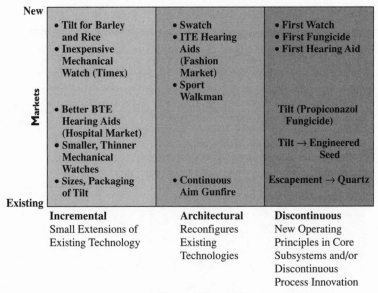

| | Incremental<br>Small Extensions of<br>Existing Technology | Architectural<br>Reconfigures<br>Existing<br>Technologies | Discontinuous<br>New Operating<br>Principles in Core<br>Subsystems and/or<br>Discontinuous<br>Process Innovation |

**Types of Innovation**

**Innovation Streams** are those multiple types of innovations through which a firm can simultaneously reap the benefits of periods of incremental change as well as shape the pace and direction of breakthrough innovation and subsequent industry standards.

Sony's Walkman is an excellent example of managing inno-vation streams. Once Sony selected the WM-20 platform for its Walkman, it went on to generate more than 30 incremental versions within the WM-20 family. Indeed, over just 10 years, Sony was able to develop four Walkman product families and more than 160 incremental versions of those four families. Such sustained attention to initiating technological discontinuities at the subsystem level (e.g., flat motor and miniature battery), closing on a few standard platforms, and leading incremental product proliferation helped Sony control industry standards in its product class and outperform its Japanese, American, and European competitors.[6] Through such proactive shaping of in-novation streams, managers build on mature technologies that provide the base from which new technology can emerge.

## BUILDING AMBIDEXTROUS ORGANIZATIONS

Organizations can sustain their competitive advantage by oper-ating in multiple modes simultaneously—managing for short-term efficiency by emphasizing stability and control, as well as for long-term innovation by taking risks and learning by doing. Organizations that operate this way may be thought of as ambi-dextrous—hosting multiple, internally inconsistent architec-tures, competencies, and cultures, with built-in capabilities for efficiency, consistency, and reliability on the one hand and experimentation, improvisation, and luck on the other.[7]

Different kinds of innovation require different kinds of or-ganizational hardware—structures, systems, and rewards—and different kinds of software—human resources, networks, and culture (see Figure 7.4). During periods of incremental change, organizations require units with relatively formalized roles and responsibilities, centralized procedures, functional structures, efficiency-oriented cultures, highly engineered work processes, strong manufacturing and sales capabilities, and relatively ho-mogeneous, older, and experienced human resources. These efficiency-oriented units have relatively short time frames and

**FIGURE 7.4**

**ORGANIZATIONAL ARCHITECTURES
AND TECHNOLOGY CYCLES**

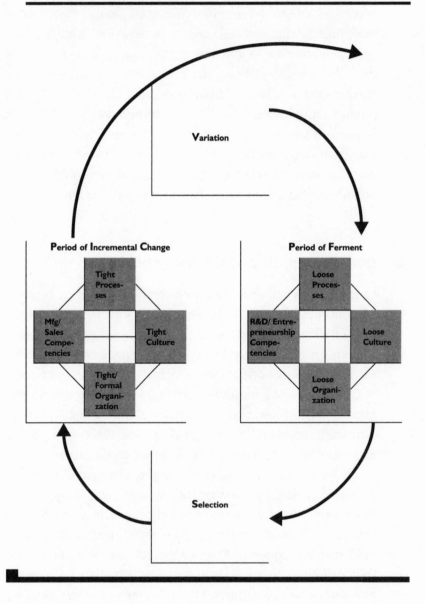

are often relatively large and old with highly ingrained, taken-
for-granted assumptions and knowledge systems. These units are

highly inertial, and often have glorious histories (e.g., SSIH, Oticon, IBM, Philips). Their cultures emphasize efficiency, teamwork, and continuous improvement.

In dramatic contrast, the discontinuous innovation during periods of ferment emerges from entrepreneurial, skunk-works types of organizations. These units are relatively small, have loose, decentralized product structures, experimental cultures, loose work processes, strong entrepreneurial and technical competencies, and relatively young and heterogeneous employees. Entrepreneurial units build new experience bases and knowledge systems; they generate the experiments, the failures, the variation from which the senior team can make bets on possible dominant designs and/or technological discontinuities. In contrast to the larger, more mature units, these small entrepreneurial units are inefficient, rarely profitable, and have no established histories. They often deliberately violate the norms valued in older parts of the organization.

The difference in the organizational configurations needed for these innovations is illustrated in a study of innovation in Japanese firms. Jiro Nonaka analyzed how large, conservative Japanese organizations can generate breakthrough innovations. He found common patterns across firms. When faced with a new technology, these companies typically establish teams of relatively young staff headed by an esteemed elder statesman and charge them with developing breakthrough products. To ensure that they are not hampered by the existing organization, the teams are moved into isolated quarters, well separated from the main firm. The group members are exhorted to violate the culture of the larger organization and do whatever it takes to develop the new product. Canon, Honda, and other established companies have used this approach as a way to overcome the disadvantages of their large sizes and conservative cultures.[8]

Ciba Crop Protection used a similar process to execute its dual strategy of supporting incremental innovation in its mature propiconazol product and developing fundamental product substitutes by building separate units for the mature fungicide product and for the genetically engineered seed. Each unit—one in Switzerland and one in the United States—had its own management team and its own structure, culture, and processes.

In building ambidextrous organizations, management teams provide the drive for incremental innovation even as they challenge other parts of the organization to re-create the future (see Figure 7.5). Ambidextrous organizations build in contradictions as they operate both for today and tomorrow. But the certainty

**FIGURE 7.5**

**MANAGING AMBIDEXTROUSLY: MULTIPLE ORGANIZATIONAL ARCHITECTURES AND INNOVATION STREAMS**

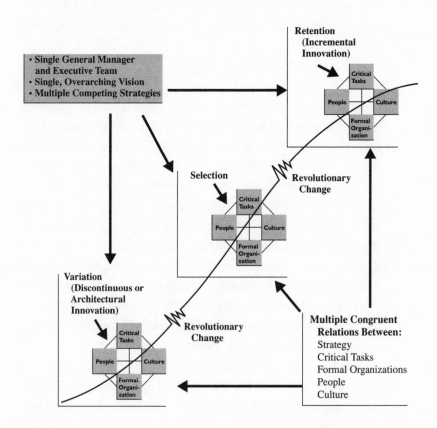

of today's incremental innovation can often destroy the potential of tomorrow's architectural or discontinuous innovation. The contradictions inherent in the multiple types of innovation create conflict and dissent between the organizational units—between those historically profitable, large, efficient, older, cash-generating units and the young, entrepreneurial, risky, cash-absorbing units. Because the power, resources, and traditions of organizations are usually anchored in the more traditional units, these units usually try to ignore, trample, or otherwise kill the entrepreneurial units. Thus, the management team must not only protect and legitimize the entrepreneurial units, but also keep them physically, culturally, and structurally separate from the rest of the organization.[9]

## MANAGING AMBIDEXTROUS ORGANIZATIONS— THE VITAL ROLE OF THE SENIOR TEAM

If the diverse capabilities of ambidextrous organizations can be harnessed, they permit the organization to lead streams of innovation. Without integration, however, the potential of ambidextrous organizations is lost. The challenge for managers and their teams, then, is to create co-existing highly differentiated *and* highly integrated organizations. Although differentiating units is easy (the central laboratories at SSIH invented both the tuning fork and the quartz movement), achieving integration is not. Three tools can help senior leadership teams achieve integration: articulating a clear, emotionally engaging, and consistent vision; building a senior team with diverse competencies; and developing healthy team processes.

A clear, emotionally engaging vision provides a strategic anchor for the contrasting requirements of innovation streams. Whether it is the HP Way, GE's requirement to be number one or two, or 3M's "be innovative and satisfy our customer," simple, direct, competitive visions provide a point of clarity within which some units master efficiency and incremental innovation even as other parts of the organization are busy destroying the very business striving for efficiency. Employees know that they can put each other out of business because the organization, and their places in it, will be secure only if they destroy their own product lines before the competition does.

Sustained, consistent commitment to a unit's vision, even as strategies and objectives change, reinforces and anchors vision. Competitive visions are further reinforced by continuity within the senior management group and its consistent behavior in support of the vision. For example, Motorola's "best in class in portable communication devices" or Ciba Crop Protection's "most dominant crop protection competitor, world-wide," were made more real through the long-term support for these visions by its senior management team. Through such clarity and consistency of vision the senior team can support internally contradictory architectures and still be seen as consistent and credible.

The composition and demography of the senior team and its ways of working together are also powerful tools for achieving integration. Effective senior teams have internal processes that enable them to handle more information and decision alternatives and deal with the conflict and ambiguity associated with contradictory architectures.

In Chapter 5 we noted that innovation (either incremental or discontinuous) stems from two component processes: those structures, people, incentives, and cultures that promote creativity and those that facilitate implementation. At the team level, creativity is enhanced by the heterogeneity among team members, which provides the fodder for alternative approaches. However, these differences also hinder implementation by slowing consensus and increasing the negative political dynamics within the team. The alternative team composition emphasizes homogeneity among team members. While homogeneous teams are more likely to agree quickly and implement decisions rapidly, they may not generate the creativity necessary for significant innovation.

To deal with the diverse needs of ambidextrous organizations, it is helpful for executive teams to be homogeneous and heterogeneous. In one study, Sylvia Flatt discovered that the most innovative firms had top management teams that were homogeneous with regard to tenure together. She also found that the most innovative firms also had heterogeneous lower level management teams (in her study, these were the vice presidents of the company); the heterogeneity that sparked the conflict and creativity came from this level and was resolved by the homogeneous senior team (the top four or five officers of the company).[10]

To avoid the negative consequences of politics and to speed decision making, team members need to be comfortable working together and understand one another's strengths and weaknesses. When teams are relatively similar with respect to service, misunderstandings and inconsistent assumptions are reduced. But this homogeneity needs to be balanced by heterogeneity with respect to background and perspective—by keeping teams relatively young, either by periodically moving teams, as HP does by changing divisional charters, or by rotating team members to offer fresh outlooks on old problems. The need for creativity must be balanced with the need for execution. Senior teams must be intellectually fresh, able to balance old and new perspectives, and not get caught up in a single viewpoint. Those that cannot resolve conflict or do not collaborate create highly unstable, politically chaotic organizations, which squander the potential of ambidextrous organizations.

In managing streams of innovation, senior teams are like jugglers, keeping several balls in the air at once—articulating a single, clear vision while simultaneously hosting multiple organization architectures without sounding confused or, worse, hypocritical. Most management teams can do one thing well, but keeping a multitude of activities going at once requires greater skill (see Figure 7.6).

## LINKING INNOVATION STREAMS AND DISCONTINUOUS ORGANIZATIONAL CHANGE

Choosing a dominant design and initiating either architectural or discontinuous innovation are windows of opportunity where

**FIGURE 7.6**

**ORGANIZATIONAL ARCHITECTURES: MANAGING AMBIDEXTROUSLY**

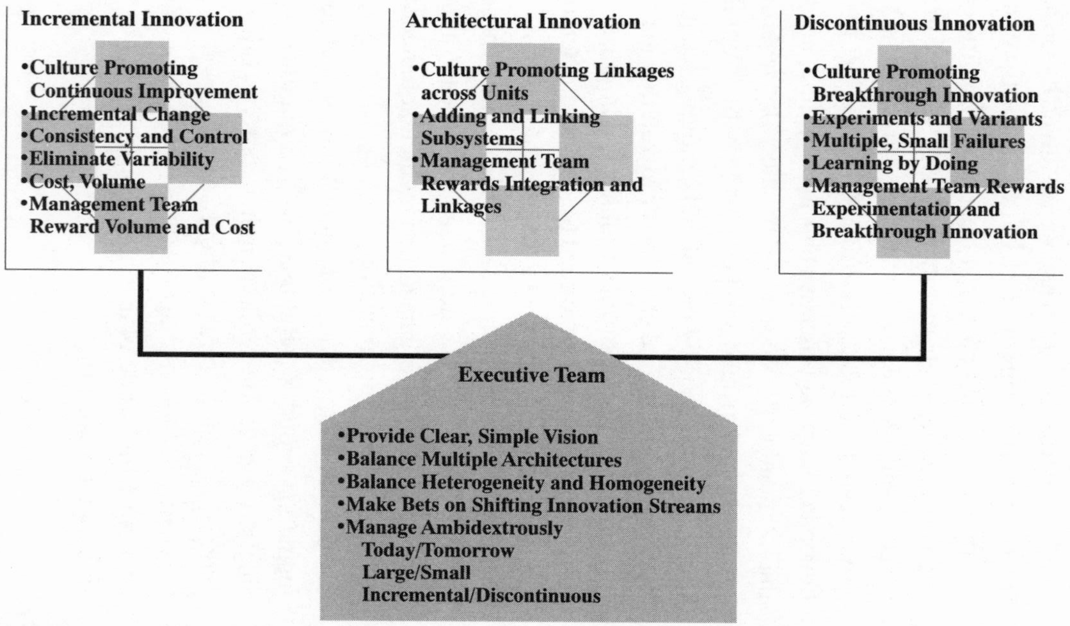

**Incremental Innovation**

- Culture Promoting
  Continuous Improvement
- Incremental Change
- Consistency and Control
- Eliminate Variability
- Cost, Volume
- Management Team
  Reward Volume and Cost

**Architectural Innovation**

- Culture Promoting Linkages
  across Units
- Adding and Linking
  Subsystems
- Management Team
  Rewards Integration and
  Linkages

**Discontinuous Innovation**

- Culture Promoting
  Breakthrough Innovation
- Experiments and Variants
- Multiple, Small Failures
- Learning by Doing
- Management Team Rewards
  Experimentation and
  Breakthrough Innovation

**Executive Team**

- Provide Clear, Simple Vision
- Balance Multiple Architectures
- Balance Heterogeneity and Homogeneity
- Make Bets on Shifting Innovation Streams
- Manage Ambidextrously
  Today/Tomorrow
  Large/Small
  Incremental/Discontinuous

managerial action can shape or reinvent an innovation stream. During periods of ferment, management can shape the closing of a dominant design. At IBM, Ciba, and Seiko, for example, internal experimentation with alternative mainframe, propiconazol, and oscillation variants led to managerial bets on the 360 series, EC250, and quartz movements. During periods of incremental change, in contrast, managers can initiate architectural innovations (e.g., Starkey's creation of the ITE hearing aid) and/or product substitutions (e.g., Ciba creating a genetically engineered seed).

Ambidextrous organizations provide the data, insight, and innovation options from which managers make bets to shape innovation streams. While one can know dominant designs and successful product substitutes after the fact (e.g., VHS over Beta, quartz over escapements), management cannot know the "right" decisions on either dominant designs or substitution events in real time. Success comes less from knowing the right answer than having the ability to pursue multiple courses of action and to move quickly to shape innovation streams.

At the closing on a dominant design, innovation within the firm shifts from major product variation to major process innovation and, in turn, to sustained incremental innovation. At product substitutions and for architectural innovation, in contrast, innovation shifts from incremental innovation to major product or process innovation. At these junctures, shifts in innovation streams must be coupled to shifts in organizational architectures. Those architectures appropriate during periods of ferment are no longer appropriate during the subsequent interval of incremental change, just as the architectures appropriate during periods of incremental change are no longer appropriate during the subsequent interval of ferment (see Figure 7.4). In Ciba's Crop Protection Division, the organizational architecture that was used to effectively produce, promote, and sell mature propiconazol will have to be completely reconfigured if and when the disease resistant seed is launched.

Shifts in innovation streams can be executed only through discontinuous organizational change. Managers can attempt to rewrite their industry's rules only if they are willing to rewrite their organization's rules. Thus Microsoft's move from DOS to Windows, Ciba's move to create EC250 as the industry standard in fungicides, and IBM's 360 decision in mainframes were accompanied by sweeping shifts in each firm's structure, controls, systems, and culture. Bold strategic moves or great technology alone lead to underperformance—these moves must be coupled with organizational shifts. Managing innovation streams is as much rooted in organizational architectures and the management of discontinuous organizational change as it is in technological prowess.

Yet the need for discontinuous organizational change runs headlong into internal inertia. Patterns in organizational evolution across industries and countries suggest that these contrasting forces cannot be managed through incremental organizational change. Incremental change benefits today's organization even as it stunts the move to tomorrow's organization. Rather, organizational renewal and shifts in innovation streams must be executed through concurrent shifts in strategy, structure, competencies, and processes. The tentative moves of Oticon and RCA into ITE hearing aids and transistors, respectively, triggered strong resistance to these shifts. Both firms were held hostage to their pasts.

Organizations evolve through long periods of incremental change punctuated by discontinuous, frame-breaking change (see Figure 7.7). Organizations can move from today's strength to tomorrow's through discontinuous organizational change. These strategic reorientations must be coupled to strategic bets on shaping innovation streams—by betting on dominant designs, architectural innovations, and product substitutions. If strategic reorientations are not proactive, they will be reactive. Reactive reorientations or turnarounds are more risky because they must be implemented under crisis conditions and under considerable time pressure, which hinder a firm's ability to learn.[11]

**FIGURE 7.7**

**ORGANIZATIONAL EVOLUTION: PERIODS OF INCREMENTAL CHANGE PUNCTUATED BY DISCONTINUOUS CHANGE**

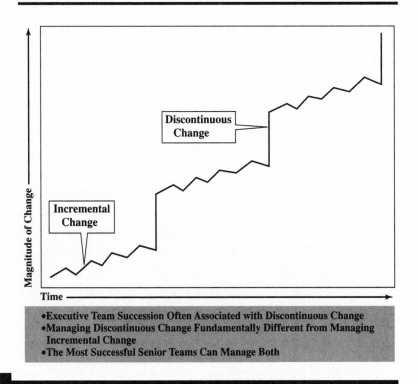

- Executive Team Succession Often Associated with Discontinuous Change
- Managing Discontinuous Change Fundamentally Different from Managing Incremental Change
- The Most Successful Senior Teams Can Manage Both

But managing both incremental and discontinuous change, managing for both today and tomorrow, is difficult. The irony, as we will see in the next chapter, is that it is always easier to introduce change in the midst of a crisis. Thus managing innovation streams requires not only building ambidextrous organizations, but also organizations capable of executing discontinuous change in the face of prior success. As Intel's Andy Grove said, "There is at least one point in the history of any company when you have to change dramatically to rise to the next performance level. Miss the moment and you begin to decline. . . . Emotionally, it's easier to change when you're hemorrhaging."[12] Indeed, managing innovation streams is as much about managing change as it is about managing technology. Given the difficulties of initiating proactive change, most are initiated under crisis conditions by new senior teams.

## HOSTING CONTRADICTIONS AND MANAGING AMBIDEXTROUSLY

Managing streams of innovation is about managing contradictions: efficiency and innovation, tactics and strategy, incremental and discontinuous as well as large and small changes for today and tomorrow. Managing innovation streams is about consistency and control as well as variability, learning-by-doing, and the creation of luck. The senior team's role is to embrace these contradictions and take advantage of the tensions and synergies that come from juggling multiple competencies simultaneously. Vision and strategy bind these dualities together. Only through clarity of vision can these multiple contradictions be reconciled and integrated, and innovation streams proactively managed.

We emphasize building executive teams and leaders throughout the organization who can simultaneously manage the strategies, structures, competencies, work processes, and cultures for short-term efficiency as well as create the conditions for tomorrow's strategic innovation. We talk not about the organizational structure or culture for innovation, but about *structures* and *cultures* for strategic innovation and change. An organization with dual capabilities is able to maximize the probability that it will be more effective in the short term and make proactive and informed strategic bets. These dual organizational capabilities, anchored by a clear vision, enable managers to create both the expertise and luck to shape their firm's future.

Even if periods of incremental change do build organizational inertia, organizations can move from strength to strength. Through the diversity inherent in ambidextrous organizations, managers develop options from which they can shape innovation streams. Organizations can, then, renew themselves through proactive strategic reorientations coupled to bets on dominant designs, architectural innovation, and/or product substitution. Like a dying vine, the prior period of incremental change provides the compost for its own seeds, its own variants, to thrive in the subsequent periods of ferment and, in turn, incremental change.

Leading innovation streams, winning through innovation, is about innovation and execution. The world is full of great technologies and innovations that were either never implemented or implemented well after the competition's. Leading innovation streams must be coupled with the ability to lead discontinuous change. Chapter 8 provides tools for effectively leading system-wide change.

# C H A P T E R 8

## IMPLEMENTING
## STRATEGIC CHANGE

UNTIL 1991, SEARS WAS THE LARGEST RETAILER IN the United States with more than 500,000 employees. By the mid-1980s, its market share had fallen 15 percent from its high in the 1970s, and the stock price had plummeted. The CEO at that time, Ed Brennan, tried to change the company's strategy, largely without success. As one observer notes, Sears was like "a runner with a 50-pound pack and Army boots competing in a marathon."[1] Service was problematic and customers fled to competitors such as Wal-Mart. One shopper in 1991 claimed after visiting Sears, "It's like shopping at a store in Russia. The people are unhelpful, the stock's not there, and you have to wait in line forever to pay."[2]

This was the challenge facing Arthur Martinez when he joined Sears as head of retail operations in 1992. Since that time Sears's stock price has doubled, operating margins are up more than 400 percent, administrative costs are down substantially, and operating profits in 1994 were $890 million compared to the $2.9 billion loss posted in 1992. How has Martinez turned Sears around?

First, recognizing that the company's strategy and structure were misaligned with the realities of retailing in the 1990s, he dramatically changed the strategy, structure, and culture of the old Sears. He focused the business, selling off insurance and financial services, closing the money-losing catalog business, and even selling the corporate headquarters building. He closed more than 100 stores, laid off more than 50,000 people, and spent more than $4 billion to remodel stores. But Martinez understands that strategy by itself isn't enough. "I think our biggest challenge has been and will be how well we execute," he says.[3]

And understanding the importance of vision, he began simply and clearly communicating the aspirations of the new Sears throughout the organization. At the new Sears one thing is clear to all employees: "Never disappoint a customer." It is up to the associate to figure out how to do this. The old Sears had 29,000 pages of policies and procedures; there is now a single folder one-eighth inch thick entitled "Rights and Obligations." Its focus is on what is referred to as the three Cs: "A compelling place to shop, a compelling place to work, and a compelling place to invest." Liam Strong, a former British Airways executive who now runs Sears in the United Kingdom, says, "People can only take away very simple ideas. . . ."[4] When communicating this new vision, Martinez often holds up as a challenge to employees the very *Fortune* article that declared Sears a dinosaur and uses this as a rallying cry for the revolution.[5]

Martinez has also instituted a revolution in the organizational alignment of Sears culture to accomplish his strategic objectives. These efforts include establishing Sears's "P.S.E. Circus" (Pure Selling Environment) to convey a sense of urgency and excitement as well as discussion groups, task forces, extensive training sessions run by Sears University, new job descriptions, new operating procedures, 360-degree evaluations, and a new pay system that ties half of executives' pay to customer satisfaction. Further, employees are educated about Sears's financials so that they can make economically informed decisions. One observer characterizes these initiatives as "Fomenting a cultural revolution, a re-education effort that would make Mao proud."[6] The point of these efforts is to help people understand exactly what attitudes and behaviors characterize the new culture, energize them, and help them feel good about the future.

But Martinez realizes that not all Sears employees agree with the need to change. "Part of the trick in getting this company moving again is not dishonoring its past but trying to honor the parts of its past that are relevant to the future."[7] Just as important, he also emphasizes that the new Sears is not for everybody. Those who can't or won't change are encouraged to leave. These efforts originate with the senior team. To break up the firm's former bureaucratic ways, Martinez even forbids managers from using the old number-oriented department references, requiring anyone who uses a number instead of a noun to put $1 in the kitty. He has also replaced 40 of the top 100 senior managers.

Will Martinez's revolution succeed? Some skeptics question whether the focus on higher margin clothing and fashion may be misdirected. Others wonder if there is the service-industry equivalent of a new dominant design emerging with category-killer stores like The Home Depot and Staples, eliminating the need for value-added department stores like Sears. But these criticisms, while reasonable, miss an important point. Under Brennan, Sears failed to execute. Whether he had the right strategy was irrelevant—the bureaucracy stifled change. Martinez has developed an integrated plan for realigning Sears to execute the new strategy. He has communicated his strategy and vision and attacked the culture head on. He has made transparent the crisis facing the company and involved the entire work force in effecting the change effort. Whether Sears's strategy is ultimately proved correct, Martinez has been successful at implementing revolutionary change.

## LEADING CHANGE

Winning through innovation involves leading change. Innovation is always disruptive to an organization. Whether it is Morison's account of the U.S. Navy at the turn of the century or the turmoil at Sears and Philips, innovation and change, particularly proactive innovation and change, are invariably associated with resistance and organizational politics. Great strategies or break-through innovations poorly executed are at the heart of many organizational disasters.

Executing change is a crucial source of competitive advantage. There is much research and tested practice on managing change. There are clear patterns that differentiate successful from unsuccessful change efforts. We discuss the role of the leader and his or her team in directing and shaping change and then focus on specific actions managers can take to shape the politics of change, to motivate individual behavior and reduce resistance to change, and to maintain control during turbulent transition periods.[8]

Managing change involves moving an organization from its current state to its desired future state through a transition period. The transition period is particularly crucial in the effective management of change. During the transition, managers and their teams take the organization apart and, component by component, move it toward the future. Given the politics, individual resistance to change, and control issues during transition periods, the shorter the period the better (see Figure 8.1).

The key to managing transition periods is to focus on the process by which a unit moves from the present to the future. These transitions are often underemphasized by managers, who often delegate or ignore the dynamics of this critical period. A common mistake is to emphasize the content of the change, carefully specifying what the future state needs to look like, but paying little attention to how the change will be implemented. Yet, the process by which the change is managed is as important as its content. A poorly managed transition process puts future organizational performance at risk.

At least part of the successes at Sears, BOC, and Alcoa are due to the personal responsibility taken by Martinez, Chow, and O'Neill, and their teams, in managing the transition periods.

**FIGURE 8.1**

## MANAGING TRANSITION PERIODS

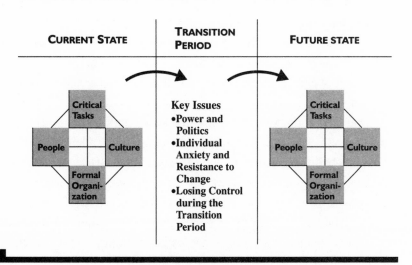

While the subject of leadership has received much attention over the years, the more specific issue of leadership during periods of significant organizational change has only recently attracted serious attention. What emerges from this research is a set of leadership behaviors and senior team characteristics that are critical during transition periods.

### Visionary Leaders

Visionary leaders are able to mobilize and sustain energy and activity within an organization by taking specific personal actions. Visionary leaders are not the popular versions of the great speech makers or television personalities. Visionary leadership is not equivalent to charisma. Rather, visionary leaders are able to emotionally engage their organization at whatever level they operate. Like Huber at Ciba's Grenzach facility, Chow at BOC Gases, or Barnevik at ABB, they influence their colleagues' values, goals, needs, and aspirations through their relentless attention to shaping interpretations and creating a sense of purpose.[9]

Visionary leaders energize the organization and find ways to motivate its members to achieve its goals. They demonstrate empathy, listen, understand, and share the feelings of others in the organization. They express their confidence in their own ability and in the ability of others to succeed. They create events to signal and celebrate transitions and turning points, expressing support for individuals grappling with the pressures of stressful change efforts and reinforcing the new vision and culture.

The behaviors associated with visionary leadership support innovation and change in several ways. Visionary leaders provide a psychological focal point for the energies, hopes, and aspirations of people in the organization. They serve as powerful role models whose actions and personal energy demonstrate the desired behaviors. Their behavior is a standard to which others can aspire. Through their commitment, effectiveness and consistency, visionary leaders build a personal bond between themselves and the organization.

## Senior Teams

An individual leader alone, no matter how heroic, is unlikely to implement change successfully. Managing change requires integrated and cohesive senior teams. These teams are the most powerful signal generators in an organization; they extend and institutionalize the leadership and management of innovation and change. There are several things successful leaders can do to develop effective, visible, and dynamic senior teams.

**EMPOWERING THE TEAM.** From the start, the team must be seen as an extension of the individual leader. Its members need to be given the autonomy and resources to serve effectively (objective empowerment), and the organization needs to be sent clear messages, through the use of titles and formal roles associated with the change, that team members are speaking for the leader (symbolic empowerment). Chow's team, for example, was the transition team in BOC Gases's transformation. Each member of this team had a formal role in both developing and executing the change agenda.

**DEVELOPING THE TEAM MEMBERS.** Empowerment will fail if the individuals on the team are not capable of performing their new leadership roles. A major problem in executing change is that the members of the senior team frequently are the products of the very systems, structures, and values that need to be changed. The need for personal change at the senior level means that the leader has to help coach, guide, and support individuals in developing their own leadership skills. Members of the senior team need not, and should not, be clones of the individual leader but should be encouraged to lead in ways consistent with their personal styles. If some individuals do not, or cannot, respond to coaching and development, the manager must make changes in the team before too much damage is done.

**FINE-TUNING THE COMPOSITION OF THE TEAM.** The need for the senior team to implement change often triggers change in the composition of the team itself. Different skills, capabilities, styles, and value orientations may be called on to lead the changes and to manage in the reconfigured organization. Senior managers should have a clear sense of the competencies required to execute the revised strategy as well as an accurate understanding of their competencies of the senior team.

**ENSURING THAT THE TEAM IS COHESIVE.** The senior team must be capable of learning about the management of the change. The challenge is to bond the team together yet avoid insularity.[10] A potential risk is that the team can become isolated from the rest of the organization, develop patterns of dysfunctional conformity, and, over time, develop patterns of learned incompetence.

One way of keeping senior teams invigorated and connected to the organization is to build in diversity in terms of the members' ages, tenures, and functional backgrounds. Diversity can be managed through job rotation as well as by including new members on a team. Such movement within the senior team provides the stability of experience but also keeps group age comparatively young. Another way of enhancing the effectiveness of the team is to expose it to outside ideas and information continually. For example, at Southwest Airlines, every year the senior team engages in a one-week exercise structured around new challenges.

**BUILDING STRATEGIC ANTICIPATION.** Executing strategic change requires the ability to anticipate significant external events. Proactive change occurs because the organization's leadership perceives competitive advantage from initiating change earlier rather than later. As a group, the senior team can scan a large number of events and potentially be more creative in analyzing the environment than can the leader alone. This requires an investment in activities that foster anticipation such as environmental scanning, experiments, probes inside the organization (frequently on the periphery), and frequent contacts with the outside environment. David Kearns at Xerox and O'Neill at Alcoa made substantial use of highly respected executive senior teams to implement their quality-oriented organizational transformations. To sharpen their change and quality skills, these teams made trips to companies in Japan and to other experienced organizations, and were involved in extensive educational and problem-solving efforts in their task forces and within their own divisions. They were, in turn, role models and champions of the change efforts in their own sectors.

**DEVELOPING LEADERSHIP IN THE ORGANIZATION.** An effective way to extend the reach of the senior team in implementing strategic change is to include the broader set of individuals who make up the upper management of the organization, including individuals several levels down from the executive team. There are two essential objectives of this effort: (1) to ensure that all

senior managers have a shared strategic perspective, not a paro-
chial or functional view of the organization, and (2) to develop
and track a talent pool capable of leading the organization in the
future. At Corning, for example, Jamie Houghton established
two groups, the Corporate Policy Group (approximately the top
35 managers) and the Corporate Management Group (about the
top 120 managers), to broaden the range of senior management.
At companies as diverse as ABB, BOC, PepsiCo, and GE, these
extended senior management teams are considered corporate
assets and the lifeblood of the future.

This expanded senior management group needs to be provided with new skills and challenged to adopt new approaches
or they may continue to rely on structures, systems, and cultures
that were successful in the past but are unsuitable for the future.
Gerstner at IBM notes this, observing, "I sensed there were too
many people inside IBM who wanted to fight the war we lost."[11]
Unless a revitalized broad set of top managers feel like active
participants in the change effort, they may feel disenfranchised
by a strong executive team, particularly if that team has been
assembled by bringing in people from outside the organization.

## IMPLEMENTING ORGANIZATIONAL CHANGE

There are three generic change problems that all managers face
in managing discontinuous change: dealing with the problem of
power and politics, dealing with individual anxiety and resistance, and maintaining control during the transition period. When
carefully managed, these three factors are powerful levers for
the successful implementation of change. If ignored, they can
easily undermine even the most reasonable change effort.

### Managing the Political Dynamics of Change

It is almost impossible to introduce major changes without
stirring up the political pot so change managers must anticipate

these dynamics and be prepared to manage them. To do otherwise is to ignore the inevitable and needlessly jeopardize the change effort.[12] Managers can directly shape organizational politics to reduce resistance, use mundane behaviors to support the change, and build in stability around those unchangeable aspects.

**SHAPE COALITIONS; MOBILIZE THE KEY PLAYERS' SUPPORT.** The key players in a change effort are those politically important individuals both inside and outside the organization who will be affected by the change. Not all individuals are equally powerful. Some individuals are powerful enough to make (or break) the change effort, others help the change, while others simply let the change happen. This political analysis must be done within the manager's unit, across the larger organization (i.e., critical peers), up with the manager's boss, and outside the organization (i.e., critical suppliers or customers).

To determine who these key individuals are and what their responses to the change might be, ask: Who has the power to make or break the change? Who controls critical resources or expertise? Then think through how the change will likely affect each of these individuals and how each is likely to react toward the change. Who will gain or lose something? What are the relationships among those affected? Are there blocs of individuals likely to mobilize against or in support of the change effort? Finally, decide what actions can be taken to minimize the impact of the opposition and to maximize the motivation of potential supporters. Managers must actively think in terms of coalitions to shape change. We ask managers to diagnose, map, and shape the networks and coalitions of their organizations in service of their change effort.

Further, what levers are available to influence the key players? In increasing order of riskiness, they include the following.

***Participation, involvement, cooptation.*** The most positive method of getting powerful individuals on board is to solicit their involvement in planning and directing the change effort. The more these individuals are involved, the greater the chance they have to put their own stamp on the change, and the more they own and become committed to it. At Jaguar of North America, Vice President Dale Gambrill and President Mike Dale did exactly this. They found the loudest dissenters and put them in charge! One of those who was coopted notes, "I was suspicious and instinctively resisted. . . . But they've really changed."[13] What's interesting is not that the senior executives had changed their plan but that the original dissenter had changed his views. Similarly, Kearns at Xerox, O'Neill at Alcoa, and Chow at BOC Gases were all careful to involve their key players in the change effort. Whatever the specific process, the psychology is the same: Participation leads to a sense of ownership. Doing is believing.

***Incentives.*** Rewards and punishments are another powerful way to shape desired behaviors. To the extent that participants see no incentive (or worse, are penalized) for supporting the change, it is reasonable for them to resist. So it is critical to be clear about what is currently rewarded versus what will be. At BOC, Chow actively measured and evaluated the behaviors required for his team's Runnymede initiative. Collaboration, teamwork, and rapid technology transfer were measured formally through revised systems and informally as Chow and his team traveled throughout the organization. With Chow's clear allocation of formal and informal rewards, key individuals quickly got the message that he was serious about the change and got behind the effort. The change manager sends mixed signals in talking about the need for change if the old reward systems remain in place.

***Exchange.*** As political systems, organizations are filled with exchange relationships: I do you a favor. You do me a favor. Indeed, reciprocity exists worldwide and tends to balance out over time. All managers need to have a bank account of favors owed them. These favors can be called in during times of change.

If managers' accounts are empty, their change efforts may be severely hampered. At Grenzach, for example, Huber reminded one of his more resistant managers of how often Huber was there for him. This manager eventually got behind the changes.

*Isolation.* To the extent that key individuals continue to resist the change, they must be either socially or physically isolated. At Anaquest, for example, a key player would not buy into the change effort even when he was asked to get involved and the reward system had been changed. After Martin McGlynn, the general manager, worked on him directly through lunches, dinners, and one-on-one meetings, the individual finally got on board. In some instances, isolation may involve keeping people out of the information loop so that they do not have the opportunity to resist the change.

*Removal or transfer.* Key antagonists who cannot be converted to supporters may have to be removed. If these politically powerful opponents are permitted to actively or passively resist the change, they may encourage others to resist and form coalitions to blunt the change. Many successful turnaround managers appreciate the importance of quickly removing opposition. To rescue Scott Paper, the new CEO removed nine of eleven senior officers. Pfeiffer at Compaq encouraged six senior executives to leave. Before the turnaround at Philips was complete, virtually the entire senior team had changed. Removal or transfer is a difficult decision and should never be taken lightly, but if it is not taken after all other influence attempts have failed, it sends a mixed signal about the importance of the change. Even with all the signals of resistance, managers are often slow to take action on important team members. After the change has been resisted, those managers often observed that they should have moved earlier.

One implication of this political approach to change is that if a key negative individual is the change manager's boss, and if he or she will not get on board, the likelihood of a successful change effort is minuscule. In this situation, the only option is to manage up: to shape the supervisor's behavior through coalitions involving other key members of the system. If, however, those senior managers cannot be persuaded to support the change, the change will not happen. Thus, in the management of strategic change, managers need to diagnose and manage down, across, up, and outside the unit.

These ideas on managing politics and coalitions are often resisted by those who want to manage change through facts and data. Scientists and engineers, for example, often resist shaping change through coalitions. But facts by themselves are never enough to manage significant change. Indeed, as Peter Drucker points out, "Anyone over the age of 21 can get facts to support his or her position."[14] Rather, facts must be made salient through political action. The most successful change managers are those who not only have the facts to motivate others, but are also careful to manage the cliques and coalitions needed to implement the change.

**REINFORCE THE MESSAGE WITH MUNDANE BEHAVIORS.** The words and actions of senior managers are critical in creating political momentum and energy in support or opposition to strategic change. While we label these "mundane," clear, unequivocal signals help reduce uncertainty and organizational politics.

Large-scale change is often derailed because of inconsistencies in words and actions: The CEO says one thing is important, but the actions of other executives suggest something else. More speeches are given, but the same actions are rewarded. Cynicism develops among those who welcome the change. Soon, even the most ardent supporters become risk-averse. The extent to which managers and their teams generate mixed messages and do not "walk the talk," cynicism and politics arise to resist change. So managers must work relentlessly to reinforce their actions with their words and vice versa, not only through symbolic activities, but also by attending to those mundane behaviors we described in Chapter 6. There are a number of mechanisms managers can use.

*Manage your calendar.* The clearest signal of what is important is how a manager spends time. Those areas to which managers give most of their time and effort are perceived as important; those areas that get little effort are not. At Anaquest, for example, McGlynn set up an innovation and change task force that met once a month. He attended every meeting, arrived prepared and on time, stayed for the entire session, and even canceled other meetings to be present. His direct reports quickly inferred that the task force was important, while other important meetings (the ones he routinely missed) were less so. When Motorola began its now widely praised quality effort, Bob Galvin, then the CEO, signaled its importance by requiring that quality be the first item on every agenda. He was known to attend meetings long enough to hear the quality report and discussions, and then leave—a signal that he meant what he said. Scrutinize any successful change effort and you will see similar signaling.

*Ask questions.* The questions that senior managers ask also clearly indicate what is important (and what is not). One reason that the strategic changes at Alcoa and Xerox were executed so well is that wherever O'Neill and Kearns went, they constantly asked questions about the progress of their change efforts. Such sustained attention to detail and consistent questioning send clear signals about what attitudes and behavior management thinks are really necessary.

*Follow up.* Just as questions from senior managers signal interest, following up conveys a seriousness of purpose. After Welch meets with managers at GE's Management Development Center, he asks for written feedback from them summarizing what it was that they learned. He marvels at how easy it is for an audience to hear things that were never said, particularly when the message is something it may not like hearing. The only way to overcome this selective hearing is through repetition and consistency. Not charisma or eloquence, but the unrelenting consistency of words and actions over time create clarity and, in turn, reduce politics.

*Take control of meeting agendas.* Another indicator of what is important is what's on the agenda at meetings. As mentioned, employees at firms like DuPont and Marriott understand the significance of safety and customer service because they are always first on the agenda. What items on the agenda are covered in great detail, what items are ignored? Over time, people soon infer that certain issues are important and others are not, regardless of the content of speeches and video tapes from senior management.

*Hold lunches, dinners, and events.* Take advantage of special opportunities to substantively and symbolically energize the change effort. For example, after the task force reported back, McGlynn and his team at Anaquest sponsored a "Spartacus" rally to thank the task force and stimulate further enthusiasm for the change effort. At the Grenzach plant, Huber held a series of lunches and dinners throughout the facility to take questions and demonstrate his personal commitment to the sweeping changes. Although these gatherings were seen at first as artificial, they soon became a valued signal of the importance of the change and an opportunity for people to celebrate their accomplishments with their spouses.

*Summarize and interpret.* At the end of many meetings, the senior person often reviews the highlights of the session. This is an opportunity to interpret and underscore the message, a chance for managers to help their colleagues understand the change effort and gain clarity as to why the change effort is important. One role of the senior team is to reduce the turbulence of transition periods by interpreting what is going on and helping others make sense of the transition. At Anaquest, BOC's chairman made a speech regarding the future of the company as a whole. Unfortunately, he was ambiguous about the future of the Anaquest division. To reduce uncertainty and the potential of increased anxiousness and resistance, McGlynn and his team actively helped Anaquest employees understand and interpret the chairman's speech with respect to the changes within the unit.

*Create heroes, stories, and myths.* All organizations have their heroes, stories, and myths. Angus McDonald at the old AT&T, Wilson at Xerox, Watson at IBM, and Mary Kay Ash at Mary Kay are exemplars. Stories about larger-than-life figures are a quick, vivid way of conveying a sense of what's important. The tales of heroic customer service at FedEx and Nordstrom, or persistence and innovation at 3M and J&J convey powerful messages about standards of behavior and performance. During transition periods, executives need to consider creating new heroes and stories to illustrate the change in standards and direction.

ABB's Barnevik says, "You have to exploit your success stories to break resistance. . . . If you want to break direction, you have to shake people up, not by threatening them, but by illustrating in a similar situation what can be accomplished."[15] Celebration is critical so people realize that the things they may have thought were impossible are not only possible but happening and being rewarded.

*Use language and symbols.* Managers do not make copiers, they do not clear checks, deliver gas, sell products, or do research. Instead, they deal with symbols, information, structures, and organizational processes. Executive teams can shape behavior and focus attention by managing symbolically. Physical locations, names, titles, and ceremonial events are powerful signals. Changing the conception of Xerox as a copier company to Xerox as the document company signals a shift in corporate vision, just as Ciba Vision's moving its headquarters from Basel to Atlanta signals the company's new view of itself as a more entrepreneurial, independent entity. At a more microlevel, offering a particular promotion (or demotion), moving an office, and eliminating the corporate dining room are small but visible signals of the future state. Calling all members of the organization associates or team members is a small thing. But over time, the use of language can affect how people think of themselves and others.

Managing mundane behavior is perhaps the least costly yet most powerful means of shaping political behavior. By themselves, these trivial actions are of little consequence to most managers. But when used together and carefully aligned, their power to focus attention and shape interpretations is considerable. The fact that separately such actions are so small only makes their combined effect more surprising and powerful.

**BUILD IN STABILITY.** A final action for reducing political behavior to change is building in stability, even as the change occurs. To mitigate the destructive aspects of political behavior, managers can begin by preparing key people for the change, providing information and detail on the change in advance, being honest and candid, and constantly sending consistent messages to lessen uncertainty. Part of this signaling is to be clear about what is not changing—what people can hold onto in the future. If some aspects of culture, physical location, and staffing patterns will not change, these anchors to the past need to be communicated and reinforced early on. At Alcoa, even in the context of wholesale change, O'Neill and his team were clear that the glorious Alcoa engineering heritage and its commitment to high-quality aluminum would not change. As Kodak refocuses, George Fisher has reemphasized the firm's commitment to the photographic market and signaled an end to diversification. Clarity about what will not change helps moderate fears of the future.

## Managing Individual Resistance

The second predictable issue faced by all managers of large-scale change is the resistance associated with individual anxiety. The psychological consequences of stress and anxiety are well known (see Figure 8.2). Overstressed individuals shut down and, in turn, resist change actively or passively. As one manager put it, whenever he attempted to introduce major organizational changes, he always had to answer the same nine questions, "Why, why, why? When, when, when? Me, me, me?" There are four practical steps all managers can take to reduce dysfunctional

**FIGURE 8.2**

**EFFECTS OF STRESS AND ANXIETY ON INDIVIDUAL PERFORMANCE**

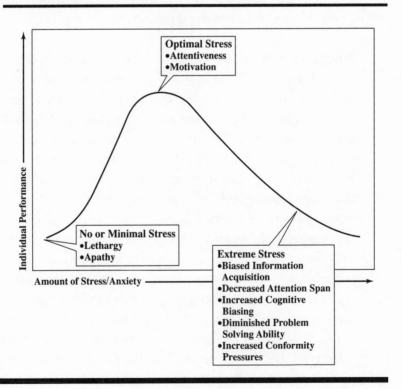

anxiety and motivate constructive behavior: create dissatisfaction with the status quo, build in participation, recognize and reward the desired new behaviors, and provide time and opportunity to disengage.

**CREATE DISSATISFACTION WITH THE STATUS QUO.** The first and most important step in motivating constructive behavior is to ensure that people understand emotionally, not just intellectually, why they have to change. Most of us become anxious when faced with new situations. Our response includes holding on to the status quo, moving slowly, and avoiding the leaps of faith revolutionary change may require. But the fact, amply documented by the organizational failures we have discussed, is that incremental change will not suffice in the face of changing innovation streams.

How do successful change managers generate the emotional energy to change? They create a credible crisis, whether the organization is failing and the crisis is immediately visible or the organization is doing well and the crisis lies up ahead. Roberto Goizueta, Coke's CEO, is succinct: "If you don't have an enemy, the best thing is you create one."[16] Brian Dumaine suggests several actions that successful change managers can take to create a crisis:[17]

- Look for evidence that a crisis is inevitable (e.g., benchmarking, customer feedback);

- Make sure the crisis is credible;

- Use simple messages to communicate the crisis;

- Give employees a vision that inspires an emotional reaction;

- Offer a plan and the resources to resolve the crisis;

- Make sure your entire team is committed (you need one vision and many missionaries); and

- Expect resistance and have a plan for overcoming it.

Several years ago when Boeing management embarked on a major change effort, it was dissatisfied with its ability to convince employees of the need to change. At the time Boeing was doing well and its employees felt little urgency to change. To engage people emotionally, senior managers hired a local Seattle TV news team. The team produced a "news story," ostensibly to be aired on the TV station reporting massive layoffs at Boeing. The video included footage of closed Boeing facilities and the impact the layoff would have on the local economy. The pictures, worth thousands of words, were successfully used as a part of the training effort to demonstrate to people the reality of the potential crisis.

Managers of change must convey both a credible reason for the change and offer a constructive channel for the release of the anxiety. Extremely anxious individuals have trouble focusing and listening so the rationale for the change needs to be simple, realistic, and overcommunicated. Until this has been done, people will wait hopefully for the crisis to pass. In the early phases of transforming ABB, Barnevik spent time delivering his "doom speech" throughout the company. He pounded home the view that as many as two-thirds of all large companies in Europe were likely to fail in the wake of European integration. The message was simple: ABB must change or it would certainly fail. Barnevik understood that before people would accept the massive changes required of them, they needed to emotionally accept the dire consequences of not changing.

**BUILD IN PARTICIPATION.** If there is one clear result from the research on change management, it is that employee participation increases individual ownership and excitement and, in turn, decreases individual resistance to change. The more people are involved, the more the change effort is their change effort. The more individuals can see that they can succeed in the future state, the more empowered they feel.

The power of involvement is visible in three major successful change efforts in the past decade—Xerox, GE, and Philips. At

Xerox, the Leadership Through Quality effort began at the top and cascaded down the organization with enormous employee involvement. Quality teams, task forces, benchmarking teams, and quality councils all generated energy and enthusiasm for the change. Nay-sayers either became convinced or left. Similarly the mandatory town meetings and Work-Out sessions at GE involved the entire organization in the process of generating speed, simplicity, and self-confidence. At Philips, Jan Timmer implemented an almost identical process, Operation Centurion, which began at the top and spread throughout the organization in a variety of ways. Timmer claims that earlier efforts at change failed because of an emphasis on systems and procedures instead of employee involvement.

To appreciate the success of these and similar efforts, consider the opposite: a change effort with no participation. Such a program would, of necessity, rely on top-down direction and formal measurement and reward systems. While useful, it could never capture the energy, ideas, and enthusiasm of the work force. It would rely completely on the wisdom and direction of senior managers—a shaky foundation. Welch says, "The only way I see to get more productivity is by getting people involved and excited about their jobs."[18] It's worth noting that participation does not mean permissiveness. Employees were not asked to participate in the crucial strategic decisions about whether to initiate quality efforts at Xerox or Alcoa, or change at BOC or Grenzach. Rather, the senior teams set the vision and strategic direction, and designed an implementation effort emphasizing extensive employee involvement.

In general, the greater the amount of participation, the better. But it is contingent on two factors: Does the organization face a crisis? and Where is the locus of crucial expertise? If a manager faces a real crisis and if a senior team has all the expertise, the team must act autocratically. If, for example, the building is burning, the last thing one wants to hear from the fire chief is, "People, we have a crisis, let's talk." Under extreme conditions, the executive team (the fire brigade) must take decisive action.

Asking uninformed individuals to participate is dangerous and lacks credibility with the people themselves. Such crisis conditions are rare, however.

While participation decreases individual anxiety and increases commitment and ownership of the change effort, these benefits are not free. Participation takes time and involves delegating increased control of the transition to employees. Once the future state is clear, widespread involvement in the development of implementation plans enhances ownership and decreases resistance to change. At Ford, for example, CEO Alex Trotman concluded that too many changes were poorly implemented because those charged with making the changes didn't understand the aims of the effort. To counteract this, he has involved hundreds of people at all levels in designing and implementing new change efforts. Even with all the talk about empowerment and the clear benefits of involvement, participation remains an underutilized lever in executing strategic organizational change.

**RECOGNIZE AND REWARD DESIRED NEW BEHAVIORS.** A third mechanism for motivating constructive behavior is the design and use of reward systems, focusing especially on those attitudes and behaviors needed during the transition. People do what they perceive they will be rewarded for. To the extent that individuals see that new attitudes and behaviors are rewarded, they will be more likely to behave accordingly. For example, as long as Torrance's laboratory managers continued to be paid for producing great technology, they were unmotivated to develop commercially successful new products. They actively resented Torrance's changes. In contrast, at BOC Gases, Chow's revised team compensation system measured and rewarded the senior team on both global and local criteria. The new reward system motivated BOC managers to get on with the global matrix organization.

One way to build a reward system in support of the change effort is to work backward from the vision to the critical tasks, beginning with clarity about what attitudes and behaviors are needed to be successful in the changed organization. Once the important attitudes and behavior are agreed upon, decide how to measure and reward them.

In addition to setting up formal rewards, management can use informal and symbolic rewards to encourage constructive behavior. Personal recognition, spending time with and paying attention to employees, and creating and attending special events are powerful signals and informal reinforcement (and punishment) as to what is important (or not important) during the transition period and in the future state. Recognizing the importance of symbolic rewards (and realizing that he did not have a large pool of substantive rewards to allocate), Huber used personal recognition, nominations for special awards, and a series of invited lunches and dinners to recognize and reward Grenzach employees in their change efforts. Similarly, CEO Frank Shrontz at Boeing began announcing all high-level promotions by sending employees letters that described why they were being advanced. This permitted him to be very clear about what competencies and values were important.

**PROVIDE TIME AND OPPORTUNITY TO DISENGAGE.** Managers can also help their colleagues disengage from the current state. To the extent that people are publicly vested in certain processes and outcomes, they may be psychologically committed to past actions. The pride that accompanies accomplishment can make it difficult to repudiate the old ways in the face of change. Individuals often respond to strategic change with a sense of personal loss. They need to let go and to mourn the passing of the old order before they become psychologically committed to the future state. Managers and their teams can facilitate this psychological transition by providing time, opportunity, and settings for individuals to let go, to celebrate the past as well as to see the promise and opportunities in the future.

Providing opportunities to disengage from the past is not done by hiring waves of psychiatrists. Instead, the use of simple events such as lunches, ceremonies, and other events during the transition period gives people the chance to honor the past as well as reinforces the new attitudes and behaviors required for success in the future. At BOC, every training session devoted to bolstering marketing and change skills was also used as a vehicle for Chow to review why BOC Gases had to change. Chow and his senior team gave employees the time to honor and celebrate BOC's past, even as they moved quickly to create the new BOC Gases.

## Maintaining Control during the Transition

Transition periods are always turbulent, uncertain, and chaotic if only because the current state is being taken apart before the full development of the future state. The executive team needs to actively manage the transition with the same degree of care and attention given to any other strategically important project. The team must do four things to maintain control during the transition period: communicate a clear image of the future state, use multiple levers to promote change, design transition management structures, and use feedback data to measure progress.

COMMUNICATE A CLEAR IMAGE OF THE FUTURE STATE. If employees lack a solid understanding of the purpose of the change and the unit's goals and organizational architecture, rumors develop, political behavior is accentuated, and the transition is jeopardized. For these reasons, it is important that the change manager and his or her team develop and relentlessly communicate as detailed a picture of the future as possible—even though the future state may still be a moving target.

For example, Federal Express developed television commercials demonstrating specific types of customer service it was attempting to provide. These vivid images gave FedEx employees and customers vivid images of the organization's desired future state. Similarly, Chow and his team developed a detailed picture of BOC Gases's future state and traveled throughout the gases business to present the specific whens, wheres, hows, and whys of the firm's transformation. Such clear, consistent, and detailed messages helped employees stay focused during the transition.

**USE MULTIPLE LEVERS TO PROMOTE CHANGE.** While incremental change usually entails the realignment of one or two organizational components (e.g., a change in the reward system), discontinuous change involves simultaneous shifts in each component—a realignment of tasks, people, culture, and the formal structure. A consistent lesson from studies of discontinuous change is that making incremental or piecemeal changes is insufficient. Focusing on a single element of the model, such as emphasizing only reengineering or retraining, won't work. To increase the chances of success, an integrated set of changes is required in which shifts in structure fit with the new training efforts, which fit with the new culture and the reengineered work process.

For instance, Operation Centurion at Philips began with agreement among senior managers about the magnitude of their problem and what it would take to ensure Philips's survival. The change effort then encompassed an array of initiatives for revitalizing every component of the organization. To gain the required competencies, significant retraining was undertaken and new people were hired. Many older Philips employees left because they either did not buy into the new vision or lacked the ability to acquire new skills. Concurrently, new structures, operating processes, and reward and promotion systems were implemented. A quality effort, as well as major restructuring and reengineering, was initiated. At the same time, explicit efforts were made to identify and reinforce the norms needed to succeed in the future and to eliminate many of the old norms that would hinder progress. The success of this sweeping effort stemmed from Timmer's use of multiple levers. A previous attempt to change Philips had failed both because of significant resistance among senior managers and the fact that the change was attempted piecemeal, giving the resistance time to derail the effort.

Success resulted not from the strategic intent but from effective implementation.

**DESIGN TRANSITION MANAGEMENT STRUCTURES.** The management of a transition period should be approached with the same rigor as that of a new product launch. Since current roles, structures, and procedures may no longer be useful and those designed for the future may not be fully in place, change managers should explicitly consider what new roles, structures, and procedures are needed to manage the transition.

*Transition managers.* Just as organizations assign a person responsibility for the introduction of a new product, so too should an individual be formally designated as the transition manager. This person should be evaluated and rewarded on the effectiveness of the change process. The more senior and more credible this person the better. Our experience indicates that transition periods are most effectively managed when the transition manager is the most senior person in the organization. Even though it is difficult to simultaneously manage the current state, build the future state, and manage the transition period, the symbolic importance of hands-on senior management responsibility for the transition cannot be overestimated. If not the most senior manager, the transition manager must have the formal and informal power and the resources to make the transition happen. At BOC and at Ciba's Grenzach facility, Chow and Huber were the respective transition managers. At Alcoa and Xerox, O'Neill and Kearns appointed respected senior executives to those posts.

*Transition teams.* No single manager can make transitions happen. He or she needs a team that shares responsibility for implementing the change. This team should also be measured and evaluated on the progress of the change effort. Since people throughout the organization will be watching to see how serious the change effort really is, it is critical that the team members be credible. The changes at BOC Gases, Grenzach, and Alcoa were effective at least partly because they were driven by highly credible, powerful transition teams.

Bob Waterman has studied the use of teams in driving organizational change and offers some very practical and insightful suggestions to maximize their effectiveness:[19]

1. Make the right start with clear, visible executive support

2. Select the right people

3. Set a tone of excitement and urgency

4. Adopt a rigorous, fact-based approach

5. Emphasize results, not reports

6. Monitor progress systematically

7. Use multiple reporting relationships

8. Minimize "us" versus "them" attitudes

9. Build trust—fight trivia.

*Transition plans.* The transition team needs to develop a realistic, achievable transition plan, preferably one that initially considers various scenarios. While one transition scenario might be aggressive in terms of speed in implementation, another might be more conservative. Each approach will have costs and benefits (e.g., level of participation versus speed). Based on a cost/benefit analysis, the transition team can choose the best approach and implement it.

Just as if the transition were a new product, the plan should include benchmarks, goals, metrics, controls, budgets, roles, and performance standards. The Xerox transition team developed detailed training and communication efforts. It also developed measures, rewards, feedback procedures, and a process for managing the transition through cascading interventions throughout Xerox. This extensive, detailed transition plan and its associated roles, systems, and processes were hammered out over weeks of full-time effort by team members in consultation with other Xerox executives. In contrast, many organizational failures are characterized by little or no attention to planning the transition.

*Transition resources.* Major changes are not cheap. Transition teams need time, resources, personal support, and often external expertise. Alcoa's transition team took the time to travel together to benchmark their transition plan and, in turn, spent weeks developing detailed plans for each Alcoa unit. The team was given resources to develop specialized training and education efforts for the top 100 Alcoa managers as well as all mid-level managers. To begin the transformation at Boeing, the CEO sent the top 200 executives on two-week benchmarking and fact-finding trips around the world. As a part of Philips's Operation Centurion, each year a "customer day" is held, in which all 250,000 employees cease their normal duties and meet to develop new ways of meeting customer needs. The cost of such efforts is immense. But without a commitment of resources and time, transition periods may not receive the attention they deserve. The cost of a failure of the strategic change effort can be fatal.

**SET TRANSITION MILESTONES AND MEASURE PROGRESS.** A final lever for maintaining control is to be systematic in measuring progress during the transition period. Again, just as if the transition were a new product, the transition team should be prepared to gather data and monitor the effectiveness of the transition. For instance, Mike Plaxton is a senior manager in the life insurance business. In 1990, he was charged with turning around the U.K. operation of a major insurance company. There was low productivity, poor delivery, and little commitment to the customer. As a part of his plan to change the organization, he developed a vision of high-performing teams accompanied by a complete change in the organization's structure and culture. He described his role as "To keep the vision in front of the team's mind, take joint responsibility for failures, and give them individual accolades when they succeeded."

Aside from spending a significant part of his time reinforcing the new culture, he recognized that a critical part the change effort was assessing progress and keeping the change on track. To do this he and his team designed an anonymous survey to assess the culture change. The items on the form reflect the specific attitudes and behaviors required by the new culture. This survey is administered periodically to all employees and the results are used to gauge the progress in the change effort. The news has been encouraging. Since 1990, the organization has reduced costs by a third, increased volume by 12 percent, improved customer service by 15 percent, and reduced staff without harming morale. Plaxton understands that the measurement and feedback of specific attitudes and behaviors is a critical element of a successful change effort.

It is vital that transition teams develop multiple, redundant methods for obtaining feedback on the transition process. Surveys, systematic interviews (often by outsiders), focus groups, and personal contact can be useful. At Anaquest, McGlynn's transition team quickly discovered that the R&D group was slow to move. The team traced the source of this resistance to the head of R&D and ultimately replaced him. At BOC Gases, after a year of progress in implementing the new vision, Chow felt that mid-level managers were slow to understand and embrace the change. Chow gathered data on this hunch and initiated a set of education and reward system changes directed at these managers.

## ASSESSING IMPLEMENTATION

Four practical but challenging criteria provide a benchmark for planning and evaluating an effective change process. First and foremost, Does the organization actually reach the future according to plan? A Harvard Business School study of 93 major organizational change efforts found that in 74 percent of the cases, unanticipated problems occurred that hindered the change effort. The study also reported that in 76 percent of the cases the change effort took longer than planned.[20]

Second, given that the future state is reached, Does the organization function as planned? Little is achieved if the change is implemented but the effort fails to work as anticipated. For Huber at Ciba, it would have been small consolation if the plant were transformed but costs and flexibility targets were not met. Only when the transformed plant met its quality, delivery, safety, and morale targets could the change effort could be considered a success.

Third, Can the change occur without undue costs to the organization? Strategic change efforts are not cheap. They cost time and money and can be disruptive to suppliers and customers. While these costs cannot be reduced to zero, a successful effort is one that minimizes them. When senior managers at Jostens, the Minnesota-based maker of class rings and yearbooks, decided to diversify in the late 1980s into computer systems, senior management lost control of the change process and destroyed a 34-year record of growth in sales and earnings.

Finally, Does the process both recognize and minimize the cost of the change to individuals, including those who leave as well as those who remain? Strategic change always affects people within the organization. The costs to individuals cannot be dropped to zero but it can be minimized. One element of Warren Buffet and Derek Maughan's effort to revive Salomon Brothers was to rein in the compensation costs of some of their traders. Their strategy was to introduce a pay system that linked risk to reward, an ideology frequently espoused by their employees and hardly controversial. Yet, the implementation of this strategy led to widespread discontent and significant turnover among employees. Alarmed at the short-term loss of crucial intellectual capital, Buffet and Maughan rescinded their plan.

While the first and second criteria are relatively objective, the third and fourth are highly subjective. Different managers will have different criteria as to what are minimal costs to individuals and organizations. While some change managers may be willing to pay substantial individual and organizational costs to get to the future state very quickly, others may not. Balancing these implementation costs will differ across individuals and competitive conditions. Whatever the weight given to individual and organizational transition costs, the fundamental challenge is to manage the change process to maximize the probability that the organization gets to its desired future state, works consistently with its plans, and does so at minimal cost to both the organization and the employees.

While there are no universal recipes or cookbooks for managing change, there are patterns that discriminate between more or less successful change efforts. We have found that while discontinuous change is difficult and complex, it can be effectively managed. And, although proactive change may be the most difficult to implement, it can be a source of great strategic advantage. To effectively implement discontinuous change, managers must engage their colleagues and employees emotionally and intellectually. This can require creating crises, building coalitions, dealing with anxiety and resistance, and, on occasion, removing those who imperil the change effort. Further, major change cannot be accomplished by a single visionary individual. It requires a committed senior team and extended leadership throughout the organization. Jack Stack of Springfield ReManufacturing puts it plainly: "It's easy to stop one person, but it's pretty hard to stop 100."[21]

# CHAPTER 9

## WINNING THROUGH INNOVATION

IN 1981, CIBA VISION WAS THE 27TH ENTRANT INTO the U.S. contact lens market. Through a strategy of acquisitions, geographical expansion, and innovation, Ciba Vision grew rapidly. By 1995, it had become a 6,000-person organization, jostling with Bausch and Lomb and Johnson & Johnson for global leadership of the contact lens/lens care market and with Alcon, Allergan, and MSD for leadership in the ophthalmics market. Led by Glen Bradley (CEO), Luzi von Bidder (head of ophthalmics), and Adrian Hunter (head of optics R&D), Ciba Vision provides a wonderful example of winning through innovation—of building an ambidextrous organization, leading innovation streams, and coupling innovation with organizational change.

Anchored by their vision of "We help people maintain and improve their vision," along with aggressive growth and profit targets, Bradley and his team knew that current products would not be sufficient to fuel tomorrow's growth. They realized that to build and sustain a market leadership position, Ciba Vision needed to pursue both incremental and radical innovation.

For mature products like conventional soft lenses and lens care products, Ciba Vision invested in incremental product and process improvements. These improvements helped grow and defend the company's market share as well as provide funding to research and develop new contact lenses and ophthalmic pharmaceuticals. The funds generated by the products of today financed those of tomorrow. So, for example, while parts of the optics organization focused on incremental innovations associated with line extensions and incremental product and process improvements, two autonomous optics teams focused on tomorrow's breakthrough innovations. One team worked on an entirely new continuous production process to radically reduce the cost of manufacturing disposable soft lenses. The other worked on an entirely new type of contact lens that could be worn safely all day and night.

The autonomous teams were comprised of people from several of Ciba Vision's functional areas: R&D, clinical and regulatory, process engineering, manufacturing, marketing, and finance. They were co-located, headed by strong project leaders, and allowed to work independently from the rest of the organization. Each team was given stretch targets and encouraged to explore several solutions to the technical challenges it faced, thereby increasing the chances of finding breakthrough solutions. The discontinuous product and process innovations have the potential to substitute for Ciba Vision's current products and processes. As in the past, with the transition from lathe production to the cast molding of contact lenses, for example, shifts in innovation streams must, in turn, be coupled with a proactive discontinuous organizational change within the firm.

Bradley, von Bidder, and Hunter observed that the main barriers to innovation are within the organization and that the key to innovation is not creating new ideas, but escaping old ones. By building their ambidextrous organization, Bradley and his team had the luxury of competing for today even as they prepared to recreate the future through breakthrough product and/or process innovation. While they knew that Ciba Vision's success was not guaranteed, the autonomous teams actually delivered the breakthroughs, providing Bradley's management team with opportunities to reshape the innovation stream in the lens market. Thus while Ciba Vision has evolved over 15 years through a range of incremental and radical innovations and through periods of incremental organizational change punctuated by discontinuous change, it looks to the outside world as having an unbroken period of sustained growth.

## WINNING THROUGH INNOVATION: OUR THEMES

We began our investigation of the success paradox with a description of how the U.S. Navy resisted innovation a century ago. Throughout the book we have illustrated how managers in the 1990s are trapped by success in much the same way—as well as how this trap can be avoided. The source of sustained competitive advantage, and a way to avoid being trapped by success, is through building and leading ambidextrous organizations. Firms like Ciba Vision compete by taking advantage of technology cycles and, in turn, driving streams of innovation. Ambidextrous organizations get today's work done—they nurture incremental innovation and increased congruence among strategy and existing structures, competencies, and culture. Ambidextrous organizations also help get tomorrow's work done—they couple incremental innovation with both architectural and discontinuous innovation. As at Ciba Vision, these shifts in innovation streams must, in turn, be coupled with discontinuous organizational change.

The ability to manage simultaneously for today and tomorrow, with contrasting alignments of people, structure, culture, and process, is the key to long-term success. In examining firms that have been successful at this such as BOC, Seiko, HP, and Ciba Vision, we have seen how excellent managers encourage both incremental and discontinuous innovation and focus on both the short term and the long term. "We like to say it's innovation and stability," says L. D. DeSimone, current CEO of 3M.[1] HP CEO Platt echoes this sentiment, "We have to be willing to cannibalize what we're doing today in order to ensure our leadership in the future."[2] In this final chapter we pull together our themes for winning through innovation.

We can learn from the actions of the many managers we have described. We have seen, for example, Pierre Urech as a lower level product champion in Switzerland, as well as Kurt Huber and John Torrance managing divisions of larger firms in Germany and the United States. We have described managers running business units, including Martin McGlynn at Anaquest, C. K. Chow at BOC Gases, Glen Bradley at Ciba Vision, as well as those leading larger corporations such as Paul O'Neill at Alcoa, Jack Welch at GE, Percy Barnevik at ABB, and Alex Krauer at Ciba-Geigy. No matter the country, industry, or level of analysis, all these managers have been dealing with issues similar to those that haunted Lt. Sims more than a hundred years ago: how to proactively lead innovation and change; how to move from today's to tomorrow's strength.

Throughout, we have emphasized how easy it is for even the best managed companies to fall behind, either because of missed strategic opportunities or a failure to implement strategic change. We offered glimpses of the tribulations of such firms as Oticon, SSIH, Philips, Sears, and IBM, illustrating how companies with powerful market positions, strong financial resources, superb technology, and presumably good managers can find themselves in trouble. We have also illustrated how some firms have created ambidextrous organizations that ensure their survival and success. To further sharpen understanding of the dynamics of managing innovation and change, we return to some of our earlier examples and show how Philips, for example, is reinventing itself, while other great firms are struggling. In doing this, we show again that success in the long term requires managers to celebrate both stability *and* change.

## Winners and Losers—Losers and Winners

In 1990, Cor van der Klugt was fired as the CEO of the Dutch electronics firm Philips. For four years he had attempted to stop Philips's downward spiral and, in the view of the supervisory board, had failed. He was replaced by Jan Timmer. Like Martinez at Sears (see Chapter 8), Timmer reengineered a turnaround. His Operation Centurion began by forcing his top one hundred managers to look honestly at the company, to agree on the root causes of its problems, and to craft a strategy and vision for solving them. The formula he used was simple: Confront people with data, establish that the problems are real, and determine how to solve them.

Having identified performance problems, Timmer involved more than 250,000 employees in the effort to reinvent Philips. Like Welch at GE and Martinez at Sears, he has cascaded this involvement throughout the organization. Management has focused the strategy, refined business practices, reduced the staff by more than 100,000, closed more than 350 manufacturing sites, and replaced 12 of the 14 executives on the top team. In doing this, Timmer simultaneously changed strategy, structure, people, and culture. As with Sears, there is no guarantee that this revolution will be successful. Some analysts remain skeptical, but the initial results are promising. From losses of $2.3 billion in 1990 Philips has returned with a profit of almost $1 billion in 1994. It has successfully entered new businesses and shortened the new product cycle time. Again, the important lesson is in the process Timmer used to reorient Philips and move beyond incremental innovation and change.

While Sears, Philips, IBM, GM, and Kodak are learning how to manage revolutionary as well as incremental change, more successful firms are sometimes stumbling. In the fourth quarter of 1995, 3M took a $600 million charge against earnings and announced a major restructuring, including the downsizing of 5,000 employees. Rubbermaid, *Fortune*'s most admired company in 1993 and 1994, has also faltered, ending a 15-year run of steadily increasing profits. As the firm's top managers began to focus more on maintaining financial performance, they over-extended the organization, angered its most important retail buyers, and were slow to recognize new competitors. Instead of lowering its financial targets in the face of rising raw material costs, Rubbermaid raised prices, alienated customers, and gave the competition an opening. "They have rested on their laurels too much," says one major retailer.[3] Even great firms like Wal-Mart and Motorola face similar challenges as their markets change and the balance between incremental and discontinuous innovation shifts.

### Lessons Learned

There are important lessons for managers in these examples and others we have tracked throughout the book.

- Vision, strategy, and objectives are the bedrock for managing innovation and change.

- Innovation is about execution, about getting it done.

- Without a performance gap, innovation is unlikely.

- Congruence is the key to diagnosis.

- Inertia kills. Managing culture is the most neglected, and highest leverage, tool for promoting innovation and change.

- Successful innovation requires skilled management of organizational politics.

- Technology cycles drive innovation streams.

- Ambidextrous organizations help compete for today and tomorrow.

- Managing innovation streams means managing discontinuous change.

- Innovation is a team sport.

**VISION, STRATEGY, AND OBJECTIVES ARE THE BEDROCK FOR MANAGING INNOVATION AND CHANGE.** Managers and their teams need be able to develop and clearly articulate a competitive vision, strategy, and objectives for their business unit. Without a clear articulation of these aspirations, ambiguity and uncertainty will plague any effort at building ambidextrous organizations and managing innovation and change. A competitive vision captures people's emotional energies and answers the question, *Why* are we doing this? But vision by itself is abstract; aspirations must be linked to concrete business unit strategies and objectives (e.g., profit, ROI, growth rates, customer satisfaction). Thus, the sustained success at Ciba Vision is partly due to its clear vision coupled with stretch objectives.

**INNOVATION IS ABOUT EXECUTION, ABOUT GETTING IT DONE.** Strategic clarity alone is not sufficient. Many competitors have similar visions and strategies. Success comes not from the articulation of vision, strategy, and objectives, but from their execution. To succeed, managers need to build organizations that are capable of accomplishing their strategic objectives more rapidly than their competitors. This requires that they build organizations to get today's work done more effectively and to anticipate tomorrow's discontinuities. Innovation results from creative ideas successfully implemented. Competitive advantage is as much about execution as it is about strategy.

**WITHOUT A PERFORMANCE GAP, INNOVATION IS UNLIKELY.** A crucial part of any manager's job is setting and clarifying today's most important organizational problems. As seen so vividly with Lt. Sims and the U.S. Navy, without engaging problems, organizations become complacent and resistant to innovation and change. Managers can define problems as real or potential gaps between strategic requirements and actual organizational performance. While it is easy to define problems when an organization is facing a crisis, it is more difficult to proactively create crises while an organization is successful. Gerstner at IBM calls this the winner's curse and says, "I was blessed by the fact that you need a crisis to focus on the need for change. Basically what I said to people around here is: We just lost $17.8 billion and 150,000 people lost their jobs, and the media is throwing us on the junkyard pile. It appears that what we're doing isn't working. Would you agree? And, therefore, we ought to try something different."[4] It is the capability to create problems or opportunities while a firm is doing well that allows the most successful managers to capitalize on incremental and discontinuous innovation and change.

**CONGRUENCE IS THE KEY TO DIAGNOSIS.** Problem definition leads to a systematic diagnosis of the performance gap's roots. This systematic problem solving was behind Huber's change efforts at Grenzach, Chow's at BOC Gases, Welch's Work-Out efforts at GE, and Timmer's Operation Centurion. Our congruence model is based on alignment among the four fundamental organizational building blocks: (1) tasks and work flows, (2) human resources, (3) organizational structure and systems, and (4) organizational culture, and provides a straightforward way to diagnose problems. These basic components are both hard (task and structure) and soft (individual and culture) levers managers can use to shape organizational capabilities and change.

**INERTIA KILLS. MANAGING CULTURE IS THE MOST NEGLECTED, AND HIGHEST LEVERAGED, TOOL FOR PROMOTING INNOVATION AND CHANGE.** Of these four organizational building blocks, culture is the most difficult to diagnose and change. Social control processes can help motivate organizational members and are a powerful way to focus behaviors in complex and changing settings. But organizational culture can also hold an organization hostage to its past. The key seems to be to create a clear vision with a limited set of core values, like Platt at HP or Bradley at Ciba Vision did, that can, in turn, host diverse cultures within the organization. In contrast, managers who do not directly attend to cultural diversity and change (like Simonsen at Oticon) pay a severe price in the management of innovation and change.

**SUCCESSFUL INNOVATION REQUIRES SKILLED MANAGEMENT OF ORGANIZATIONAL POLITICS.** Long-term innovation involves linking innovation streams, market requirements, and organizational capabilities. This requires building functional competencies, such as technology, marketing, or distribution, and linking them to develop products or services that meet customer requirements. Since managing innovation involves linking diverse competencies across multiple boundaries, executive teams must manage organizational processes down within their units, across with their peers, up with more senior managers, and outside the firm with important suppliers, vendors, alliance partners, and customers. These external linkages often require managers to work without formal power or control. As such, managing across multiple boundaries requires managers to be politicians, negotiators, and network builders. For example, Pierre Urech was as successful as he was with Tilt because he was able to forge tight linkages to powerful actors in central R&D, in his larger division, and in the geographic regions.

**TECHNOLOGY CYCLES DRIVE INNOVATION STREAMS.** Technologies evolve through cycles: periods of variation, selection of a dominant design, followed by periods of incremental technological change punctuated by a subsequent technological breakthrough. The most successful firms are able to influence these technology cycles; they are able to shape dominant designs (like Seiko did with the quartz movements) and are able to trigger new technology cycles by proactively initiating breakthrough product or process innovations (like Ciba Vision's extended wear lens). Through shaping technology cycles, managers can create streams of innovation—incremental, architectural, and discontinuous. By leading innovation streams managers can simultaneous win for today as well as set the standards for tomorrow.

**AMBIDEXTROUS ORGANIZATIONS HELP COMPETE FOR TODAY AND TOMORROW.** Strategic innovation and the need to create incremental, architectural, and discontinuous innovation require managers to balance contradictory pressures. This means building, like Ciba Vision, the organizational competencies to simultaneously host the multiple strategies, structures, processes, and cultures needed to be successful today and to create the conditions for discontinuous innovation in the future. Clear, simple visions are an important tool to reconcile the contradictions built into ambidextrous organizations. It is through such internal diversity and experimentation that managers generate data from which to make strategic bets. Luck is, then, an important ingredient in managing innovation over time. While managers cannot guarantee it, they can create organizations that can be systematically luckier than the competition.

**MANAGING INNOVATION STREAMS MEANS MANAGING DISCON-TINUOUS CHANGE.** Innovation streams involve organizational change. Whereas incremental innovation can be managed within the current organizational configuration, as we have seen in Oticon, Ciba Vision, and with Lt. Sims, both architectural and discontinuous innovations involve systemwide organizational change. These innovation types are disruptive; they tear at the political, structural, and cultural fabric of an organization. In organizations as varied at Xerox, Alcoa, SMH, and Ciba Vision, managing streams of innovation involves managing incremental as well as revolutionary organizational change. Having the right technology is not enough. Innovation must be implemented in the context of an often indifferent, if not hostile, organization. Understanding the fundamental dynamics of integrated change management is a crucial determinant of successful innovation. This means shaping the politics of change, dealing with individual anxiety and resistance, and maintaining control during transition periods.

**INNOVATION IS A TEAM SPORT.** Whether it is Ciba Crop Protection, Anaquest, or BOC Gases, the management team is where winning through innovation begins. If the organization is to be able to handle the contradictory demands of incremental, architectural, and discontinuous innovation, the manager and his or her direct reports must be able to embrace these tensions. The team must have the competencies and processes to host internal diversity coupled with a clear, shared vision. This group, the entire senior team, is a powerful signal generator that is closely observed by the rest of the organization. If it preaches one message and practices another, people quickly translate this contradiction into confusion, incompetence, or dishonesty. To be consistent, the whole team must be clear about what is important and relentless in reinforcing its message. To avoid the intellectual inertia that accompanies success often means keeping the group's age young, either through rotation or replacement. It is no accident that most successful revolutions are driven by new senior teams.

Strategic innovation dictates that senior managers themselves be ambidextrous and adjust their leadership styles and their team's competencies to manage the contrasting demands of short-term efficiency and long-term adaptation. At Ciba Vision, for example, Bradley created entrepreneurial teams to run the breakthrough areas of the firm even as he promoted more efficiency-oriented, cost-focused managers to run the mature product areas. These portfolios of managerial characteristics, integrated with a common vision and clear objectives, are important levers for leading innovation streams.

## WINNING THROUGH INNOVATION: EMBRACING CONTRADICTIONS FOR ORGANIZATIONAL RENEWAL

Winning through innovation is about managing contradictions, managing for both today and tomorrow. It is about taking advantage of technology cycles to proactively shape today's and tomorrow's innovation streams. As we saw with Lt. Sims, C. K. Chow in BOC's Gases business, and Glen Bradley at Ciba Vision, the difficulties of managing innovation are deep and worldwide. Managing innovation is rooted more in leadership and organizational capabilities than it is in technological prowess. Winning through innovation is led by managers who can build, embrace, and take advantage of the contradictions inherent in ambidextrous organizations. These managers are able to take advantage of, yet not get trapped by, today's culture and the firm's historical success.

Winning through innovation is also about managing change. The world is full of inspiring visions, grand strategies, and breakthrough innovations that were either never implemented or implemented too late. Winning through innovation hinges on the manager's ability to implement change in often complacent or inertial organizations. As innovation and change are intertwined, we have focused on managing change within and across organizations; we have coupled managing innovation streams with managing politics, organizational control, and individual resistance to change.

Our book presents several distinct images of managers leading innovation and change. Whether at the top of a firm—for example, Chow at BOC—or a project manager—for example, Urech in Ciba's Crop Protection Division—managers are simultaneously organizational architects, network builders as well as jugglers (see Table 9.1). The manager as architect uses strategy, structures, competencies, and cultures as tools to build ambidextrous organizations. Yet innovation streams also involve discontinuous change. Our second image focuses on the manager as a network builder and politician, building cliques and coalitions in service of innovation and change. Finally, we have portrayed managers as artists or as jugglers—building in and integrating the tensions and contradictions inherent in ambidextrous organizations and in managing for today and tomorrow. The best managers have the competencies and behavioral flexibility to balance the diverse management skills required to lead innovation streams and organizational renewal.

The business press is full of both clichés and the truth about the pace of change facing today's executives. As we learned from Lt. Sims in Chapter 1, it is difficult for successful organizations

**TABLE 9.1**

## MANAGERIAL ROLES IN LEADING INNOVATION AND CHANGE

| The Manager As: | Role: |
| --- | --- |
| Architect | • Building fit, consistency and congruence of structures, human resources, and cultures to execute critical tasks in service of strategy, objectives, and vision. |
| Network Builder | • Managing strategic change by shaping networks and coalitions down, across, up, and outside the manager's unit. |
| Juggler | • Hosting contradictory strategies, structures, competencies, and cultures in service of incremental, architectural, and discontinuous innovation, as well as integrating these contradictions with a clear vision. |

to reform themselves. All over the world, successful organizations stumble because managers were unable to lead innovation streams. We have focused on how to understand the dynamics of innovation and change and how to avoid the tyranny of success. While it may be true, as Tom Peters has claimed, that there are no excellent organizations, our experience is that there are excellent managers—those men and women who have learned how to build diverse executive teams and use social control and diverse cultures in creating ambidextrous organizations. They are the individuals from whom we have learned how organizations can go from today's to tomorrow's strength; they have mastered the architectural, network, and juggling skills necessary to win through innovation.

# Notes

## Chapter 1

1. See *Fortune*'s annual articles on "America's Most Admired Companies" and "Corporate Reputations."
2. See Loomis 1993, 36–42.
3. See Sager 1995b, 116–120; and Sherman, 1994.
4. See Abrahamson, 1996.
5. We build on substantial research on innovation and change, including Burgelman, 1991; Christensen and Bower, 1996; Eisenhardt and Tabrizi, 1995; Foster, 1985; Henderson, forthcoming; Hurst, 1995; Iansiti and Clark, 1994; Leonard-Barton, 1995; Morone, 1993; Nadler and Tushman, forthcoming; Utterback, 1994; and Van de Ven, Angle, and Poole, 1989.
6. The following account draws on Morison, 1966.
7. Lublin and Markels 1995, 131.

## Chapter 2

1. See Foster, 1986.
2. For an extensive discussion of the watch industry, see Glassmeier, 1991; Landes, 1983; and Taylor, 1993.
3. See Cooper and Smith 1992, 92–120, for more detail on the response of leading firms to technological change.

   Patterns in organizational evolution have been described in detail by Lawrence and Dyer, 1983; Meyer, Brooks, and Goes, 1990; Miller, 1990, 1994; Miller and Friesen, 1984; Tushman, Newman, and Romanelli, 1986; and Van de Ven and Grazman, forthcoming.
4. See Gould, 1987a, 1987b.
5. See Baum and Singh, 1994; Carroll and Hannan, 1995; and Hannan and Carroll, 1992.
6. See also Chakravarthy, 1981; Greenwood and Hinings, 1993; Hurst, 1995; Miles and Cameron, 1982; Nadler, Shaw, and Walton, 1995; Pettigrew, 1985; Quinn and Cameron, 1983; and Strebel, 1992, for more on organizational response to environmental jolts.
7. Rebello, Burrows, and Sager, 1996.
8. For more detail on technology cycles, see Chapter 7 as well as Abernathy and Clark, 1985; Dosi, 1982; Tushman and Anderson, 1986; Tushman and Rosenkopf, 1992; Utterback, 1994; and Wade, 1995.
9. See Abernathy 1978 for more details on the automobile industry.

10.   See Miller, 1993; and Nadler and Tushman, 1992, forthcoming.

11.   See Hays, 1994.

12.   See Kotter and Rothbard, 1993.

13.   Quoted in *Fortune* 1991, 31.

14.   See Leahy, 1990.

15.   See Sager and Cortese 1994, 96.

16.   See Strom, 1992.

17.   See Deutschman 1994, 90.

18.   See Machiavelli 1974, p. 44.

19.   See Sherman 1993, 58.

## CHAPTER 3

1.   There is a large literature on problem definition. See, for example, Bartunek, 1984; Dutton, Fahey, and Narayanan, 1983; Louis and Sutton, 1991; March and Simon, 1958; Milliken and Lant, 1991; and Weick, 1979.

2.   For more detail on understanding strategic context in service of setting strategy, objectives, and vision, see Chandler, 1990; Collins and Porras, 1994; Hamel and Prahalad, 1994; and Porter, 1980.

3.   Kets de Vries and Miller, 1984; Milliken and Lant, 1991; and Weick, 1979.

4.   For more detail on technology strategy, see Burgelman and Rosenbloom, 1989.

5.   See the extensive literature on vision and strategic intent, including Collins and Porras, 1994; and Hamel and Prahalad, 1989, 1994.

6.   Collins and Porras 1994, 57.

7.   For greater detail on Alcoa, see Kolesar, 1993.

8.   Collins and Porras 1994, 65.

9.   See March and Simon, 1958; Nadler and Tushman, 1988; and Van de Ven and Ferry, 1980 for more detail on problem definition.

10.   See also Eisenhardt, 1989; Hamel and Prahalad, 1994; Hurst, 1995; and Strebel, 1992.

## CHAPTER 4

1.   This chapter builds on Nadler and Tushman, 1980, 1992, forthcoming.

2.   See also other approaches to the notion of fit or congruence, including Davis and Lawrence, 1977; Galbraith, 1973; Gresov, 1989; Miles and Snow, 1994; Miller, 1993 and 1986; and Peters and Waterman, 1983.

3.   See Taylor, 1991.

4.   This mode of problem solving is consistent with the work on TQM and organizational learning. See, for example, Cohen and Sproul, 1996; Huber, 1991; Kano, 1993; Kolesar, 1993; Levitt and March, 1988; Nonaka, 1993; Senge, 1990; and Walton, 1986.

5.   See also Argyris and Schon, 1978; and Weick, 1979.

6.   Describing tasks and associated work processes is also the initial step in any reengineering, information technology, or TQM effort. See Ettlie and Reza, 1992; Hammer and Champy, 1993; and Lucas, 1996.

7. See Gresov, 1989; Gresov, Drazin, and Van de Ven, 1989; Tushman and Nadler, 1978; and Van de Ven and Drazin, 1985.
8. See Thompson, 1967; and Wageman, 1995.
9. See Bartlett and Ghoshal, 1989, 1990; Doz and Hamel, 1995; and Quinn, 1992.
10. See Allen, 1977; Iansiti and Clark, 1994; Morone, 1993; and Schoonhoven and Eisenhardt, 1990.
11. See Bartlett and Ghoshal, 1991; and Quinn, 1992.
12. See Pfeffer, 1994 for more detail on human resource issues.
13. See Kidder, 1982.
14. See Chatman and Barsade, 1995; and O'Reilly and Chatman, 1994.
15. See Ancona, 1990; Jackson, 1992; O'Reilly, Caldwell, and Barnett, 1989; O'Reilly, Snyder, and Booth, 1993; Virany, Tushman, and Romanelli, 1992; and Wiersema and Bantel, 1992.
16. See Nonaka, 1995; and Westney and Sakakibara, 1986.
17. See Taylor, 1991.
18. This section builds on Nadler and Tushman, 1988, forthcoming.
19. See Davis and Lawrence, 1977; Galbraith, 1973; Galunic and Eisenhardt, 1994; and Nadler and Tushman, 1988, forthcoming.
20. See Chandler, 1962 and 1990.
21. See also Bartlett and Ghoshal, 1989; Davis and Lawrence, 1977; Galbraith, 1973; Lorenzoni and Baden-Fuller, 1995; Nadler, Gerstein, and Shaw, 1992; Nohria and Eccles, 1992; and Quinn, 1992.
22. Gresov, 1989; Tushman, 1978; and Wageman, 1995.
23. See Kerr, 1995; Lucas, 1996; and O'Reilly and Weitz, 1980.
24. See Foulkes, 1991.
25. There is a large literature on informal organization and culture upon which we build. See, for example, Kotter and Heskett, 1992; O'Reilly and Chatman, 1996; and Schein,1996.
26. See Barnard, 1938; Homans, 1950; and Katz and Kahn, 1966.
27. See Collins and Porras, 1994; and Tichy and Sherman, 1993.
28. There is a large literature on networks, informal roles, and informal power. See, for example, Ancona and Caldwell, 1992, forthcoming; Barley, 1990; Brown and Eisenhardt, 1995a; Burkhardt and Brass, 1990; Finkelstein, 1992; Gargiulo, 1993; Ibarra and Andrews, 1993; Krackhardt, 1990; and Pfeffer, 1992.
29. See Allen, 1977; and Katz, Tushman, and Allen, 1994.

## CHAPTER 5

1. There is an interesting research literature attesting to the importance of commitment and identification as a source of motivation. See, for example, Bellah, Madsen, Sullivan, Swidler, and Tipton, 1985; O'Reilly and Chatman, 1986; and Rousseau, 1995.
2. Ash, 1995.
3. Quoted in Collins and Porras 1994, 56.

4. There is a large and contentious academic literature on the concept of culture. Some authors contend that culture is, by its nature, not easily accessible to its adherents. In this sense, culture can be seen as the implicit or unspoken assumptions held by people in an organization (e.g., Schein, 1985). Other academics contend that culture is inherently fragmented and, as such, it makes little sense to talk about organization-wide cultures (e.g., Martin and Siehl 1983, 52–64). Our own view is that although these may be interesting academic arguments, a focus on norms is a useful perspective for studying organizations and one that permits practitioners to use culture for managerial ends.

5. For a useful review of cross-cultural norms, see Hofstede, 1991; Redding, 1995; and Smith and Ford, 1994.

6. For a brief overview of the social psychology of persons and situations, see Ross and Nisbett, 1991; and Zimbardo and Leippe, 1991.

7. Ingrassia and White, 1994.

8. Hof, 1992.

9. O'Reilly and Chatman, 1996.

10. Waterman, 1994.

11. Katsumata, 1994.

12. See Vedin, 1994, for a sample of the studies that have been done.

13. Caldwell and O'Reilly, 1995.

14. Numerous examples are offered in Jasinowski and Hamrin, 1995; and Levering and Moskowitz, 1993.

15. Levering and Moskowitz, 1993, 124.

16. Levering and Moskowitz, 1993, 101.

17. Tichy and Sherman, 1993b.

18. Levering and Moskowitz, 1993, 149.

19. Sherman, 1993.

20. The examples and quotes in this paragraph are drawn from Levering and Moskowitz, 1993.

## CHAPTER 6

1. Comer and Laird, 1975; and Tomsho, 1992.

2. For a superb treatment of this psychology, see Cialdini, 1993.

3. Although much has been written about NUMMI, the best single source is Adler, 1993. Pfeffer 1994 also describes some of NUMMI's practices.

4. Henkoff, 1994.

5. Levering and Moskowitz 1993, 72.

6. Tichy and Sherman, 1993b.

7. For a good overview of how direct sales organizations motivate their members, see Biggart, 1989.

8. Sellars, 1993

9. Pfeffer, 1981.

10. Stewart, 1990; and Kolesar, 1993.

11. Chatman and Barsade, 1995.

12. Kraar, 1989.

13. Levering and Moskowitz 1993, 125.

14. Farnham, 1993.

15. The following describe a variety of the techniques 3M uses to promote and celebrate innovation: Kelly, 1991, 59–62; Labich, 1988, 51–64; and Mitchell, 1989, 58–64.

16. Waterman, 1994.

17. For a discussion of the concept of social learning see Bandura, 1977; and Zimbardo and Lieppe 1991, 44–52.

18. For a discussion of the social learning effects of punishment, see Mitchell and O'Reilly 1983, 201–234; and O'Reilly and Weitz 1980, 445–448.

19. For a comparison of the recruitment procedures of strong culture organizations, see Chatman 1991, 459–484; and O'Reilly and Chatman 1996, 167–210.


## CHAPTER 7

1. Zellner 1995, 66.

2. Loeb 1995, 217.

3. There is a burgeoning literature on the competitive importance of innovation and the linkage among innovation, technology cycles, and organization renewal. See Brown and Eisenhardt, 1995; Burgelman, 1994; Christensen and Bower, 1996; Damanpour, 1996; Foster, 1987; Henderson and Clark, 1990; Iansiti and Clark, 1994; Leonard-Barton, 1995; Morone, 1993; Rosenbloom and Christensen, 1994; Schoonhoven and Eisenhardt, 1990; and Utterback, 1994.

4. For more detail on technology cycles and dominant designs, see Anderson and Tushman, 1990; Baum and Korn, 1995; Cusumano, Mylonadis, and Rosenbloom, 1992; Cusumano and Selby, 1995; David, 1985; McGrath, MacMillan, and Tushman, 1992; Noble, 1984; Teece and Pisano, 1994; Tushman and Anderson, 1986; Tushman and Rosenkopf, 1992; Utterback, 1994; and Wade, 1995.

5. For more detail on subsystems, linkages, and architectural innovation, see Henderson and Clark, 1990; and Rosenkopf and Tushman, 1994. For greater insight on the watch industry, see Glassmeier, 1991; and Landes, 1983.

6. See Sanderson and Uzumeri, 1995.

7. See Duncan, 1976; and Eisenhardt and Tabrizi, 1995.

8. See Nonaka, 1988, 1990, 1995.

9. See also Brown and Eisenhardt, 1995; Cooper and Smith, 1992; Nadler and Tushman, forthcoming; and Tushman and Nadler, 1986.

10. For more detail on the senior team's role in innovation, see Ancona, 1990; Finkelstein and Hambrick, 1992; Flatt, 1993; Garbarro, 1987; Gersick, 1994; Hamel and Prahalad, 1994; Kearns and Nadler, 1992; Morone, 1993; and Virany, Tushman, and Romanelli, 1992.

11. For more on the linkages between innovation and organizational change, see Gersick, 1991; Greenwood and Hinings, 1993; Hurst, 1995; Iansiti and Clark,

1994; Meyer, Goes, and Brooks, 1993; Miller, 1990; Nadler, Shaw, and Walton, 1995; Pettigrew, 1985; and Romanelli and Tushman, 1994.

12. See Sherman, 1993.

## CHAPTER 8

1. Quoted in Caminiti 1996, 90.
2. Quoted in Diamond, 1991.
3. Quoted in Strom, 1992.
4. Quoted in Buckley, 1994.
5. Loomis 1993, 36–42.
6. Dobrzynski, 1996.
7. Sellars 1995, 98.
8. We build on much literature on managing change. In particular, see Beer, Eisenstadt, and Spector, 1990; Huber and Glick, 1993; Jick, 1991; Kanter, Stein, and Jick, 1992; Nadler and Tushman, 1989, 1992, 1990, forthcoming; Nadler, Gerstein, and Shaw, 1992; Nadler, Shaw, and Walton, 1995; Pettigrew and Whipp, 1991; and Tichy, 1983.
9. For more detail, see Ancona and Nadler, 1989; Barnard, 1938; Collins and Porras, 1994; Hamel and Prahalad, 1989; House, Spangler, and Wyecke, 1991; Hurst, 1995; Nadler and Tushman, 1990; and Tichy and Sherman, 1993.
10. There is an interesting literature on the role of the top management team and how cohesiveness can affect its performance. See, for example, Finkelstein and Hambrick, 1996.
11. Sager 1995a, 142.
12. See Pfeffer, 1992a, for an extensive discussion of politics and change.
13. Fisher 1995, 124.
14. Pfeffer 1992a, 248.
15. Schares 1993, 208.
16. *Fortune* 1995, 98.
17. Dumaine 1993, 123–130.
18. Tichy and Sherman, 1993b.
19. Waterman, 1991.
20. Jick, 1991; see also Kanter, Stein, and Jick, 1992.
21. Stack 1992, 2.

## CHAPTER 9

1. Stewart 1996, 94.
2. Deutschman 1994, 90.
3. Schiller, 1995.
4. Sager 1995b, 120.

# BIBLIOGRAPHY

Abernathy, W. 1978. *The Productivity Dilemma.* Baltimore: Johns Hopkins University Press.

Abernathy, W., and K. Clark. 1985. "Innovation: Mapping the Winds of Creative Destruction." *Research Policy* 14: 3–22.

Abernathy, W., and J. Utterback. 1978. "Patterns of Industrial Innovation." *Technology Review* 80: 40–47.

Abrahamson, E. 1996. "Management Fashion." *Academy of Management Review* 21: 254–285.

Adler, P. 1988. "Managing Flexible Automation." *California Management Review* (Spring): 34–55.

———. 1993. "The Learning Bureaucracy: New United Motors Manufacturing, Inc." In *Research in Organizational Behavior,* edited by B. Staw and L. Cummings. Greenwich, Conn.: JAI Press.

Aitken, H. 1985. *The Continuous Wave.* Princeton: Princeton University Press.

Allen, T. 1977. *Managing the Flow of Technology.* Cambridge, Mass.: MIT Press.

Ancona, D. 1990. "Top Management Teams: Preparing for the Revolution." In *Social Psychology in Business,* edited by J. Carroll. Hillsdale, NJ: Erlbaum.

Ancona, D., and D. Caldwell. 1992. "Bridging the Boundary: External Processes in Organization Teams." *Administrative Science Quarterly* 37: 634–665.

———. Forthcoming. "Making Teamwork Work: Boundary Management in Product Development Teams." In *Managing Strategic Innovation: A Collection of Readings,* edited by M. Tushman and P. Anderson. New York: Oxford.

Ancona, D., and D. Nadler. 1989. "Top Hats and Executive Tales." *Sloan Management Review* 30: 19–28.

Anderson, P., and M. Tushman. 1990. "Technological Discontinuities and Dominant Designs: A Cyclical Model of Technological Change." *Administrative Science Quarterly* 35: 604–633.

———. 1991. "Managing Through Cycles of Technological Change," *Research and Technology Management* 34: 26–31.

Argyris, C., and D. Schon. 1978. *Organizational Learning.* Reading, Mass.: Addison-Wesley.

Ash, M. K. 1995. *Mary Kay: You Can Have It All.* Rocklin, Calif.: Prima Publishing.

Bandura, A. 1977. *Social Learning Theory.* Englewood Cliffs, N.J.: Prentice-Hall.

Barley, S. 1990. "The Alignment of Technology and Structure through Roles of Networks." *Administrative Science Quarterly* 35, no. 1: 61–103.

Barnard, C. 1938. *Functions of the Executive.* Cambridge, Mass.: Harvard University Press.

Barnett, W. 1994. "The Liability of Collective Action: Growth and Change Among Early American Telephone Companies." In *Evolutionary Dynamics of Organizations,* edited by J. Baum and J. Singh. New York: Oxford University Press.

Barnett, W., and G. Carroll. 1995. "Modeling Internal Organization Change." *American Review of Sociology* 21: 217–236.

Bartlett, C., and S. Ghoshal. 1989. *Managing Across Borders.* Boston: Harvard Business School Press,

———. 1990. "Managing Innovation in the Transnational Corporation." In *Managing the Global Firm,* edited by C. Bartlett, Y. Doz and B. Hedlund. New York: Oxford University Press.

Bartunek, J. 1984. "Changing Interpretative Schemes and Organizational Restructuring." *Administrative Science Quarterly* 29: 355–372.

Baum, J. 1996. "Organization Ecology." In *Handbook of Organization Studies,* edited by S. Clegg, C. Hardy, and W. Nord. London: Sage.

Baum, J., and H. Korn. 1995. "Dominant Designs and Population Dynamics in Telecommunications Services." *Social Science Research* 24: 97–135.

Baum, J., and J. Singh. 1994. *Evolutionary Dynamics of Organizations.* New York: Oxford University Press.

Beer, M., R. Eisenstadt, and B. Spector. 1990. *The Critical Path to Organization Renewal.* Boston: Harvard Business School Press.

Bellah, R., R. Madsen, W. Sullivan, A. Swidler, and S. Tipton. 1985. *Habits of the Heart: Individualism and Commitment in American Life.* Berkeley: University of California Press.

Biggart, N. 1989. *Charismatic Capitalization; Direct Selling Organization in America.* Chicago: University of Chicago Press.

Boeker, W. 1989. "Strategic Change: Effects of Founding and History." *Academy of Management Journal* 32: 489–515.

Brass, D., and M. Burkhardt. 1993. "Potential Power and Power in Use." *Academy of Management Journal* 36: 441–470.

Brown, J. 1991. "Research that Reinvents the Corporation," *Harvard Business Review* (January–February): 102–111.

Brown, S., and K. Eisenhardt. 1995a. "Product Development: Past Research, Present Findings, and Future Directions." *Academy of Management Review* 20: 343–378.

———. 1995b. "Product Innovation as Core Capability: The Art of Dynamic Adaptation." Stanford University Working Paper, Stanford, Calif.

Buckley, N. 1994. "Break-Out: A New Fashion at Sears." *Financial Times,* September 28.

Burgelman, R. 1991. "Intraorganizational Ecology of Strategy Making and Organizational Adaptation." *Organization Science* 2, no. 3: 239–262.

———. 1994. "Fading Memories: A Process Theory of Strategic Business Exit." *Administrative Science Quarterly* 39: 24–56.

Burgelman, R., and R. Rosenbloom. 1989. "Technology Strategy: An Evolutionary Perspective." In *Research on Technological Innovation,* edited by R. Rosenbloom and R. Burgelman. Greenwich, Conn.: JAI Press.

Burkhardt, M., and D. Brass. 1990. "Changing Patterns or Patterns of Change: Effects of Technology Change on Social Network Structure and Power." *Administrative Science Quarterly,* 35, no. 1: 104–127.

Caldwell, D., and C. O'Reilly. 1995. "Promoting Team-Based Innovation: The Use of Normative Influence." Paper presented at the 54th Annual Meetings of the Academy of Management, Vancouver, B.C., August.

Caminiti, S. 1996. "Sears Need: More Speed." *Fortune,* February 13.

Carroll, G., and M. Hannan. 1989. "Density Dependence in the Evolution of Populations of Newspaper Organizations." *American Sociological Review* 54: 524–541.

———. 1995. *Organization in Industries.* New York: Oxford University Press.

Chakravarthy, B. 1981. *Managing Coal.* New York: SUNY Press.

Chandler, A. 1962. *Strategy and Structure.* Cambridge, Mass.: MIT Press.

———. 1990. *Scale and Scope.* Cambridge, Mass.: Harvard University Press.

Chapman, R. 1986. *New Dictionary of American Slang.* New York: Harper Collins.

Chatman, J. 1991. "Matching People and Organizations: Selection and Socialization in Public Accounting Firms." *Administrative Science Quarterly* 36: 459–484.

Chatman, J., and S. Barsade. 1995. "Personality, Organization Culture, and Cooperation." *Administrative Science Quarterly* 40: 423–443.

Christensen, C., and J. Bower. 1996. "Customer Power, Strategic Investment, and the Failure of Leading Firms." *Strategic Management Journal* 17, 197–218.

Cialdini, R. 1993. *Influence: The Psychology of Persuasion.* New York: Quill Press.

Clark, K., and T. Fujimoto. 1991. *Product Development Performance.* Boston: Harvard Business School Press.

Clark, K., and S. Wheelwright. 1992. "Organizing and Leading 'Heavyweight' Development Teams." *California Management Review* (Spring): 9–27.

Cohen, M., and L. Sproul, eds. 1996. *Organizational Learning.* London: Sage.

Cohen, W., and D. Levinthal. 1990. "Absorptive Capacity: A New Perspective on Learning and Innovation." *Administrative Science Quarterly* 35: 128–152.

Collins, J., and J. Porras. 1994. *Built to Last.* New York: Harper Business.

Comer, R., and J. Laird. 1975. "Choosing to Suffer as a Consequence of Expecting to Suffer: Why Do People Do It?" *Journal of Personality and Social Psychology* 32.

Cooper, A., and C. Smith. 1992. "How Established Firms Respond to Threatening Technologies." *Academy of Management Executive* 6, no. 2: 55–70.

Cusumano, M., Y. Mylonadis and R. Rosenbloom. 1992. "Strategic Maneuvering and Mass Market Dynamics: The Triumph of VHS Over Beta." *Business History Review* (Fall): 51–93.

Cusumano, M., and R. Selby. 1995. *Microsoft Secrets.* New York: Free Press.

Damanpour, F. 1996. "Organizational Complexity and Innovation: Developing and Testing Contingency Models." *Management Science* 42, no. 5: 693–701.

D'Aveni, R. 1994. *Hypercompetition*. New York: Free Press.

David, P. 1985. "Clio and the Economics of Qwerty." *American Economic Review* 75 no. 2: 332–337.

Davis, S., and P. Lawrence. 1977. *Matrix*. Reading, Mass.: Addison-Wesley.

Day, D. 1994. "Raising Radicals: Different Processes for Championing Ventures." *Organization Science* 5: 148–172.

De Meyer, A. 1991. "Tech Talk: How Managers Are Stimulating Global R&D Communication." *Sloan Management Review* (Spring): 49–58.

Deschamps, J., and P. Nayak. 1995. *Product Juggernauts*. Boston: Harvard Business School Press.

Deutschman, A. 1994. "How HP Continues to Grow and Grow." *Fortune,* May 2.

Diamond, S. 1991. "Sears Biggest Problem May Be Its Service." *Los Angeles Times,* February 2.

Dobrzynski, J. 1996. "Yes, He's Revived Sears. But Can He Reinvent It?" *New York Times,* January 7.

Donaldson, L. 1995. *American Anti–management Theories of Organization*. Cambridge, England: Cambridge University Press.

Dosi, G. 1982. "Technological Paradigms and Technological Trajectories." *Research Policy* 11: 147–162.

Dougherty, D., and T. Heller. 1994. "The Illegitimacy of Successful Innovation in Established Firms." *Organization Science* 5: 200–218.

Doz, Y., and G. Hamel. 1995. "The Use of Alliances in Implementing Technology Strategies." In *Managing Technology and Innovation for Corporate Renewal,* edited by Y. Doz. New York: Oxford University Press.

Dumaine, B. 1993. "Times Are Good? Create a Crisis." *Fortune,* June 28.

Duncan, R. 1976. "The Ambidextrous Organization: Designing Dual Structures for Innovation." In *The Management of Organizational Design,* edited by R. Kilman and L. Pondy. New York: North Holland.

Dutton, J., L. Fahey, and V. Narayanan. 1983. "Toward Understanding Strategic Issue Diagnoses." *Strategic Management Journal* 4: 307–323.

Ehrnberg, E. 1995. "On the Definition and Measurement of Technological Discontinuities." *Technomation* 5: 437–452.

Eisenhardt, K. 1989. "Making Fast Strategic Decisions in High Velocity Environments." *Academy of Management Journal* 32: 543–576.

Eisenhardt, K., and B. Tabrizi. 1995. "Acceleration Adaptive Processes: Product Innovation in the Global Computer Industry." *Administrative Science Quarterly* 40: 84–110.

Ettlie, J., and E. Reza. 1992. "Organizational Integration and Process Innovation." *Academy of Management Journal* 35: 795–827.

Farnham, A. 1993. "Mary Kay's Lessons in Leadership." *Fortune,* September 20.

Finkelstein, S. 1992. "Power in Top Management Teams." *Academy of Management Journal* 35: 505–538.

Finkelstein, S., and D. Hambrick. 1996. *Strategic Leadership: Top Executives and Their Effects on Organizations.* New York: West.

Fisher, A. 1995. "Making Change Stick." *Fortune,* April 17.

Flatt, S. 1993. "The Innovation Edge: How Top Management Demography Makes a Difference." Ph.D. diss., University of California, Berkeley.

Florida, R., and R. Kenney. 1990. *The Breakthrough Illusion.* New York: Basic Books.

*Fortune.* 1991. "Today's Leaders Look to Tomorrow." March 26.

⸻. 1995. "A Conversation with Roberto Goizueta and Jack Welch." December 11.

Foster, R. 1986. *Innovation: The Attacker's Advantage.* New York: Summit Books.

Foulkes, F. 1991. *Executive Compensation: A Strategic Guide for the 1990s.* Boston: Harvard Business School Press.

Gabarro, J. 1987. *The Dynamics of Taking Charge.* Boston: Harvard Business School Press.

Galbraith, J. 1973. *Designing Complex Organizations.* Reading, Mass.: Addison-Wesley.

Galunic, C., and K. Eisenhardt. 1994. "Reviewing the Strategy-Structures-Performance Paradigm." In *Research in Organization Behavior,* edited by B. Staw and L. Cummings. Greenwich, Conn.: JAI Press.

Gargiulo, M. 1993. "Two–Step Leverage: Managing Constraint in Organizational Politics." *Administrative Science Quarterly* 38: 1–19.

Gersick, C. 1991. "Revolutionary Change Theories: A Multi–Level Exploration of the Punctuated Equilibrium Paradigm." *Academy of Management Review* 16: 1–32.

⸻. 1994. "Pacing Strategic Change: The Case of New Ventures." *Academy of Management Journal* 37: 9–45.

Glassmeier, A. 1991. "Technological Discontinuities and Flexible Production Networks: The Case of Switzerland and the World Watch Industry." *Research Policy* 20: 469–485.

Gomory, R. 1989. "From the Ladder of Success to the Product Development Cycle." *Harvard Business Review* (November–December): 110–115.

⸻. 1991. "The Technology–Product Relationship: Early and Late Stages." In *Technology and the Wealth of Nations* , edited by N. Rosenberg, R. Landau, and D. Mowery. Stanford, Calif.: Stanford University Press.

Gould, S. 1987a. "The Panda's Thumb of Technology." *Natural History* 1:14–23.

⸻. 1987b. *Time's Arrow, Time's Cycle.* Cambridge, Mass.: Harvard University Press.

Greenwood, R., and H. R. Hinings. 1993. "Understanding Strategic Change." *Academy of Management Journal* 6: 1052–1081.

Gresov, C. 1989. "Exploring Fit and Misfit with Multiple Contingencies." *Administrative Science Quarterly* 34: 431–453.

Gresov, C., R. Drazin and A. Van de Ven. 1989. "Work Unit Uncertainty, Design and Morale." *Organization Science* 10: 45–62.

Grinyer, R., and P. McKiernan. 1990. "Generating Major Change in Stagnating Companies." *Strategic Management Journal* 11: 131–146.

Hambrick, D., and R. D'Aveni. 1988. "Large Corporate Failures as Downward Spirals." *Administrative Science Quarterly* 33: 1–28.

Hamel, G., and C.K. Prahalad. 1989. "Strategic Intent." *Harvard Business Review*, 67: 63–76.

———. 1994. *Competing for the Future*. Boston: Harvard Business School Press.

Hammer, M., and J. Champy. 1993. *Reengineering the Corporation*. New York: Harper Business.

Hannan, M., and G. Carroll. 1992. *Dynamics of Organizational Populations*. New York: Oxford University Press.

Hannan, M., and J. Freeman. 1989. *Organizational Ecology*. Cambridge, Mass.: Harvard University Press.

Haveman, H. 1992. "Between a Rock and a Hard Place: Organization Change Under Conditions of Fundamental Environment Transformation." *Administrative Science Quarterly* 37: 48–75.

Hays, L. 1994. "Gerstner Is Struggling to Change Ingrained IBM Culture." *Wall Street Journal*, May 13.

Henderson, R. Forthcoming. "Of Life Cycles Real and Imaginary: The Unexpectedly Long Old Age of Optical Lithography." *Research Policy*.

Henderson, R., and K. Clark. 1990. "Architectural Innovation: The Reconfiguration of Existing Product Technologies and the Failure of Existing Firms." *Administrative Science Quarterly* 35: 9–30.

Henkoff, R. 1994. "Finding and Keeping the Best Service Workers." *Fortune*, October 3.

Herstatt, C., and E. von Hippel. 1992. "Developing New Product Concepts via the Lead User Method: A Case Study in a 'Low–Tech' Field." *J. of Product Innovation Management* 9:213–221.

Hof, R. 1992. "Inside Intel." *Business Week*, June 1.

Hofstede, G. 1991. *Cultures and Organizations*. New York: McGraw-Hill.

Hollander, S. 1965. *Sources of Efficiency*. Cambridge, Mass.: MIT Press.

Homans, G. 1950. *The Human Group*. Orlando, Fla.: Harcourt Brace.

House, R., W. Spangler, and J. Wyocke. 1991. "Personality and Charisma in the U.S. Presidency." *Administrative Science Quarterly* 36: 364–396.

Howard, R. 1992. "The CEO as Organizational Architect: An Interview with Xerox's Paul Allaire." *Harvard Business Review* (September–October): 107–119.

Huber, G. 1991. "Organization Learning: Contributing Processes and the Literature." *Organization Science* 2: 88–115.

Huber, G., and W. Glick, eds. 1993. *Organizational Change and Design*. New York: Oxford University Press.

Hughes, T. 1983. *Networks of Power*. Baltimore, Md.: Johns Hopkins Press.

Hurst, D. 1995. *Crisis and Renewal*. Boston: Harvard Business School Press.

Iansiti, M., and K. Clark. 1994. "Integration and Dynamic Capability." *Industry and Corporation Change* 3:557–606.

Ibarra, H. 1993. "Network Centrality, Power and Innovation Involvement." *Academy of Management Journal* 36: 471–501.

Ibarra, H., and S. Andrews. 1993. "Power, Social Influence, and Sense Making: Effects of Network Centrality on Employee Perceptions." *Administrative Science Quarterly* 38: 277–303.

Imai, K., I. Nonaka, and H. Takeuchi. 1985. "Managing the New Product Development Process: How Japanese Firms Learn and Unlearn." In *The Uneasy Alliance,* edited by K. Clark, et al. Boston: Harvard Business School Press.

Ingrassia, P., and J. White. 1994. *Comeback: The Fall and Rise of the American Automobile Industry.* New York: Simon & Schuster.

Jackson, S. 1992. "Consequences of Group Composition for the Interpersonal Dynamics of Strategic Issue Processing." *Advances in Strategic Management* 8: 345–382.

Jackson, S., and S. Dutton. 1988. "Discerning Threats and Opportunities." *Administrative Science Quarterly* 33: 370–387.

Jasinowski, J., and R. Hamrin. 1995. *Making It in America: Proven Paths to Success from 50 Top Companies.* New York: Simon & Schuster.

Jellinek, M., and C. Schoonhoven. 1990. *The Innovation Marathon.* New York: Blackwell.

Jick, T. 1991. "Implementing Change." Case 9–491–114. Boston: Harvard Business School Publishing.

Kano, N. 1993. "A Perspective on Quality Activities in American Firms." *California Management Review* (Spring): 12–30.

Kanter, R., J. North, L. Richardson, C. Ingols, and J. Zolner. 1991. "Engines of Progress: Designing and Running Entrepreneurial Vehicles in Established Companies; Raytheon's New Product Center, 1969–1989." *Journal of Business Venturing* 6.

Kanter, R., B. Stein, and T. Jick. 1992. *The Challenge of Organizational Change.* New York: Free Press.

Katsumata, M. 1994. "Interview with Ciba-Geigy Japan President Paul Dudler." *The Nikkei Weekly,* November 14.

Katz, D., and R. Kahn. 1966. *Social Psychology of Organizations.* New York: Wiley.

Katz, R. Forthcoming. "Managing Professional Careers: The Influence of Job Longevity and Group Age." In *Managing Strategic Innovation,* edited by M. Tushman and P. Anderson. New York: Oxford University Press.

Katz, R., M. Tushman and T. Allen. 1995. "Dual Ladder Promotions in R&D." *Management Science* 41: 848–863.

Kearns, D., and D. Nadler. 1992. *Prophets in the Dark.* New York: Harper.

Kelly, K. 1991. "3M Run Scared? Forget About It." *Business Week,* September 16.

Kerr, S. 1995. "On the Folly of Rewarding A., While Hoping for B." *Academy of Management Executive* 9: 7–14.

Kets de Vries, M., and D. Miller. 1984. "Neurotic Style and Organization Pathology." *Strategic Management Journal* 5: 82–104.

Kidder, T. 1982. *The Soul of a New Machine*. Boston: Little, Brown.

Kimberly, J., and R. Miles. 1980. *The Organization Life Cycle*. San Francisco: Jossey–Bass.

Kolesar, P. 1993. "Vision, Values, and Milestones: Paul O'Neil Starts Total Quality at Alcoa." *California Management Review* (Spring): 133–165.

Kotter, J., and Heskitt, J. 1992. *Corporate Culture and Performance*. New York: Free Press.

Kotter, J., and N. Rothbard. 1993. "Cultural Change at Nissan Motors." Case 9-491-079, Harvard Business School Publishing.

Kraar, L. 1989. "Japan's Gung-Ho U.S. Car Plants." *Fortune,* January 30.

Krackhardt, D. 1990. "Assessing the Political Landscape: Structure, Cognition and Power." *Administrative Science Quarterly* 35: 342–369.

Labich, K. 1988. "The Innovators." *Fortune,* June 6.

Landes, D. 1983. *Revolution in Time*. Cambridge, Mass.: Harvard University Press.

Lant, T., F. Milliken, and B. Batra. 1992. "The Role of Managerial Learning and Interpretation in Strategic Persistence and Reorientation." *Strategic Management Journal* 13: 585–608.

Lawler, E. 1986. *High-Involvement Management: Participative Strategies for Improving Performance*. San Francisco: Jossey-Bass.

Lawrence, P., and D. Dyer. 1983. *Renewing American Industry*. New York: Free Press.

Lawrence, P., and J. Lorsch. 1967. *Organizations and Environments*. Boston: Harvard Business School Press.

Leahy, J. 1990. "Changing the Culture at British Airways." Case 9-491-009, Harvard Business School Publishing.

Lee, J., D. O'Neil, M. Pruett, and H. Thomas. 1995. "Planning for Dominance: A Strategic Perspective on the Emergence of a Dominant Design." *R&D Management* 25: 3–15.

Leonard–Barton, D. 1992. "Core Capabilities and Core Rigidities: A Paradox in Managing New Product Development," *Strategic Management Journal* 13: 111–125.

———. 1995. *Wellsprings of Knowledge*. Boston: Harvard Business School Press.

Levering, R., and M. Moskowitz. 1993. *The 100 Best Companies to Work for in America*. New York: Currency Doubleday.

Levitt, B., and J. March. 1988. "Organization Learning." *American Review of Sociology* 14: 319–340.

Loeb, M. 1995. "Leadership Lost—and Regained." *Fortune,* April 17.

Loomis, C. 1993. "Dinosaurs?" *Fortune,* May 3.

Lorenzoni, G., and C. Baden-Fuller. 1995. "Creating a Strategic Center to Manage a Web of Partners." *California Management Review* 37, no. 35: 146–162.

Louis, M., and R. Sutton. 1989. "Switching Cognitive Gears: From Habits of Mind to Active Thinking," In *Advances in Organizational Sociology,* edited by S. Bacharach. Greenwich, Conn.: JAI Press.

Lublin, J., and A. Markels. 1995 "How Three CEOs Achieved Fast Turnaround." *Wall Street Journal,* July 21.

Lucas, H. 1996. *The T–Form Organization.* San Francisco: Jossey–Bass.

Lynn, Gary S., Joe Morone and Albert S. Paulson. Forthcoming. "Marketing and Discontinuous Innovation: The Probe and Learn Process." In *Managing Strategic Innovation,* edited by M. Tushman and P. Anderson. New York: Oxford University Press.

Machiavelli, N. 1985. *The Prince.* Translated by L.P.S. de Alvarez. Dallas: University of Dallas Press.

March, J., and H. Simon. 1958. *Organizations.* New York: Wiley.

Martin, J., and C. Siehl. 1983. "Organizational Culture and Counterculture: An Uneasy Symbiosis." *Organizational Designs* 12: 52–64.

McGrath, R., I. MacMillan and M. Tushman. 1992. "The Role of Executive Team Actions in Shaping Dominant Designs: Towards Shaping Technological Progress." *Strategic Management Journal* 13: 137–161.

Meyer, A., G. Brooks, and J. Goes. 1990. "Environmental Jolts and Industry Revolutions." *Strategic Management Journal* 11:93–110.

———. 1993. "Organizations' Reaction to Hyperturbulence." In *Organization Change and Redesign,* edited by G. Huber, and W. Glick. New York: Oxford University Press.

Meyer, M., and V. Gupta. 1994. "The Performance Paradox." *Research in Organization Behavior,* 309–369.

Meyer, M., and J. Utterback. 1993. "Product Family and the Dynamics of Core Capability." *Sloan Management Review* 34: 29–47.

Mezias, S., and M. A. Glynn. 1993. "Three Faces of Corporate Renewal: Institution, Revolution and Evolution." *Strategic Management Journal* 14: 77–101.

Miles, R., and K. Cameron. 1982. *Coffin Nails and Corporate Strategy.* Englewood Cliffs, N.J.: Prentice Hall.

Miles, R., and C. Snow. 1994. *Fit, Failure and the Hall of Fame.* New York: Free Press.

Miller, D. 1986. "Configurations of Strategy and Structure: Towards a Synthesis." *Strategic Management Journal* 7: 233–249.

———. 1990. *The Icarus Paradox: How Exceptional Companies Bring About their Own Downfall.* New York: Harper.

———. 1993. "The Architecture of Simplicity." *Academy of Management Review* 18: 116–138.

———. 1994. "What Happens After Success?" *J. of Management Studies* 31: 325–358.

Miller, D., and P. Friesen. 1984. *Organizations: A Quantum View.* Englewood Cliffs, N.J.: Prentice–Hall.

Milliken, F., and T. Lant. 1991. "The Effect of an Organization's Recent History on Strategic Persistence and Change." In *Advances in Strategic Management,*

Vol. 7, edited by J. Dutton, A. Huff, and P. Shrivastava. Greenwich, Conn.: JAI Press: 129–156.

Mintzberg, H., and F. Westley. 1992. "Cycles of Organization Change." *Strategic Management Journal* 13: 39–59.

Mitchell, G., and W. Hamilton. 1988. "Managing R&D as a Strategic Option." *Research and Technology Management* (May–June): 15–22.

Mitchell, R. 1989. "Masters of Innovation." *Business Week,* April 10.

Mitchell, T., and C. O'Reilly. 1983. "Managing Poor Performance and Productivity Organizations. " In *Research in Personnel and Human Resources Management,* Vol. 1. Greenwich, Conn.: JAI Press.

Mokyr, J. 1990. *Lever of Riches.* New York: Oxford University Press.

Morison, E. 1966. *Men, Machines, and Modern Times.* Cambridge, Mass.: MIT Press.

Morone, J. 1993. *Winning in High Tech Markets.* Boston: Harvard Business School Press.

Nadler, D., and M. Tushman. 1980. "A Model for Diagnosing Organization Behavior." *Organization Dynamics* (Spring):148–163.

———. 1988. *Strategic Organization Design.* New York: Harper.

———. 1989. "Organization Frame–Bending: Principles for Managing Reorientation." *Academy of Management Executive* 3: 194–204.

———. 1990. "Beyond Charismatic Leaders: Leadership and Organization Change." *California Management Review,* Winter, 1990, 77–90.

———. 1992. "Designing Organizations that Have Good Fit." In *Organization Architecture,* edited by D. Nadler: San Francisco: Jossey Bass.

———. Forthcoming. *Competing by Design: The Power of Organizational Architectures.* New York: Oxford University Press.

Nadler, D., M. Gerstein and R. Shaw. 1992. *Organization Architecture.* San Francisco: Jossey–Bass.

Nadler, D., R. Shaw and E. Walton. 1995. *Discontinuous Change.* San Francisco: Jossey–Bass.

Nelson, R. 1995. "Recent Evolutionary Theorizing About Economic Change." *Journal of Economic Literature* 33: 48–90.

Nelson, R., and S. Winter. *An Evolutionary Theory of Economic Change.* Cambridge, Mass.: Harvard University Press, 1982.

Noble, D. 1984. *Forces of Production.* New York: Knopf.

Nohria, N., and R. Eccles, eds. 1992. *Networks and Organizations.* Boston: Harvard Business School Press.

Nonaka, I. 1988a. "Creating Order Out of Chaos: Self Renewal in Japanese Firms." *California Management Review* 30, no. 3: 57–73.

———. 1988b. "Toward Middle–Up–Down Management: Accelerating Information Creation," *Sloan Management Review* (Spring): 9–18.

———. 1990. "Redundant, Overlapping Organization: A Japanese Approach to Innovation." *California Management Review* 32: 27–38.

————. 1993. *The Knowledge Creating Company.* New York: Oxford University Press.

O'Reilly, C. 1989. "Corporations, Culture and Commitment: Motivation and Social Control in Organizations." *California Management Review* 31: 24–38.

————. Forthcoming. "Organization Culture and Managing Innovation." In *Managing Strategic Innovation,* edited by M. Tushman and P. Anderson. New York: Oxford University Press.

O'Reilly, C., and J. Chatham. 1986. "Organizational Commitment and Psychological Attachment: The Effects of Compliance, Identification, and Internalization on Prosocial Behavior." *Journal of Applied Psychology* 71: 492–499.

————. 1995. "Working Smarter and Harder: A Study of Managerial Success." *Administrative Science Quarterly* 39: 603–627.

————. 1996. "Culture as Social Control: Corporations, Cults, and Commitment." In *Research in Organization Behavior,* edited by B. Staw and L. Cummings. Greenwich, Conn.: JAI Press.

O'Reilly, C., D. Caldwell, and W. Barnett. 1989. "Work Group Demography, Social Integration and Turnover." *Administrative Science Quarterly* 34: 21–37.

O'Reilly, C., J. Chatman, and D. Caldwell. 1991. "People and Organizational Culture." *Academy of Management Journal* 34:487–516.

O'Reilly, C., R. Snyder and J. Booth. 1993. "Effects of Executive Team Demography and Organizational Change." In *Organizational Design and Change,* edited by G. Huber and W. Glick. New York: Oxford University Press.

O'Reilly, C., and B. Weitz. 1980. "Managing Marginal Employees: The Use of Warnings and Dismissals." *Administrative Science Quarterly* 25: 467–484.

Pascale, R. 1990. *Managing on the Edge.* New York: Simon & Schuster.

Perrow, C. 1970. *Organizational Analysis.* Belmont, Calif.: Wadsworth.

Peters, T., and R. Waterman. 1983. *In Search of Excellence.* New York: Free Press.

Pettigrew, A. 1985. *The Awakening Giant: Continuity and Change at ICI.* Oxford, England: Blackwell, 1985.

Pettigrew, A., and R. Whipp. 1991. *Managing Change for Competitive Success.* Oxford, England: Basil Blackwell.

Pfeffer, J. 1981. "Management as Symbolic Action." In *Research in Organizational Behavior,* edited by B. Staw and L. Cummings. Greenwich, Conn.: JAI Press.

————. 1992a. *Managing with Power.* Boston: Harvard Business School Press.

————. 1992b. "Understanding Power in Organizations," *California Management Review* (Winter): 29–50.

————. 1994. *Competitive Advantage through People.* Boston: Harvard Business School Press.

Porter, M. 1980. *Competitive Strategy: Techniques for Analyzing Industries.* New York: Free Press.

Prahalad, C. 1993. "The Role of Core Competencies in the Corporation," *Research and Technology Management* (November–December): 40–47.

Quinn, J. 1992. *Intelligent Enterprise.* New York: Free Press.

Quinn, R., and K. Cameron. 1983. "Organization Life Cycles and Shifting Criteria of Effectiveness." *Management Science* 29: 33–51.

———. 1988. *Paradox and Transformation.* Cambridge, Mass.: Ballinger Publications.

Redding, G. 1975. *International Cultural Differences.* Aldershot, England: Dartmouth.

Robello, K., P. Burrows, and I. Sager. 1996. "The Fall of an American Icon." *Business Week,* February 5.

Roberts, E., and C. Berry. 1985. "Entering New Businesses: Selecting Strategies for Success." *Sloan Management Review* (Spring): 3–17.

Romanelli, E., and M. Tushman. 1994. "Organization Transformation as Punctuated Equilibrium." *Academy of Management Journal* 37: 1141–1166.

Rosenbloom, D., and C. Christensen. 1994. "Technological Discontinuities, Organization Capabilities, and Strategic Commitments." *Industry and Corporate Change* 3: 655–686.

Rosenkopf, L., and M. Tushman. 1994. "The Coevolution of Technology and Organization." In *Evolutionary Dynamics of Organizations,* edited by J. Baum, and J. Singh. New York: Oxford University Press.

Ross, L., and R. Nisbett. 1991. *The Person and the Situation: Perspectives of Social Psychology.* New York: McGraw-Hill.

Rousseau, D. 1995. *Psychological Contracts in Organizations.* Thousand Oaks, Calif.: Sage.

Royston, G., and C. Hinings. 1993. "Understanding Strategic Change: The Contribution of Archetypes." *Academy of Management Journal* 30, no. 5: 1052–1081.

Sager, I. 1995a. "The View from IBM." *Business Week,* October 30.

———. 1995b. "We Won't Stop . . . Until We Find Our Way Back." *Business Week,* May 5.

Sager, I., and A. Cortese. 1994. "Lou Gerstner Unveils His Battle Plan." *Business Week,* April 4.

Sakakibara, K., and E. Westney. 1991. "Japan's Management of Global Innovation: Technology Management Crossing Borders." In *Technology and the Wealth of Nations,* edited by N. Rosenberg, R. Landau, and D. Mowery. New York: Oxford University Press, 1991.

Sanderson, S., and M. Uzumeri. 1995. "Product Platforms and Dominant Designs: The Case of Sony's Walkman." *Research Policy* 24: 583–607.

Sastry, A. Forthcoming. "Problems and Paradoxes in a Theoretical Model of Punctuated Organization Change." *Administrative Science Quarterly.*

Schares, G. 1993. "Percy Barnevik's Global Crusade." *Business Week Enterprise.*

Schein, E. 1977. *Process Consultation.* Reading, Mass.: Addison-Wesley.

———. 1985. *Organizational Culture and Leadership: A Dynamic View.* San Francisco: Jossey–Bass.

———. 1996. "Culture: The Missing Concept in Organization Studies." *Administrative Science Quarterly* 41, no. 2: 229–240.

Schiller, Z. 1995. "The Revolving Door at Rubbermaid." *Business Week,* September 18.

Schoonhoven, K., and K. Eisenhardt. 1990. *Managing Complexity in High Technology Organizations.* New York: Oxford University Press.

Schoonhoven, K., K. Eisenhardt, and K. Lyman. 1990. "Speeding Products to Market. *Administrative Science Quarterly* 35, no. 1 :177–207.

Sellars, P. 1993. "Companies That Serve You Best." *Fortune,* May 31.

———. 1995. "Sears: In with the New: Out with the Old." *Fortune,* October 16.

Senge, P. 1990. *The Fifth Discipline.* New York: Doubleday.

Sherman, S. 1993. "Andy Grove: How Intel Makes Spending Pay Off." *Fortune,* February 22.

———. 1994. "Is He Too Cautious to Save IBM." *Fortune,* October 3.

Smith, D., and R. Alexander. 1990. *Fumbling the Future.* New York: Harper.

Smith, M. R., and L. Marx. 1994. *Does Technology Drive History?* Boston: MIT Press.

Smith, P., and M. Ford. 1994. *Social Psychology Across Cultures.* Boston: & Bacon.

Spender, J. C. 1989. *Industry Recipes: An Enquiry into the Nature of Managerial Judgment.* New York: Blackwell.

Stack, J. 1992. *The Great Game of Business.* New York: Currency/Doubleday.

Stewart, T. 1990. "A New Way to Wake Up a Giant." *Fortune,* October 22.

———. 1994. "How to Lead a Revolution." *Fortune,* November 28.

———. 1996. "3M Fights Back." *Fortune,* February 5.

Strebel, P. 1992. *Breakpoints: How Managers Exploit Radical Business Change.* Boston: Harvard Business School Press.

Strom, S. 1992a. "Further Prescriptions for the Convalescent Sears." *New York Times,* October 10.

———. 1992b. "Signs of Life at Sears, Roebuck." *New York Times,* October 25.

Taylor, W. 1991. "The Logic of Global Business: An Interview with ABB's Percy Barnevik." *Harvard Business Review* (March–April): 91–105.

———. 1993. "Message and Muscle: An Interview with Swatch Titan Nicholas Hayek." *Harvard Business Review* (March–April): 99–110.

Teece, D. 1987a. "Capturing Value from Technological Innovation: Integration, Strategic Partnering, and Licensing Decisions." In *Technology and Global Industry,* edited by B. Guile and H. Brooks.

———. 1987b. "Profiting from Technological Innovation." In *The Competitive Challenge,* edited by D. Teece. New York: Harper & Row.

Teece, D., and G. Pisano. 1994. "Dynamic Capabilities of Firms." *Industry and Corporate Change* 3: 537–556.

Thompson, J. 1967. *Organizations in Action.* New York: McGraw-Hill.

Tichy, N. 1983. *Managing Strategic Change.* New York: Wiley.

Tichy, N., and S. Sherman. 1993a. *Control Your Destiny or Somebody Else Will.* New York: Currency/Doubleday.

———. 1993b. "Jack Welch's Lessons for Success." *Fortune,* January 25.

Tomsho, R. 1992. "Worm Turns Out to Have Many Uses Few Can Appreciate." *The Wall Street Journal,* March 4.

Tushman, M. 1978. "Task Characteristics and Technical Communication in R&D." *Academy of Management Journal* 21: 624–645.

Tushman, M., and P. Anderson. 1986. "Technological Discontinuities and Organization Environments." *Administrative Science Quarterly* 31: 439–465.

Tushman, M., and D. Nadler. 1978. "Information Processing as an Integrating Concept in Organization Design." *Academy of Management Review* 3: 613–624.

———. 1986. "Organizing for Innovation." *California Management Review* 28, no. 3:74–92.

Tushman, M., and E. Romanelli. 1985. "Organization Evolution: A Metamorphosis Model of Convergence and Reorientation." In *Research in Organization Behavior,* Vol. 7, edited by B. Staw and L. Cummings. Greenwich, Conn.: JAI Press.

Tushman, M., and L. Rosenkopf. 1992. "On the Organizational Determinants of Technological Change: Towards a Sociology of Technological Evolution." In *Research in Organization Behavior,* Vol. 14, edited by B. Staw and L. Cummings. Greenwich, Conn.: JAI Press.

Tushman, M., P. Anderson, and C. O'Reilly. Forthcoming. "Technology Cycles, Innovation Streams and Ambidextrous Organizations." In *Managing Strategic Innovation,* edited by M. Tushman, and P. Anderson. New York: Oxford University Press.

Tushman, M., W. Newman and E. Romanelli. 1986. "Convergence and Upheaval: Managing the Unsteady Pace of Organizational Evolution." *California Management Review* (Fall): 29–44.

Tyre, M., and W. Orlikowski. 1993. "Exploiting Opportunities for Technological Improvement in Organizations." *Sloan Management Review* (Fall): 13–26.

Utterback, J. 1994. *Mastering the Dynamics of Innovation.* Boston: Harvard Business School Press.

Van de Ven, A., and R. Drazin. 1985. "The Concept of Fit in Contingency Theory." In *Research in Organization Behavior,* Vol. 4, edited by B. Staw and L. Cummings. Greenwich, Conn.: JAI Press.

Van de Ven, A., and D. Ferry. 1980. *Organization Assessment.* New York: Wiley.

Van de Ven, A., and R. Garud. 1994. "The Coevolution of Technical and Institutional Events in the Development of an Innovation." In *Evolutionary Dynamics of Organizations,* edited by J. Baum, and J. Singh. New York: Oxford University Press.

Van de Ven, A., and D. Grazman. Forthcoming. "Evolution in a Nested Hierarchy." *Strategic Management Journal.*

Van de Ven, A., H. Angle, and M. Poole. 1989. *Research on the Management of Innovation.* New York: Harper.

Vedin, B. 1994. *Management of Change and Innovation.* Alderhot, England: Dartmouth.

Virany, B., M. Tushman, and E. Romanelli. 1992. "Executive Succession and Organization Outcomes in Turbulent Environments." *Organization Science* 3: 72–92.

Von Hipple, E. 1988. *Sources of Innovation*. New York: Oxford University Press.

Wade, J. 1995. "Dynamics of Organizational Communities and Technological Bandwagons." *Strategic Management Journal* 16: 111–133.

Wageman, R. 1995. "Interdependence and Group Effectiveness." *Administrative Science Quarterly* 40: 145–180.

Walton, M. 1986. *The Deming Method*. New York: Dodd Mead.

Waterman, B. 1991. *Adhocracy: The Power to Change*. New York: Norton.

———. 1994. *What America Does Right: Learning from Companies That Put People First*. New York: Norton.

Weick, K. 1979. *The Social Psychology of Organizing*. Reading, Mass.: Addison-Wesley.

Westney, E., and K. Sakakibara. 1986. "The Role of Japan-Based R&D in Global Technology Strategy." *Technology and Society* 7: 315–330.

Wiersema, M., and K. Bantel. 1992. "Top Management Team Demography and Corporate Strategic Change." *Academy of Management Journal* 35: 91–121.

Zellner, W., R. Hof, R. Brandt, S. Baker, and D. Greising. 1995. "Go-Go Goliaths." *Business Week,* February 13.

Zimbardo, P., and M. Lieppe. 1991. *The Psychology of Attitude Change and Social Influence*. New York: McGraw-Hill.

# INDEX

# ABOUT THE AUTHORS

**Michael L. Tushman** is the Philip Hettleman Professor of Management at the Graduate School of Business at Columbia University, and has directed the Managing Strategic Innovation and Change Program at Columbia for ten years. He has also been a visiting professor at MIT's Sloan School of Management and INSEAD. He has extensive experience teaching executive education seminars, and he has consulted with organizations worldwide on managing innovation and change. Professor Tushman is also a director of Delta Consulting Group, the coauthor of *Competing by Design: The Power of Organizational Architecture,* and the author or coauthor of more than sixty articles and book chapers. Professor Tushman serves on the boards of many scholarly journals and is an active leader in the Academy of Management.

**Charles A. O'Reilly** is the Frank Buck Professor of Human Resources and Organizational Behavior at the Graduate School of Business at Stanford University. He previously taught at the Haas School of Business and the Institute of Personality Research at University of California at Berkeley and the Anderson Graduate School of Management at UCLA. He consults to a variety of public and private firms in the United States, Europe, and Japan. His most recent study examined how CEOs and executive teams deal with periods of crisis and transition. Professor O'Reilly has published over 70 papers on topics such as corporate culture, employee commitment, executive compensation, organizational demography, and human resources management.